A YANKEE'S ODYSSEY

JOEL BARLOW

Portrait by Charles Willson Peale, 1807. Used by permission of the owner, Joel Barlow of Washington, D. C., a descendant of Joel Barlow's brother Aaron.

A Yankee's Odyssey

THE LIFE OF JOEL BARLOW

By JAMES WOODRESS

GREENWOOD PRESS, PUBLISHERS
NEW YORK

FOR
ROBERTA

Contents

CONTENTS

Illustrations

ACKNOWLEDGMENTS

I have received a great deal of help in writing this book, and I wish to thank the many individuals and institutions who placed their knowledge and resources at my disposal.

First of all, I am grateful to the Guggenheim Foundation for the fellowship which gave me the leisure to write this life of Joel Barlow and the funds to visit distant libraries, and to my own institution, Butler University, for granting me a leave of absence. I wish also to thank the Huntington Library for a grant-in-aid which enabled me to spend a summer using its rich resources. I am further indebted to Duke University where I was a research associate when I embarked on this project and to the Modern Language Association, which gave me a research grant for microfilm.

Next I wish to thank the libraries I visited, many of which also supplied me with microfilm, and the librarians who assisted me. I am particularly grateful to Miss Carolyn E. Jakeman and William A. Jackson of the Houghton Library at Harvard University, Miss Mary Isabel Fry and Leslie E. Bliss of the Huntington Library, Robert H. Land of the Library of Congress, Robert F. Metzdorf of Yale University. I also wish to thank the following institutions and their staffs: the National Archives in Washington, D.C., Duke University Library, the American Philosophical Society, the New-York Historical Society, the Boston Public Library, the Boston

13

Athenaeum, the American Antiquarian Society, the Massachusetts Historical Society, the Connecticut State Library, the Connecticut Historical Society, Northwestern University Library, the Library Company of Philadelphia, the Hugh Wallace Collection in the United States Embassy Library in Paris, the Bibliothèque Nationale and the Archives Nationales in Paris.

Besides the above institutions and librarians I am grateful to these libraries which I did not visit but which supplied me with microfilm or copies of documents: the New York Public Library, Haverford College Library, the Historical Society of Pennsylvania, the Maryland Historical Society, and Princeton University Library.

For permission to publish extracts from manuscripts owned by various libraries, I wish to thank Harvard University, the Huntington Library, the New-York Historical Society, the American Antiquarian Society, the Massachusetts Historical Society, the Charles Roberts Autograph Collection in the Haverford College Library, Yale University, the Boston Public Library, the New York Public Library, Northwestern University, and the Connecticut Historical Society.

My debts to individuals are large and varied. Leon Howard and M. Ray Adams loaned me notes that they had used in their own work on Barlow. Mrs. R. K. Van Mater put at my disposal the rich collection of Barlow papers that she since has given to the Huntington Library. Irving Brant, Owen Aldridge, Lewis Leary, John Dos Passos, Frederick B. Tolles, Gilbert Chinard, Maury A. Bromsen, Stephen Larrabee, and Mrs. Carrie C. Autrey encouraged, advised, and gave me information drawn from their own knowledge of Barlow, his manuscripts, his period, and his friends. Dr. Margaret Schlauch of the University of Warsaw and Jan Lukasiewicz of Kielce, Poland, supplied me with data on Barlow's last days. My colleague Howard Baetzhold did some investigating for me in the Brown University Library. Russell Porter, American lawyer in Paris, helped me search for Barlow's land title in Paris.

For permission to use illustrations and for help in obtaining photographs, I am indebted to Samuel L. M. Barlow of New York City, Joel Barlow of Washington, D.C., M. O. Anderson, Superintendent of Independence Hall National Historical Park, Miss Penelope Roy-

ACKNOWLEDGMENTS

all of the United States Embassy Library in Paris, the American Antiquarian Society, and Harvard University. Also I wish to thank Laura Thoe for the drawings I have used and the Frick Art Reference Library in New York City for photographs.

My final debts are to my colleague Allan J. McCurry, who read my manuscript from the viewpoint of an American historian; to George Stevens of J. B. Lippincott Company, who edited my manuscript expertly and sympathetically; and to Roberta Woodress, whose services as editorial assistant, critic, and wife I am unable to acknowledge adequately.

Paris
March, 1958

Drawing by Laura Thoe

The Redding, Connecticut, farmhouse where Barlow was born in 1754

A YANKEE'S ODYSSEY

Prologue

Man's inhumanity to man and the cruel indifference of nature made December, 1812, a time of bitter memory in Northern Europe. Napoleon's troops lay bleeding and freezing on the icy battlefields of Russia, while their commander-in-chief raced incognito towards Paris to outrun the news of his disaster. The Emperor's grand design had ended in rout on the steppes of Russia, and the retreat from Moscow was under way against staggering odds. Pursued murderously by flying columns of Cossacks, most of the Grand Army never returned from the debacle. Hundreds of thousands of men and their horses died along the roads of White Russia, Poland, and Lithuania, buried only by the snow and ice of the coldest winter survivors could remember.

On November twentieth rumors had circulated among the diplomatic corps in Wilna, ancient Lithuanian capital where Napoleon planned to winter, that the French armies were retreating. They were said to be forty leagues west of Smolensk, without cavalry and under incessant flanking attack by swarms of Cossacks. The Duc de Bassano, French foreign minister, reassured the diplomats that all was well, but nine days more passed without news from the front. On the twenty-ninth dispatches finally arrived reporting that Napoleon was eighteen leagues beyond Minsk and sixty-five from Wilna. Bassano still insisted the Emperor would arrive in about six days to set up winter headquarters.

Five more days of silence passed. Then a half-frozen courier slipped into the troop-jammed city with news that Napoleon had fought and lost the bloody Battle of Berezina and was now in full flight. There was no longer any question of his wintering in Lithuania. The Russians were closing in fast, and any Frenchman overtaken there could expect no quarter. Headlong retreat was the only course. Even the diplomats were alarmed at the prospect of being caught behind the enemy lines, and on the afternoon of the fifth their carriages joined the procession of wagons and foot soldiers crowding the roads west.

For weeks the old city had been packed with soldiers, horses, wagons, and ordnance, and the streets were so congested that it took an hour and a half to maneuver through the traffic to the city gate. It seemed to one observer that a thousand wagons loaded with sick and dying were trying to pass through Wilna. In fact, the traveler from the West reported that the whole country from Kovno to Wilna was strung out with cartloads of maimed and sick troops through a countryside utterly devastated. Entire villages had been deserted and houses burned by the Russians in their scorched-earth retreat of the previous spring, and the thatch of houses that had escaped the fire had gone to fodder Napoleon's horses. Beside the road at frequent intervals lay abandoned equipment, hasty, shallow graves, and rotting horses.

In late November one could pass six hundred wagons in a day's journey towards Wilna. Then the weather had been mild, and the wretched horses dragged their miserable cargoes through seas of mud. The soft mud had been hell on the horses but a blessing for the wounded, for it cushioned their ride. The wagons were little more than open, naked planks laid on wheels with never a canopy shutting out the weather and only occasionally a little straw to lie on. The wounded frequently ended their tortures by dying on the wagons and lightening the load for the exhausted horses. The horses frequently died in their traces, whereupon they were cut loose and eaten raw by the starving troops. During the first week of December, when the bottom seemed to drop out of the thermometer, the roads froze in hard, ugly ruts; the sick and wounded suffered like damned souls and began freezing to death on the carts.

East of Wilna the carnage was even more appalling. "It grows worse & worse & worse & worse the nearer you approach to the theatre of glory," wrote one diplomat. Survivors of the debacle straggled back reporting the loss of entire units. Colonels returned without a single man in their regiments, and when the Grand Army under Murat finally reached Königsberg, only about one thousand out of the original six hundred thousand remained. A Polish count who fought his way back to Warsaw by the middle of December reported that there were one hundred and fifty thousand dead horses and fifty thousand bodies of unburied soldiers between Wilna and Moscow. Of the fifteen hundred fine artillery pieces that had passed the Niemen River during the autumn march into Russia, scarcely one remained.

Among the retreating diplomats who joined the exodus from Wilna on the fifth of December was the American minister to France, Joel Barlow. He had sailed for Europe the year before to negotiate settlement of some long-standing scores between Napoleon and the United States. After a year of futile talks in Paris, the Duc de Bassano had invited him to come to Wilna to obtain Napoleon's signature on an important treaty. He had set off hopefully, only to reach Lithuania as the Emperor lost his last desperate gamble with fate. Traveling with Joel Barlow were two passengers, his nephew Tom Barlow, who had come along as secretary, and Jean Baptiste Petry, a minor official of the French foreign ministry.

The retreating diplomats rode day and night in sub-freezing temperatures, scarcely getting out of their upholstered carriages. They hoped the emaciated little post horses, "not much larger than rats," could pull them to safety before the Russians overran the country. The Danish minister, even with thirteen horses, got stuck ten miles out of town and had to be helped by the Americans who followed behind, but Joel Barlow's French-built carriage, lighter and drawn by six horses, arrived safely in Warsaw on the twelfth after a journey of seven days. Except for a day's wait at Grodno where the bridge over the Niemen was out and the ice not quite thick enough to cross, the American minister made the two-hun-

dred-and-fifty-mile trip without incident. While he traveled towards Warsaw, Napoleon arrived in Wilna, stayed only a few
hours, and raced on westward, traveling with sleigh runners on his
carriage and without army escort. The American minister wrote
his wife in code that the Emperor was fleeing from assassination by
his own troops. Napoleon passed the Americans at night three days
out of Wilna as they broke their almost non-stop flight for a few
hours' sleep at a post house.

By the middle of December, as the remnant of Napoleon's army
struggled back towards France far behind their Emperor, who already was crossing into Germany, heavy snows blanketed Poland
from the Baltic to the Carpathians. On the sixteenth the mercury
dropped to minus twelve in Warsaw. Rutted dirt roads leading
south towards Krakow, the ancient Polish capital, and eventually
to Vienna and Paris, filled with ice and froze hard. The country
stretched away in all directions—one vast, empty, white wasteland.
No one without compelling business dared venture outdoors, but
at four o'clock on the morning of the eighteenth, the American
minister's tightly closed carriage slipped away from the southern
outskirts of Warsaw. The coachman on the outside seat whipped
up his scrawny horses and shivered under his several flannel waist-
coats, double pantaloons, fur-lined boots, fur cap, and three great-
coats, while inside, numb also with cold, sat the two Americans and
the Frenchman.

On the nineteenth of December the American minister caught
cold and rode all day chilled to the bone in the frigid carriage.
They now had climbed out of the low Vistula River valley and
were in the snowy, fir-covered hills around Kielce. Except for the
thatched cottages huddled in the upland villages, the scene might
have passed for a New England winter landscape. On the twentieth the minister's cold grew worse and was accompanied by head-
ache and fever; but there was no refuge in the bleak Polish
countryside, and the carriage jolted ahead over the endless snow
and ice. The minister's pelisse of six wolfskins, his footbag, marten
mittens, and long-wooled, sheepskin carpet seemed preferable to a
Polish village inn during the dead of winter. On the morning of
the twenty-first, however, after the carriage had traveled only six

leagues, the hills and fir forests opened on the town of Zarnowiec, a cluster of houses thrown protectively about a parish church. Joel Barlow said he could go no further.

The village of Zarnowiec was an ancient settlement of perhaps a thousand inhabitants built around a ruined castle on the Pilica River. A Polish prince had erected a church there in the thirteenth century, and the town long had served as a market center for a marginal farming area. Though it was burned by Swedish invaders in the seventeenth century and long in recovering, by 1812 Jewish settlers had begun rebuilding. Joel Barlow's carriage stopped at the center of the village, and Monsieur Petry took charge of finding lodging among Zarnowiec's meager resources. The chief man of the town, John Blaski, mayor and postmaster, took the stricken American minister into his home.

A day's rest in a warm house did not improve the patient's condition. By the next day he was totally unable to travel. His companions then summoned a doctor from a neighboring town. To no avail. On the twenty-third and twenty-fourth the minister grew steadily worse. On Christmas Day he was in critical condition, and another doctor with a greater reputation from twelve leagues away was called; but when the second physician arrived, he immediately confirmed the prognosis of the first: there was no hope. Pneumonia had developed; the patient was unconscious; the end could not be far off. On the following day at noon Joel Barlow died in Zarnowiec, Olkuski County, Department of Krakow, Poland. Monsieur Petry and Tom arranged a hasty funeral and burial in the parish churchyard and departed once more for Paris a few hours ahead of Cossack columns reported pillaging the neighboring country. Thus ended an eventful life at the untimely age of fifty-eight, in alien soil, far from home, wife, and friends. Barlow's death left the treaty negotiations unfinished and the United States without a minister in France during an important part of the War of 1812. In a real sense Barlow was another of the victims of Napoleon's mad dream of conquest.

This story, which ends in the hills of southern Poland, begins inauspiciously on a rocky Connecticut farm in 1754. The tale is an American success story—the saga of a poor New England plow-

boy who climbed to wealth and reputation in Europe and Americ
Horatio Alger's yarns are more prosaic than this life that spans thr
continents and the germinal decades of American history. This
a career that leads from the Colony of Connecticut to the Americ
Revolution. It is a tale that unfolds in London and Paris during t
French Revolution and continues among the Barbary pirates in A
giers during Washington's presidency. It is a life that touches si
nificantly the career of Robert Fulton and operates backstage in t
national capital of Jefferson and Madison, and finally it stops
midflight during one of the great tragedies of history—the shatte
ing winter retreat of the French army from Moscow.

Joel Barlow played a bit part in the same American drama th
featured the colossi of American history, and his rôle, while le
important, is nonetheless fascinating. Like a Franklin, he rose fro
a humble background to fortune through a canny New Englar
sense of how to turn a dollar. Like a Jefferson, he was a passiona
Republican and anti-Federalist in the early years of the Unit
States. And like both a Franklin and a Jefferson, he took all know
edge for his province, interested himself in science, patronized t
arts, and believed that one of man's first obligations was to do go
to his fellow men. But unlike his more illustrious countryme
Barlow's career covered more ground, touched at firsthand mo
history in the making, embraced a wider diversity of experienc
and suffered more failures. His tragedy and triumph lie in his ve
satility, for he was preacher of the Gospel, small-city lawyer, lar
salesman, shipping broker, political pamphleteer, confidant of pres
dents, diplomat, and finally (most significantly, he hoped) poet.

Barlow's hold on posterity customarily derives from his membe
ship in the circle of Connecticut Wits, that group of Yale graduat
who wrote satiric verse in Hartford immediately after the Revol
tion. But this base of his reputation is far too narrow. Barlo
himself is largely to blame if literary historians remember him d
risively as the last American poet rash enough to write an ep
poem. He placed an inflated value on his *Columbiad*, lavished gre
energy on it, and failed completely to realize that his humoro
Hasty Pudding alone gave him a chance to be remembered as
poet.

24

PROLOGUE

Barlow the poet was also Barlow the politician, and his reputation as versifier got mixed up with his reputation as pamphleteer. If the Republicans praised his poetry, the Federalists had to disparage it. The impossibility of separating the man from his poetry was a tribute to his importance as a political writer during the furious controversies of the early republic. In the perspective of a century and a half, however, we can see him as a minor poet and a major prose writer. We can also see this able man who never quite achieved real greatness as the progenitor of us all. As poet trying to articulate America's future importance, as cosmopolite trying to place his country in the world community, as enlightened defender of democracy, as promoter of cultural enterprises, and as businessman, Barlow mirrors most of the impulses and experiences that make up the United States.

CHAPTER I

The Foreground

1: *Antecedents and Early Education*

In 1754 the stolid yeomen farmers of Connecticut gave their loyalty
to the Puritan God and to King George. Already more than a century of history had been recorded since the first Englishmen appeared in the Connecticut River Valley. Only five years after
Governor Winthrop planted the Massachusetts Bay Colony, restless
immigrants from Massachusetts founded Hartford, Windsor, and
Wethersfield. And soon after that, other settlers landed at New
Haven. Long before the middle of the eighteenth century seacoast
villages and river valley towns had been consolidated into a single
administrative unit as the Colony of Connecticut under a charter
from Charles II. These hard-working farmers prospered, owned
their land in fee simple, and by midcentury had settled the entire
state.

The original theocratic nature of New England society in the
seventeenth century gradually relaxed, but in Connecticut the old-
time religion gave ground slowly. Just a decade before this story
begins a famous Connecticut boy, Jonathan Edwards, from his pulpit in near-by Northampton, Massachusetts, fired the valley with
new religious fervor in the Great Awakening. And in this year,
1754, Edwards published his most important work, a primary docu-

ment in Calvinist theology: *Freedom of Will*. The village churches, throughout the colony, enforced an austere discipline. They allowed no processions, lighted no candles, suffered no bishops, used no mitres, crucifixes, or censers. They uttered their prayers extempore, fearing an act of idolatry if they committed them to paper. They had no organs in the meetinghouse, used no music in their worship.

Yet the devil remained at work in New England, and man's sinful nature was hard to curb. Rustic New England customs like bundling existed side by side with the blue laws, and during the period of the Great Awakening, in one town at least, the incidence of shotgun marriages jumped alarmingly. In another village some sixty-six couples over a fourteen-year period confessed publicly to fornication before marriage. Despite the anguished outcries of Connecticut historians in the nineteenth century, the notorious Samuel Peters, the Tory clergyman who fled the state during the Revolution, was not writing fiction when he wrote his history of the colony and recited its blue laws.

In Connecticut church membership was a practical, though not legal, qualification for voting; adultery *could* be punished by death; Quakers were banished, whipped, or imprisoned; priests might be seized without a warrant by anyone. It was a statutory offense to woo a maid without her father's consent, and there was no drinking or sporting allowed from Saturday sunset until after the Sabbath. As time went on, many of these blue laws were more honored in the breach than the observance, but the laws on keeping the Sabbath, at least, grew stricter as the eighteenth century advanced. Moreover, when the statutes were revised as late as 1769 many parts of the harsh old code were retained. Yet the rigors of New England existence, or what seems rigorous to the twentieth century, were not apparent to the Connecticut farmers who tilled their rocky acres, raised their large families, and managed to enjoy simple, useful lives.

One of these farmers was Samuel Barlow, who bought one hundred and seventy acres in Redding about 1750 and settled there with his children and second wife, Esther Hull. Samuel was descended from John Barlow, who had come from England a hundred years before and bought land at near-by Fairfield. The Barlows were unpretentious folk in their first century in America and produced no scholars or statesmen. Samuel, like his forebears, farmed his hilly land modestly and did his part to populate Connecticut. Esther, a Redding girl, promptly added four sons and a daughter to the four children of her husband's first marriage, the next to last being Joel, who was born on March 24, 1754. Samuel did not give his son the advantage of starting life in a log cabin, but his clapboard, salt-box farmhouse stood amid scenery grand enough to inspire a poet and rocky enough to build character.

Redding, now a well-tended center of exurbia, lies inland about forty-five miles northeast of New York City. The township, which consists of Redding Center, West Redding, and Redding Ridge, escapes the endless antlike streams of motorists along the coastal Merritt Parkway. A pleasant place then and now, it drew Mark Twain there to live in his old age and retains today an unspoiled rural appearance. As part of Fairfield County, Redding sprawls across three long parallel ridges running roughly north and south. The glaciers of the ice age rounded off the hills and neatly plowed out the watercourses between them. Handsome stands of elm, maple, sycamore, and oak cover the uplands, while the Saugatuck River, the chief stream in the area, nourishes the bottom land.

Farming in Redding township today is a less serious occupation than it was in 1750 when Samuel Barlow settled his family on the westernmost ridge. As New England farmland goes, Samuel had a valuable piece of property worth even then about one thousand pounds. He probably planted thirty or forty acres in rye, oats, Indian corn, potatoes, and turnips, much of which he fed his family and livestock, and let the rest of his cleared land grow up in grass. Hay was a Connecticut farmer's chief cash crop and was sold loose from the barn or bailed for whatever city market could be reached most easily by water transportation. Only a few of Samuel's fields were more or less flat; the rest ran off into the hills, which provided abundant supplies of wood for all purposes. He fenced his land with stones rolled out of the fields, and plowed with both oxen and horses.

Life on a Connecticut farm a generation before the Revolution was healthful, active, and plain. Eight of Samuel Barlow's nine children grew to adulthood and survived their father, who lived to be sixty-three. There was always work to be done in those days of hand labor, and a farmer with one hundred and seventy acres needed plenty of strong sons to cultivate the land, feed the stock, harvest the crops, and chop the firewood. In return, the farm maintained its proprietors generously with dairy products, poultry, various grains, some fruits and vegetables. The diet and cooking were simple; salt was the chief condiment and molasses the main sweetening. Especially plentiful was that nutritious New England staple, made of Indian meal and served with milk—hasty pudding.

Young Joel Barlow's rôle in this scheme of farm life was for many years routine and unexceptional. He had few companions as a child, for only his brother Sam, two years older, was nearly enough his own age to be a playmate. Even Aaron, Sam's immediate predecessor and Joel's closest family tie in after years, was four years older. His half brothers and sister were mostly grown before he was breeched, but there was the incessant round of farm chores and never a shortage of appropriate tasks for a boy of any age. Joel later remembered:

> From morn to noon, from noon to night,
> I daily drove the plow,
> And foddered like an honest wight,
> Sheep, oxen, horse, and cow.

He might have added that he also had hoed and picked corn, dug potatoes, cut hay, milked the cows, and helped his father and brothers at slaughtering time.

Though New England farm life was narrow and the family self-sufficient, there was some social life. The Sunday visit to the village meetinghouse had its social overtones, for youngsters could not be compelled to ponder predestination rather than girls, even though they had to listen to endless sermons. Connecticut farm boys kissed their girls furtively among the corn rows while they gathered roasting ears, and in October after the creaking carts had dumped their loads of corn in the barns, both youths and maidens gathered for husking bees. Under the light of whaleoil lamps "brown, corn-fed nymphs and strong, hard-handed beaux" sat in circles about the grain to shuck corn and play post office. They husked energetically only until someone found a red ear. A lucky male then kissed all the girls; a lucky maiden had to walk blushingly around the circle to choose her particular youth. The girl who husked a smut ear, however, could whack the nearest boy over the head with it.

Joel Barlow's primary-school education and adolescent years may only be conjectured. He lived on his father's farm until he was nineteen and walked three miles twice a day to receive his early lessons in the Reverend Nathaniel Bartlett's village school. Parson Bartlett, the shepherd of the Redding flock, was a graduate of Yale, as were most of the Connecticut clergy at that time, and apparently he saw promise in Joel. Local tradition holds that Joel began spontaneously to write verse that excited the parson, who then determined that his pupil must go to college. Such may have been the case, but the decision that Samuel Barlow made to give one of his sons a higher education came late. Joel was no infant prodigy like another Connecticut poet, John Trumbull, who is supposed to have taken his entrance exams for Yale at the age of seven sitting on the president's knee.

Joel no doubt learned at the normal age to read, write, and cast sums. Then during the years that a boy normally goes to high school, he perhaps developed on his own a taste for books. Both his father and mother were literate and certainly possessed a Bible, catechism, and "other good books," as required by Connecticut law, but Joel's interest in letters must have been largely *sui generis*. If he wrote verse as a schoolboy, none of it has survived, but it took him only a year as Parson Bartlett's special student to prepare himself for an academy that would prepare him for college. This he did in 1772-1773, and when he was nineteen, he set off in the autumn on horseback with his father to enroll in school. His father had selected Moor's Indian School at Hanover, New Hampshire.

A journey of one hundred and eighty miles into the howling wilderness to attend a school founded to make educated Christians out of savages requires some explanation. The founder of the academy was the well-known Eleazar Wheelock, a Yale graduate and

Connecticut clergyman who earlier had opened a school for Indian youth in his native state. Success in his undertaking had led to fund-raising in England, a large gift of land in New Hampshire, and expansion of the project. Several years before the Barlows journeyed north, Wheelock had enlarged the scope of his Indian school and founded Dartmouth College.

A New England farmer's lack of ready money apparently had dictated this choice of schools, for Samuel Barlow was able to strike up a barter arrangement to pay for Joel's education. Wheelock's backwoods institution needed someone capable of "overseeing, superintending, and directing the affair of cooking for the college & school and managing the prudentials thereof," and Joel's father knew of a Fairfield woman, Elizabeth Burr, willing to take the place. Under the agreement struck up, as Wheelock's diary records, the elder Barlow was to hire and support the chief cook and housekeeper in return for Joel's room, board, and tuition. Joel was also to "officiate as a waiter on the table at mealtime . . . be at the beck of Miss Elizabeth . . . to perform such errands & incidental services as she shall have occasion for in her business."

The course of education charted hopefully in September grounded on an unexpected reef in December. After concluding his bargain with Wheelock, Samuel Barlow bade his son goodby and made the long trek back to Redding. It was the final parting between father and son, for three months later Samuel Barlow died. The boy learned of his loss about the same time that Hanover read the sobering news of the Boston Tea Party. The following March Miss Burr left her position in Hanover, ending the reciprocal trade of service for tuition, and Joel soon afterwards concluded his stay in New Hampshire. Before he left, however, he entered the freshman class at Dartmouth during the following August and began his college career.

Why Joel began college at Dartmouth and transferred to Yale three months later is not clear from the record. Apparently an infant college in a frontier town a long way from home did not suit his fancy, though it had been the best his father could afford, at least during his lifetime. After Samuel Barlow's death the probate court at Fairfield appointed Esther Barlow her son's guardian, and

under terms of the father's will Joel could receive his portion of the estate before his majority. "Whereas I expect my son Joel will have a liberal education and therefore may need his portion before he arrives to the age of twenty-one years," the will read, "my wish is that his portion of my estate be divided out to him at the discretion of the person that may be his guardian." Perhaps Joel persuaded his mother that he should go to Yale; perhaps it was her desire that he study nearer home.

In all events, Joel left Dartmouth in early November carrying with him a letter of recommendation from President Wheelock to President Daggett of Yale. It was patently untrue that Joel was leaving Hanover for the reason Wheelock cited in his letter: "By means of his father's death his outward circumstances are straitened." The fact was that his share of the estate came to about one hundred pounds, approximately enough to see him through to graduation, in either Dartmouth or Yale. Wheelock seems to have shed no tears over losing Joel, for though his recommendation was strong enough to get the boy into Yale, it was not enthusiastic. He spoke of his scholar's "sober, regular, and good behavior" while at Moor's School and Dartmouth but characterized him only as "a good genius & a middling scholar to be admitted by you into the freshman class if you shall judge his acquirements entitle him to it." And Wheelock concluded: "I hope he will be a comfort to you and an ornament to your seminary."

However it came about, Joel's decision to enter Yale was crucial. Redding had been a farming community with a limited horizon, and Hanover, even with its new college, was still a remote and isolated pioneer village. By modern criteria New Haven was a country town, but in 1774 it was the metropolis of Connecticut and by colonial standards a busy, cosmopolitan, thriving city. For the farm boy, it was a window on a larger world: an important seaport, a community of more than eight thousand persons, the seat of Yale College, and beyond question the intellectual center of Connecticut. Moreover, Joel arrived in New Haven as the Revolution boiled towards its beginning and the first Continental Congress was meeting in Philadelphia.

2: *College*

By 1774 Yale College, Connecticut's "great nurse of learning," had climbed dripping out of one slough of trouble but stood poised on the brink of another. Though it had already survived seventy-three years, the college not long before had floundered through hard times that reduced enrollments once to a mere forty students and the institution to near bankruptcy. Inept teaching, maladministration, and a musty curriculum resulted in a breakdown of discipline, a wave of student hell-raising, and a resistance to learning. Old graduates feared their alma mater was about to go under. The immediate future, moreover, held in store the dislocations, alarms, and problems of the Revolution. Even a dispersal of the college to places of safety would ultimately be necessary to weather the times. But during the lull of 1774, when Joel Barlow transferred from Dartmouth, the college was well attended and fairly prosperous.

Student life at Yale on the eve of the Revolution was infinitely more regimented and circumscribed than it is today. The college was an all-male community aiming at a kind of monastic life dedicated to learning. The authorities levied fines for a wide variety of disciplinary breaches, imposed daily prayers on their students, and enforced a regimen of early hours with few diversions. An undergraduate on a typical day of the academic year followed a schedule something like this: rise at 5:30; attend prayers and recitation lasting till 7:30; breakfast and walk if the weather is good till 8:15; study till 11; recite from 11 to 12; dine at 12; walk or take other exercise till 3; study again till 6; go to prayers and supper; spend evening in conversation; retire at 9. There was no organized extracurricular activity, except for two literary societies, and the only social function of the year occurred at commencement when the authorities allowed visiting, dancing, and fireworks.

The students slept and studied in their rooms in Old College or Connecticut Hall. They split their own wood, built their own fires, and slipped shivering in and out of doors to visit the pump or the necessary. Everyone ate in the commons from pewter utensils (students could not be trusted with glass or crockery) under the vigilant eyes of the tutors, who sat on daises to keep order. Before meals the cooks exacted menial service from undergraduates, such as shelling peas, but after eating, the students could gather in the buttery (the campus store), which occupied a first-floor room of Old College. For a century Yale appointed a college butler who dispensed the soft drinks of the eighteenth century—cider, beer, metheglin (fermented honey and water)—in an effort to keep undergraduates from drinking hard liquor in their rooms.

Repressing the animal spirits of one hundred and forty post-adolescents, however, was more than the faculty, which consisted of only two professors and five tutors, could accomplish perfectly. The existing records of faculty judgments abound in punishments meted out to high-spirited youths. Students were fined for pulling out the bung of a barrel of cider stored by an unpopular tutor in the cellar of Connecticut Hall. They were disciplined for upending the president's privy and for traveling to college on the Sabbath. They were rusticated for profanely mimicking the president as he conducted prayers in chapel. They were fined for stealing chickens from Widow Brochet's henhouse and being caught eating the loot in the dormitory. And one ebullient freshman who rang the chapel bell at nine p.m. was sentenced to "have his ears boxed by the president"—punishment that was administered promptly.

The curriculum at Yale, dry and narrow, aimed at turning out right-thinking, orthodox members of the New England community. Latin and Greek, not taught as literature but as language exercises, occupied an inordinate amount of the students' time. Undergraduates laboriously translated Cicero, Virgil, Horace, spent three years turning the New Testament from Greek into Latin, and parroted back their knowledge in perfunctory recitation. For all but the really inquiring minds this was dull business, pretty superficial, and conferred little lasting benefit. A good preparatory or high school today inculcates as much learning as Yale undergraduates obtained during their first three years. Students were not encouraged to browse in the library or read independently; in fact, the library was a rental collection beyond the means of many an indigent scholar.

In addition to the "tongues," as the classics were called, the course of study at Yale embraced a few other subjects. English composition had just barely infiltrated the curriculum. Mathematics and natural science held a secure place, though neither subject went much beyond the rudiments, and if a student managed to master algebra and geometry, he probably learned more than the average. By the time Barlow entered, the scientific side of the program had been greatly strengthened by the appointment of Nehemiah Strong, first professor of mathematics and natural philosophy. Theological instruction, of course, figured prominently in any Yale undergraduate's life. All students studied the Westminster Confession of Faith and recited their catechism. Freshmen and sophomores digested William Ames' *Medulla Theologiae* and juniors fed on Johannes Wollebius' *Compendium Theologiae Christianae*. The Yale faculty and corporation tried mightily to water their garden from the pure springs of Puritanism unpolluted by heresy.

Though the quality of instruction in the first three years was low, the last year was tough and challenging. The seniors devoted their efforts to metaphysical studies, using Locke's *Essay Concerning Human Understanding* as a basic text. God, the author of all knowledge, and scriptural revelation, of course, were not questioned, but Locke's system was drilled into students who thus learned to reason empirically. Besides Locke, Jonathan Edwards' *Freedom of Will* served as the text for theology, and William Wollaston's *The Religion of Nature Delineated* instilled proper moral philosophy. The books studied in the senior year were designed to stretch the student's mind, to make him think, but in no sense to shake him loose from the moorings of Connecticut conservatism and orthodoxy.

As Joel Barlow rode into New Haven on horseback that autumn day in 1774, his eye first caught sight of the slim spire of the new brick chapel rising one hundred and twenty-five feet above the college. This building, which also contained the library, was the newest and handsomest structure on the campus. As he drew closer, he also saw the huge, barnlike wooden hulk of Old College, a faded sky-blue building which rose three stories and a cupola above College Street. This antique, he was to learn, combined dormitory, assembly hall, and dining room. It also housed the college kitchen, which had been off-limits to students since the poison plot of '64 when an undergraduate introduced strong physic into the food. Old College would not last much longer, but it was supplemented by the comparatively new Connecticut Hall, built in 1752 and still standing. The chapel, Old College, and Connecticut Hall made up the entire physical plant of Yale College in 1774. In addition to the buildings, Barlow noted as he arrived, the campus and adjoining streets lacked shade trees. Yale would be dusty in summer, muddy in winter, but beyond the college lay the village green, larger than the school grounds and pretty even in November.

Despite the treeless campus, Barlow's first glimpse of the academic community was indelible. The newcomer saw President Daggett and Professor Strong passing down College Street garbed in black robes, white wigs, and high cocked hats. He saw tutors and graduate students crossing the campus in less pretentious silk gowns, but he noted that they were accorded much respect and addressed as "Sir." Most of the student body seemed to wear gowns when they appeared on the streets. But as Barlow crossed the college yard, he observed a group of plain young men dressed in ordinary clothes who seemed awed by the gentlemen in gowns. These turned out to be the freshmen, who could be sent on errands and assigned duties at any time by their lords, the sophomores. Barlow might have overheard this actual order: "Nevill, go to my room, middle story of Old College, No. ——, and take from it a pitcher, fill it from the pump, place it in my room, and stay there till I return."

Though the hazing by sophomores was a constant irritation to a freshman, the endless procession of rigorous college regulations probably seemed normal and endurable. The rules governing Dartmouth students had been strict and no doubt cast from the same mold; hence Barlow gave scant heed to the laws of decorum exacted by Yale. Rule number one was short and to the point: "If any scholar shall be guilty of blasphemy, cursing, robbery, fornication, forgery, or any such atrocious crime, he shall be immediately expelled." Number two threatened expulsion for denying holy writ or uttering heretical opinions. From that point on, the laws of the college proscribed and prescribed in minute detail, even to the extent of including a two-shilling fine for any student who should "make an indecent rout, tumult, noise, or hallowing . . . in the presence of the president or a tutor."

As soon as Barlow matriculated, he met an eloquent young man three years his senior, Joseph Buckminster, the newest tutor, who was assigned to instruct the freshman class. Buckminster became Barlow's close friend and encouraged him when he began to write poetry. Even after resigning his position later to accept a pastorate in New Hampshire, Buckminster kept track of his pupil with an enthusiastic, though didactic, correspondence. Because he stayed with the same class through most of its course, Buckminster deserves great credit for the success of the graduates of 1778. Barlow's class of thirty-five assayed high in distinguished judges, scholars, and statesmen. There were Noah Webster, America's schoolmaster and lexicographer; Oliver Wolcott, Secretary of the Treasury; Uriah Tracy, United States Senator; Josiah Meigs, President of the University of Georgia; Zephaniah Swift, Noah Smith, and Stephen Jacob, all supreme court justices in Connecticut and Vermont.

The rumblings of approaching revolution echoed in New Haven during Barlow's first year. The previous commencement audience had listened to a dialogue on "The Rights of America and the Unconstitutional Measures of the British Parliament," and in December some of the students voted to give up drinking tea to protest unfair duties. Soon afterwards the students organized a militia company, petitioned the town council for permission to store arms, and began drilling on the village green. When George Washington and his staff passed through New Haven en route to Boston, the entire community, town and gown, turned out. Part of the General's escort was the college militia company with Noah Webster at the head playing the flute. The *Connecticut Journal* reported that the "young gentlemen belonging to the seminary" made a handsome appearance and their "expertness in the military exercises gained them the approbation of the generals."

Even before General Washington visited New Haven, news of the Battle of Lexington, two days after the action, electrified the Yale undergraduates. Ebenezer Fitch, a sophomore, wrote in his diary that the "tidings of the battle . . . rendered it impossible for us to pursue our studies to any profit." His statement was literally true, for President Daggett had to dismiss the students the next day to begin their spring vacation two weeks early. When college convened again at the end of May, excitement still ran high. A junior who was rash enough to utter pro-British sentiments was publicly ostracized by the rest of the student body. Then came further sensational intelligence: superior British forces had overwhelmed the defenders of Bunker Hill in the war's first bloody engagement.

About this time Barlow sent off a message to his mother asking for money to pay his bills and discussing affairs at the college. It is his earliest extant manuscript:

> Yale College, 6th of July 1775
>
> HONORED MOTHER:
>
> . . . I have heard nothing from Aaron & Samuel [brothers in the army], nor from home. The students are sensably [*sic*] affected with the unhappy situation of publick affairs, which is a great hindrance to their studies; and for that reason there has been talk of dismissing college; but whether they will tis uncertain. . . .

The undergraduates were not sent home again till after commencement in early September, but nonetheless Barlow's freshman year ended abruptly. His letter home concluded with an ominous postscript: "If your circumstances are such as to want me at home, send a horse at any time & I shall be ready to come." His apprehension became fact sometime in August. The call came, and the young man rode home to the farm to see his mother for the last time. He had begun his first year away from home in New Hampshire with the death of his father, and he ended his freshman year at Yale with the loss of his mother. Esther Barlow died on the twenty-eighth at Redding in the fifty-fifth year of her life.

During September Barlow, as executor, settled his mother's estate, then in October returned to college for his sophomore year. Redding was unbearably lonesome that fall, for his older brothers, Nathaniel, Aaron, and Samuel, were in Canada with General Montgomery. Of his own brothers and sisters, only his little sister Huldah, who was fourteen, remained at home when his mother died.

It must have been a relief to plunge into another period of study at Yale, but Barlow's sophomore year of college was no less unsettled than the preceding one. Personal bereavement again, as well as the "unhappy situation of publick affairs," broke in upon his studies. In January Sam died at Poughkeepsie as he returned home from the unsuccessful Quebec assault that cost Montgomery's life. Some consolation perhaps was the public news two months later that the British had been forced to evacuate Boston.

Notwithstanding the intrusions of the year, Barlow began writing poetry as a Yale sophomore. His compositions have not survived, except for a prose outline and one line of a single poem, but he apparently celebrated in mock heroic verse, in the manner perhaps of Pope's *Rape of the Lock*, a snowball fight among Yale undergraduates. The poem derived its fun from the introduction of supernatural machinery, gods and goddesses of classic mythology who intervened on behalf of freshmen and sophomores. The only extant line is this:

And Jove descends in magazines of snow.

The loss of this imitation of the Queen Anne wits is certainly no cause for tears. But the verses are biographically significant because the ex-Redding plowboy very quickly made a name for himself as undergraduate poet. When his poems began attracting attention, he began to think he might win a reputation beyond the cloisters. Among students and faculty at Yale in 1776, there was plenty of encouragement for a novice poet, but there was no competent criticism.

3: *Paths of Glory*

Meanwhile, events of major importance were taking place in Philadelphia where the Second Continental Congress was assembled. During the winter Yale had read and applauded Tom Paine's *Common Sense*, but the sentiment in New Haven already was strong for independence. When Richard Henry Lee on behalf of the Virginia delegation moved in Congress that the united colonies are and ought to be free and independent states, the Yale community agreed wholeheartedly. The final draft of the Declaration, adopted in Philadelphia on July fourth, reached New England the next week. Ezra Stiles, soon to become president of Yale, wrote in his diary:

> This I read at Noon, & for the first time realized Independency. Thus the CONGRESS have tied a Gordian Knot which the Parliament will find they can neither cut, nor untie. The *thirteen united Colonies* now rise into an *Independent Republic*. . . . May the . . . Lord . . . shower down his Blessings upon it. . . . And have I lived to see such an important & astonishing Revolution?

Excitement over the Declaration soon was tempered with the ominous news of British movements. In the north, following the failure of Arnold and Montgomery to capture Quebec in December, the American forces had been falling back steadily. By June they were back to Crown Point on the west shore of Lake Champlain. There was rejoicing, however, when news circulated northward that Colonel Moultrie's makeshift fort of palmetto logs had thwarted British efforts to take Charleston, but this was the last good news for six months. The next report reaching Yale described the imminent danger of New York City from invasion. General Washington faced the impossible task of deploying about seventeen thousand men all the way from the present sites of Coney Island to Jersey City, from the Battery to the Bronx, to face the superior forces of General Howe on Staten Island.

Washington called for men, and in response Governor Trumbull of Connecticut issued a broadside proclamation on August twelfth. "Be roused therefore & alarmed to stand forth in our just and glorious cause," urged the governor's message, which further directed citizens to form themselves into companies. The proclamation, he declared, was to be their warrant. His call to arms coincided with the early dismissal of Yale because of the prevalence of "camp distemper," which threatened a typhoid epidemic in New Haven. Yale undergraduates and the entire state of Connecticut rallied to Trumbull's call. Somewhere among these marching men from Connecticut was Joel Barlow. The colonels of Connecticut militia received their orders about the fifteenth, and three days later several thousand men passed through New Haven en route to New York. West of the Connecticut River thousands more under the command of Oliver Wolcott, father of Barlow's Yale classmate, also marched toward New York. Unfortunately, the raw, half-trained militia that poured into the city two weeks before the Battle of Long Island provided unreliable support for General Washington's defenses.

As Barlow marched towards New York with the volunteers from Connecticut, Washington's army braced itself for the assault. On August twenty-second Howe landed twenty thousand men, including Hessian mercenaries, at Gravesend Bay and prepared to attack the fortifications commanded by Israel Putnam at Brooklyn Heights. Washington ferried additional militia across the East River to reenforce the Brooklyn garrison, but even so, the defenders were badly outnumbered, about two or three to one. The white tents of the British and Hessians dotted the plain for several miles between Gravesend Bay and the hills. For four days Howe's forces feinted and reconnoitered in preparation, but on the night of August twenty-sixth they moved north along four roads, three of which led directly towards the American positions.

The Battle of Long Island was lost before it began. The British Highland regiments moving along the coastal Gowanus Road and the Hessians on the direct Bedford and Flatbush roads made contact with the American defenses on the morning of the twenty-seventh. A sharp, evenly matched battle began on this sector. But hardly had the issue been joined before General Sullivan, who faced the Hessians, was attacked from the rear by a larger force than he was already fighting. Three divisions under Cornwallis, Clinton, and Percy had slipped through an undefended pass in the hills east of Brooklyn and in a brilliant maneuver turned the American flank. Meantime, Lord Stirling, who commanded the American troops defending the Gowanus Road, fought four hours, then also was attacked from the rear. The battle became a rout, and the only question that remained was how many Americans could escape from the trap to reach the fortifications. Several thousand succeeded, some across the exposed salt marshes, but the American casualties by late afternoon stood at two thousand men, killed, wounded, and captured, including two generals. How much action Barlow saw that day, the record does not say, but he was somewhere near the panicked events that cost the American army a humiliating defeat.

Fortunately, Howe did not follow up his victory by an immediate attack on the fortifications, and General Washington was able to evacuate his entire army from Brooklyn. During the night of the twenty-ninth he collected every boat, sloop, yacht, fishing smack, yawl, scow, and rowboat he could lay his hands on from the Battery to Hellsgate. These he manned with soldiers who were Marblehead and Gloucester fishermen in civilian life. By seven a.m. on the thirtieth the army had crossed to Manhattan without losing a man. Barlow's experience during the withdrawal was perhaps similar to this report of a fellow New England volunteer: "We were strictly enjoined not to speak, or even cough, while on the march. All orders were . . . communicated to the men in whispers. . . . We marched off in the same way that we had come. . . . Some were of the opinion that we were to endeavor to get . . . in the rear of the enemy." The scuttlebutt, of course, was wrong, and the account continues: "We marched on, however, until we arrived at the ferry, where we immediately embarked on board the batteaux, and were conveyed safely to New York, where we landed about three o'clock in the morning, nothing against our inclination."

During Barlow's next two months in the militia the American forces fell back slowly before Howe's armies. After offering unacceptable peace terms, the British took Manhattan in mid-September and faced Washington's army across the Harlem River. Although the Americans held strong positions, they could not prevent Howe's flanking them by sailing up the Hudson to attack from the rear. Washington was forced to withdraw well into Westchester County to find defensive positions he could hold effectively. On October twenty-eighth in the sharp engagement at Chatterton Hill, known as the Battle of White Plains, Howe found he could not dislodge the American defenders.

By the time the disastrous campaign of 1776 ended Joel Barlow had finished his brief military service. During the autumn retreat across New Jersey Barlow was back in New Haven beginning his junior year of college. When he marched from New Haven to New York in August, he may have intended to replace his brother Sam in the service of the United States, but sometime during Washington's slow withdrawal from Manhattan to White Plains he took sick and had to return home. Once out of the struggle, he remained out for four years to finish his college course and take a master's degree.

During the next year the Yale Corporation kept the college open with the greatest of difficulty. After having to raze part of decrepit Old College Hall, they packed the grumbling students four to a room in Connecticut Hall. As the Revolution inflated prices and disrupted the normal flow of food from farm to market, Yale authorities found it impossible to keep the commons dining hall open. Before the year ended, the ineffectual President Daggett gave up the struggle and resigned, and by spring the corporation had been forced to move the students from New Haven to Farmington, Glastonbury, and Wethersfield. With the classes dispersed the problem of feeding the undergraduates shrank to manageable size.

Barlow returned from the war something less than a docile undergraduate. He soon joined the student clamor over the scarcity and monotony of the food and helped speed the resignation of the unpopular Naphtali Daggett. He wrote a parody on the biblical book of Chronicles that delighted the students and exasperated the president:

1. And it came to pass on the third day of the tenth month, that there went forth a decree from Naphtali, the son of Zebulon, that all the captives throughout his dominion should depart for a little season, into the land of their nativity, to buy themselves some bread.

2. For it was so, that in the days of Naphtali, there was no bread in all that country round about, insomuch that there was a famine throughout all the land of Naphtali.

3. Now Naphtali was a great man and ate much bread, insomuch that the famine was very sore.

4. Moreover, there were beans in great abundance in that land; so that Naphtali said, peradventure my captives that are in this land will eat the beans thereof.

5. Howbeit, the captives were not accustomed to eat beans in their own country; therefore they murmured against the hand of their master, saying give us some bread to eat.

6. Wherefore Naphtali assembled all the sons of his captivity, and lifted up his voice in the midst of them, and said, O ye sons of my captivity, hear ye the words of Naphtali.

7. Forasmuch as the famine is sore in the land, insomuch there is hardly bread enough for me and my household:

8. Wherefore ye sons of the captivity of Naphtali, behold you may return to your houses in the land of your nativity, where ye can get some bread, lest ye die.

9. Nevertheless, when you shall hear the voice of my decree in the land of your fathers, saying unto you, return into the land of Naphtali.

10. Then it shall come to pass, that ye shall return and sojourn again in the land of captivity.

11. Thus was it done according to all the words of Naphtali.

January 16, 1777.

From the end of May until early September Barlow and the junior class boarded in Glastonbury, near Hartford, and pursued their studies under their tutor Joseph Buckminster. No doubt the rustication offered tranquility for study, but the students were restive under the dislocations of war. They did not like the crowded living conditions in Glastonbury and petitioned to be housed only two to a room the next year. As they began their senior year, however, the corporation ordered them back to New Haven to finish their course. Some of the students liked this move even less than staying at Glastonbury.

Barlow and four of his classmates rebelled. They refused to follow the corporation's order to return to New Haven and in complete defiance of the college laws took jobs teaching school. The corporation was obliged to meet in January and cite the five seniors for contempt before it broke the resistance. The recalcitrant five ultimately appeared for classes but not until January, and the entire class was dismissed a month later for a long vacation lasting until late June. When the class of 1778 graduated in July, they had barely completed four months of instruction as seniors, and Barlow plus the other dissident four had been in school only two months of that time.

The college's undisciplined drifting stopped abruptly in June when Ezra Stiles, one of Yale's great presidents, took office. As all four classes assembled in New Haven, undergraduate life returned to something like normal. Stiles took personal charge of the seniors' instruction, and the graduating class in turn requested the president to give them two recitations a day instead of the usual one. But only a month remained before graduation, too short a period to make up much of the lost time. The final year, normally the crucial one in the intellectual life of a Yale undergraduate, was for the class of 1778 a period of meager accomplishment. But on Wednesday, July twenty-second, Stiles' diary notes, the seniors finished volume two of Locke, and their wartime college course came to an end.

Senior exercises the following day mirrored the upturn of Yale's fortunes and the hopeful progress of the Revolution. The formal installation of Stiles in July occurred almost at the same time as the withdrawal of the British from Philadelphia and the arrival off New York of the French fleet. On the morning of the twenty-third the seniors stood their public examinations, "touching their knowledge and proficiency in the learned languages, the liberal arts and sciences, and other qualifications requisite for receiving a bachelor's degree." In the afternoon the president, fellows, tutors, students, and "other gentlemen of liberal education" met in the library for speaking and recitations. After Josiah Meigs delivered a learned Latin oration, Joel Barlow, the class poet, mounted the platform to read his first ambitious poem, "The Prospect of Peace." Stiles, in his customarily precise manner, records in his diary that Barlow's poem began at 3:59 p.m. and ended twelve minutes later.

Barlow was a good debater and no doubt rattled off his lines with a fine display of patriotic fervor to the warm applause of his listeners. A New Haven printer promptly thought enough of the poem to publish it in pamphlet form. But the performance is not very remarkable. Written in endless heroic couplets, it starts with America's struggle for independence and ends with a vision of the millennium—appropriately laid, of course, in the United States.

> Long has Columbia rung with dire alarms,
> While Freedom call'd her injur'd sons to arms,

begins Barlow, but the battle progresses successfully, "crowds of patriots bless the happy land," and peace lurks just over the horizon. Under the aegis of the "Church elect," meaning New England Congregationalism, he concludes:

> THEN love shall rule, and Innocence adore,
> Discord shall cease, and Tyrants be no more.

Commencement exercises at American colleges throughout the United States were producing these visionary poems, full of optimism and the idea of progress. In Barlow's case the poem anticipates another commencement poem he was asked to read at Yale three years later, and, following that, his pretentious long poems—the *Vision of Columbus* and the *Columbiad*. Poetically, he spent his career summing up the meaning of American experience and crystal-ball gazing into the future. When Barlow sent a copy of the poem to his former tutor Buckminster, that worthy man praised it extravagantly. He urged: "I advise you to encourage and cultivate your turn for poetry. I should think myself particularly honored if you will favor me with a view of some of your fugitive lucubrations."

After commencement Barlow returned home to await the formal awarding of diplomas at Yale in early September. He had traveled figuratively a long distance since entering college four years before, but his education was only beginning. One can see clearly in retrospect that Yale failed to anchor him in the harbor of Connecticut conservatism and orthodoxy. He somehow managed to begin the liberal education that his father's will planned for him. While most of his classmates remained New England conservatives and ardent Federalists, he was to move from Federalism to Jeffersonian liberalism, from Lockean empiricism to deism. He was to grow as a kind of political sport from Yale's educational garden. Perhaps because he missed important weeks of instruction during the times that tried men's souls, Yale influenced him less than it did Timothy Dwight and John Trumbull, two other Connecticut Wits who graduated before the war. Perhaps because he already had passed his twenty-second birthday by the summer he fought with Washington on Long Island, Yale molded him less than it did his classmate Noah Webster, who graduated at seventeen and never lost the orthodox Yale imprimatur. Perhaps because in the final analysis Barlow confronted life on a longer and more devious road than any of his classmates, his empiricism was tested far more widely.

CHAPTER II

Chaos and Order

1: *Young Man in Limbo*

Only a few careers were suitable for Yale graduates in 1778, and they were chiefly the learned professions. Therefore, Uriah Tracy and Zephaniah Swift studied law; Oliver Wolcott read law and served as aid to his father, the general; Josiah Meigs prepared to become a Yale tutor. Other members of the class entered the traditional vocation of the Yale alumnus, the ministry. Because an eighteenth-century college graduate was a gentleman and scholar, he was exempted by common consent from menial tasks. He was not likely to join the army unless he had a commission. Nor would he enter business unless he came from a mercantile family and planned to take over his father's responsibilities. The crafts and trades still recruited new blood via the ancient apprentice system. All of the acceptable occupations, therefore, demanded additional study or family connections. Noah Webster and Joel Barlow, both impecunious young men, chose the one respectable means of support immediately open to them: they became schoolmasters.

Four months after graduating, Barlow was teaching school in New Haven and hating it. He felt a little sorry for himself because the small patrimony that had seen him through college was gone and he was now on his own. He made a brave show of resolution when he wrote Webster in midwinter: "You and I are not the first men in the world that have broke loose from college without friends and without fortune to puff us into public notice. Let us show the world a few more examples of men standing upon their own merit and rising in spite of opposition." But he added that he was at a loss for a vocation and unhappy not knowing what he could or should do.

Barlow suffered from his hopeless ambition to be a poet. He aspired to write poetry for a living in an era when there was no profession of letters. He was born a hundred years too soon to live by writing, but even if he had lived in the twentieth century, he could have supported himself only as a prose writer. American poets frequently starve unless they combine writing with teaching school, practicing law, or selling insurance. Unfortunately for Barlow, his friends encouraged him incessantly to write poetry and pestered their friends to help him. One of his enthusiasts was David Humphreys, Washington's aide-de-camp and later Connecticut Wit, who wrote after meeting Barlow: "He is in reality one of the most considerable geniuses in poetry which we have ever had rise up amongst us." Humphreys even recorded this opinion publicly in his own inimitable verse:

> *Barlow* I saw, and here began
> My friendship for that spotless man;
> Whom, though the world does *not yet* know it,
> Great nature form'd her loftiest poet.

If Barlow wasted the months after graduation in futile efforts to write a poem beyond his capabilities, his well-meaning friends deserve some of the blame. He was an ambitious, eager young man who wanted to conquer the world, but his genius was neither poetic nor ready for the harvest.

When he quit teaching school in the winter of 1778-1779, he persuaded his older brother Nathaniel to stake him to another year at Yale. He planned to devote himself to study for a master's degree and to write poetry. The latter activity, rather than graduate work itself, sent him back to college. A graduate student had the run of the library without fee and paid no tuition; he had only to attend lectures and prayers and manage to pay his board. Barlow returned to Yale when the winter recess ended and immediately planned an epic poem.

What to write about, however, gave him a great deal of trouble. He outlined and wrote a few lines of an epic celebrating the exploits of Cyrus the Great before inspiration flagged and the vein petered out. Then his old tutor Buckminster suggested the story of Daniel, which for a moment he thought possible, but unfortunately Timothy Dwight's ponderous and still unpublished *Conquest of Canaan* already had pre-empted biblical subjects (with patriotic allegory) for American epic poets. The subject of Christianity itself, the Messiah, really was Barlow's first choice, but unfortunately again, Milton had beaten him to that. Finally he hit upon the subject of Columbus. In a letter to Buckminster written on March nineteenth he first broached the topic that was to occupy him for nearly thirty years: "The discovery of America made an important revolution in the history of mankind. It served the purpose of displaying knowledge, liberty, and religion . . . perhaps as much as any human transaction." This idea was the germ of the *Vision of Columbus* (1787) and the *Columbiad* (1807).

The enthusiasm of his friends kept Barlow in a state of anxiety for a full year after the plan for the great poem had been conceived. Dwight, who kept school in Northampton, invited him to be an usher there for the summer of 1779. Barlow was to work for his board while at the same time mapping out the epic under Dwight's critical eye. This he did, and during his brief stay in Massachusetts he made the first detailed plan of the *Vision of Columbus*. Others among Barlow's friends naïvely thought that businessmen could be persuaded to subsidize the poet while he wrote his epic, and they introduced him to John Perkins, Norwich merchant, and Titus Hosmer, Connecticut member of the Continental Congress. Perkins listened respectfully but declined to pay Barlow's bills. "Go into business for a living, and make poetry only an amusement for leisure hours," Perkins advised. Hosmer was sympathetic, so much so that Barlow later wrote an elegy on his death, but the great man also kept his strongbox locked.

The young man's friends sent him on one futile errand after another to seek a patron in Revolutionary America. He even made a trip to New London in a January snowstorm to talk to businessmen there, and he returned, as usual, empty-handed. He finally realized that American merchants could not be substituted for the noble lords who sometimes supported European poets. He wrote disgustedly after this journey: "The people of New London . . . attend more to commerce than any town in this state. This branch of business . . . leads the mind to a particular narrowness of thought. . . . The price of insurance and the property of a good sailing vessel are the usual topics." He compared New Londoners to Dutchmen, whose brains were "said to be too fat for the play of genius or refinement of taste."

As the year 1780 began, Barlow's hopes and prospects touched bottom. Another loan from his older brother was tiding him over the winter in his second year of graduate study, but he certainly could not ask Nathaniel to support him much longer. He tried therefore to get Ezra Stiles to appoint him tutor at Yale, but that possibility fizzled out leaving him despondent: "I have now got to the end of my line. . . . I have not a plan that will carry me an inch out of this town and know not which way to ride. I have nothing to go after, nobody to go to see and nothing to do." Some weeks later he declared: "I am as uncertain as ever where I shall spend the winter. . . . God knows . . . whether he intends I shall drag out a life of wretchedness or whether I shall return soon to the dust." And the next month: "Though the Devil is not allowed to afflict my body with disease, yet he is left to invade the more sovereign empire of the soul."

Depression, however, was never one of Barlow's problems for long, and even while he was feeling abandoned and forlorn, his spirits bounded back. He visited his classmate Mac Swift at Colchester and was cheered up by listening to his friend damn the world. Joel wrote to Wolcott after the visit with Swift: "He is the greatest misanthropist that ever lived and I am determined to love mankind if they kill me."

After two years of backing and filling, Barlow finally had to adopt a legitimate profession. Buckminster had urged him early in 1779 to enter the ministry. He would have time, argued the former tutor, to write poetry while carrying on his pastoral duties. Barlow replied that while he liked the study of theology, he could not see himself as a minister. He knew better than his friends what he was not suited for, and he was surely right in adding: "I can better serve mankind in some other way." A year after this exchange, however, the would-be poet was not quite so hard to please, and when he received a letter urging him to become an army chaplain, he suddenly was interested.

The correspondent was Abraham Baldwin, his graduate school roommate, who had left a Yale tutorship to join Washington's army. "Come and be chaplain to our other brigade," the letter urged, "for I have them both to preach to. . . . Depend upon it, there is not a situation in the army [that] would be more agreeable. . . . If you won't believe me, come and see." Baldwin's suggestion that a commission was ripe for the plucking now excited Barlow. When he answered that he would like to follow up the proposal, Baldwin was enthusiastic. "I will pull every string," he wrote, and at the same time he admonished his friend, as prospective clergyman, to "begin to put on the long face." Securing an appointment proved easy, though not in the same unit, and Barlow became chaplain of the Third Massachusetts Brigade.

Only one obstacle remained between Barlow and his new position: he was not a minister. It was true that he had studied theology at Yale, but his bachelor's degree was not a license to preach. He had to pass the critical eye of the ministerial association; yet he already had obtained the chaplaincy. The appointment was so easy to get that Barlow was embarrassed by the improper sequence of events. He cautioned Abraham Baldwin's sister Ruth: "Don't communicate a word, for the Association are not to know I have the offer (if I should have it), till I am done with them." The association, however, made no trouble, for after Barlow had crammed six weeks, he passed the test with ease. Ezra Stiles' diary for August fourteenth notes: "This day the special Association sat in the college library, called for examining Sir Barlow, whom they licensed as a candidate for the ministry." The blistering heat of that summer, which passed ninety-eight in New Haven on August sixth, was more rigorous than the examination. A few days later the Reverend Joel Barlow mounted his horse and rode off to camp.

2: *Chaplain*

West Point in 1780 was the anchor of General Washington's defensive lines flung out for forty miles along the Hudson River. On the present site of the United States Military Academy French engineers in 1778 had supervised construction of forts to guard the approach to upstate New York. Commanding a sharp bend in the river, where the Point and Constitution Island thrust out towards each other from opposite shores, the fortifications seemed impregnable. North of the Point the river widens, but downstream for several miles it narrows and slices through mountains, the highest being Bear Mountain, which rises thirteen hundred feet above the river. In New York City, fifty miles to the south, British troops were holed up as they had been ever since evacuating Philadelphia two years before. In July Benedict Arnold obtained command of West Point.

The Revolution by autumn had become a war of endurance, for neither Washington nor Clinton was sufficiently strong to dislodge the other. The addition of French sea and manpower to the patriot armies had made the war costly and burdensome to England, but like a bulldog the British hung grimly on to their colonies. The Continental Congress continued to dump printing-press money into an already inflated economy, Washington's soldiers grew poorer and poorer, and the speculators in Philadelphia and Boston privateered and profiteered. The outlook for the American cause was not black, but it was certainly a little gray. The Battle of Yorktown was still a year off.

The American army in September was stretched out parallel to the Hudson from Morristown, New Jersey, to Newburgh, New York. Washington's troops needed everything: shelter, clothes, food, weapons. Conditions never seemed to improve. Scarcely a week passed during the fall that the army did not go without meat

ne or two days. Food had to be wrung by threats of confiscation
om embittered farmers. Although the army supposedly had four
ounted regiments, most of its horses were widely scattered for
rage. Fortunately for the quartermaster, the winter of 1780-1781
as mild, but there was no end of trouble. On January third a
essenger from General Wayne galloped into Washington's head-
uarters at New Windsor to report that Pennsylvania troops had
utinied and were marching on Philadelphia.

Joel Barlow, chaplain of the Third Massachusetts Brigade, rode
is horse into camp near Hackensack on a rainy Saturday night,
eptember second. Too late to find indoor quarters, he crawled
ripping into a tent and slept on a wet bed of bark. The next day
e looked up Baldwin, whose regiment was stationed near by, and
e two friends agreed to bunk and mess together as long as their
nits were close. On Monday the army marched several miles to
aramus, repitched their tents, and Barlow and Baldwin found
uarters in a Dutchman's house. There Joel made ready to preach
is first sermon the next Sunday.

The duties of a chaplain in camp were anything but arduous. He
ad to preach one sermon on Sunday, conduct an occasional funeral,
nd perform a marriage ceremony once in a while. The rest of the
haplain's time was free for reading, writing, or visiting with officers
 his own or other regiments. Revolutionary War soldiers did not
ke their personal problems to the brigade chaplain for sympathy
 amateur psychiatric treatment. Barlow wrote home from camp:
After all my bad feelings I have certainly done right in coming
to the army. My duty is extremely easy and is not disagreeable;
ey certainly treat me with attention." He was writing, he said,
hile he sat snugly at the Dutchman's fireside with Baldwin snoring
eside him.

The two friends were not able to live together long, for the Third
assachusetts moved on the twenty-third to an old camp near the
udson, but the new living arrangements also pleased Barlow.
When Baldwin went into his general's mess, Barlow also joined his
wn commanding officer, Colonel Bailey, "a good, easy, sensible
an." After making the change, Joel wrote: "I have taken lodgings

55

in an old Dutchman's bedroom, as snug as a poker, and have as go
a study as ever lived." After still another move, he later wrote:
have the knack of turning Dutch folks out of their bedrooms—b
they love to oblige the *Domine*." And in the same letter: "A bea
tiful morning . . . I am just called up to a fine breakfast of but
and honey, which we generally have with our tea."

Outside the Dutch farmhouse lay the farmer's big barn that do
bled as meetinghouse for divine services on Sunday. On all si
soldiers of Washington's army camped, fourteen brigades in t
immediate vicinity of Barlow's quarters. "They don't make a b
figure," Barlow thought as he looked out of his study at the pleasa
countryside. His opinion was re-enforced a few hours later wh
commanding officers called out their men for a great parade of t
entire army. The chaplain turned out to watch the spectacle, whi
he reported, "was indeed *grand*."

On Sunday, the tenth, Barlow mounted the brigade pulpit f
the first time. Though his knees knocked a little, he opened
mouth wide and let fly a sermon that seemed to satisfy his listene
"I really did *well*, far beyond my expectations," he confided ir
letter home, "and I find it all a joke . . . 'to be in awe of sucl
thing as myself.' I now feel hearty and well, and begin to gr
fat and talk Dutch." The weekly sermons soon became routine, a
after the second performance, he wrote again: "Yesterday I h
another preachment, which kept me awake awhile—whether it h
the same effect upon others I am not certain." And the day bef
his third sermon, he was saying: "The worst difficulty is . . . S
bath days come rather too thick; there will be one upon my he
now before I finish this letter." Barlow's heart was not in his prea
ing, and except for special occasions, he conducted his duties p
functorily. One regimental surgeon who heard him make a pray
in public thought his performance "very ordinary." When t
surgeon commented on the prayer, he was told that Barlow "h
not been much accustomed to public performance, and that he w
more calculated to attain to eminence in the art of poetry, than
the clerical profession."

Funerals and weddings obtruded on the chaplain's reading a
writing only infrequently. Barlow's first funeral, which he attend

mourner, was the last rite for General Enoch Poor. The ceremony took place soon after Barlow joined his brigade and was conducted with great solemnity and military parade. All the officers
of the army, perhaps five hundred, with a regiment of infantry, a
regiment of dragoons, and a band playing the funeral dirge, marched
in the procession. At the head of the cortege walked the general's
horse saddled with the usual trappings and holsters, boots fitted into
the stirrups, but with no rider, "a perfect picture of bereavement."
Then followed the coffin with the general's sword and pistols attached, after which came the particular mourners, the regiments,
and finally at the end of the mile-long procession General Washington. In sharp contrast two weeks later was Barlow's first wedding, which he had to perform rather than witness. While he was
writing home, into his room in the Dutchman's farmhouse walked
a pair of folks requesting to be joined in matrimony. On talking
with them, Barlow realized that a preacher's lot is beset with problems: the couple had first laid eyes on each other only the day before. "But they will take no denial," he wrote; "they are here in
my study and I must link them, but I'll warrant them I'll not kiss
the bride."

Three weeks after Barlow joined the brigade, the treason of Benedict Arnold stunned General Washington's headquarters. Historians no longer think the loss of West Point might have cost
America victory, but one can imagine Washington's shock on discovering a traitor among the highest officers in his army. President
Lincoln might have felt the same emotion if General Grant had
been caught turning the national capital over to the Confederacy,
or General Eisenhower, too, if George Patton had offered to trade
the Third Army to Hitler for five million marks and a castle on the
Rhine. At the time, the treachery of Arnold seemed incredible and
potentially fatal. News of the capture of Major André and the escape of Arnold to the British warship *Vulture* anchored off Haver-
straw rocked all the brigades up and down the river. On October
first Barlow mounted his pulpit for the fourth time. "I gave them
a . . . flaming political sermon, occasioned by the treachery of
Arnold," he wrote. So much patriotic indignation was packed into
his sermon that news of it spread. During the following two weeks

57

"several gentlemen who did not hear it and some who did hav
been to read it; they talk of printing it." Barlow decided agains
publication, though he admitted it "would be sweet mortification
to my reverend fathers, the Association, to see their heretic so
given such applause." He did not want, he added, to be known a
a declaimer.

The day after delivering the sermon, Barlow rode to West Poin
to witness the execution of André. Almost all the general and field
officers, except Washington and his staff, he noted, were drawn up
on horseback around the gallows. The condemned man dressed in
full regimentals walked out of the stone guardhouse between two
subalterns. All eyes turned on André, but he betrayed no fear
smiled, and bowed at several men he knew. When he saw the gallows, he recoiled momentarily.

"Why this emotion, Sir," said an officer by his side.

"I am reconciled to my death, but I detest the mode," replied the
young British officer. He had requested to be shot, but General
Washington had refused to depart from the usual method of exe-
cuting spies.

When André reached the wagon drawn up under the gallows,
he hesitated a moment, swallowed hard, then climbed up. He immediately recovered his composure and said audibly: "It will be
but a momentary pang." Then he took off his hat and stock, band-
aged his own eyes. He worked with such firmness that he "melted
the hearts, and moistened the cheeks, not only of his servant, but of
the throng of spectators." Barlow, sitting among the crowd, reported that he was thrown into a flutter at the sight. The sobering
spectacle was soon over. André slipped the noose over his own
neck, adjusted it, and said: "I pray you to bear me witness that I
meet my fate like a brave man." The wagon was jerked away and
the spy died quickly. Summing up the experience that evening,
Barlow thought he had never seen "a politer gentleman or a greater
character of his age," who met his fate with such "an appearance
of philosophy and heroism."

Indelible experiences followed in quick succession during Barlow's first few weeks as chaplain. General Washington apparently

heard of the "flaming political sermon" against Arnold, for he soon sent the obscure new chaplain an invitation to dinner. Two weeks after riding to West Point to the execution, Barlow retraced his steps. "How do you think I felt," Joel wrote, "when the greatest man on earth placed me at his right hand, with Lord Stirling at his left, at table." Barlow returned grace and felt during the meal "perfectly easy & happy." The occasion was memorable. "There were many gentlemen there," he reported, one of whom was now his friend as well as Washington's aide. This was Colonel Humphreys, the man who thought Barlow was destined to be nature's "loftiest poet." After dinner Humphreys made his guest promise to lend him the plan of the *Vision of Columbus* and the completed first book to read at headquarters. Barlow rode back to his brigade that evening delighted with his situation and the vistas that opened before him.

The immediate vista was a place to spend the winter. About the first of November the army went into winter quarters, leaving Barlow free to spend the next seven months wherever he pleased. Weekly sermons to the troops between November and May formed no part of the chaplain's obligations. Hence he soon packed his saddlebags and departed for a round of visits in New Haven, Redding, and Litchfield. In January, 1781, he began drawing rations in Hartford, where he lived until time to return to camp at the end of May. For the next two years, except for a few excursions out of the orbit, he followed the same procedure: in camp from June through October, in Connecticut from November through May. In the third summer, 1783, he reported to camp for perhaps five weeks, then departed for good. Soon thereafter the army disbanded, the Revolution was over, the problems of independence had begun.

Any way one looks at Barlow's chaplaincy, the experience was easy, agreeable, and profitable. He probably did not preach more than three dozen sermons during the entire time he was with the Third Massachusetts Brigade, though he did supply an occasional pulpit back in Connecticut during the winter. He enjoyed congenial company among the officers of the army and a situation that was like a summer bivouac in a resort country. All the time he was

59

with the army the fighting was going on in the Carolinas and Vir
ginia. His pay, meantime, was a comfortable twenty-two pound
a month for twelve months a year, which allowing even for massive
inflation was more money to spend than he ever had possessed be
fore. This situation was a far cry from the abortive campaign o
1776 which ended in ignominious defeat and illness. It is no wonde
that Barlow was able in this period to write nearly six thousand line
of poetry and to get married.

3: *Courtship and Marriage*

When Joel Barlow tied his horse outside the president's office an
entered the Yale freshman class in 1774, he was a very rough dia
mond indeed. But the raw-boned Redding farm boy caught o
quickly. In addition to studying his catechism and translating clas
sic texts, he devoted a good deal of extracurricular activity to gal
lanting the girls about New Haven. He soon mastered the soft ar
of tea-table conversation and became something of a beau. His tal
ent for rhyming was no liability in this pursuit, for Connecticu
belles in the eighteenth century were especially susceptible to
neat heroic couplet. The young man from Redding, with seriou
address and newly acquired elegance, captured the hearts of at leas
three handsome girls: Betsy Stiles, daughter of the Yale president
Elizabeth Whitman, Connecticut poetess; and Ruth Baldwin, the
vivacious daughter of a blacksmith. Though Betsy Stiles placed
poor third in the contest for Joel's affections, the other two girl
were for a while serious rivals.

Elizabeth Whitman was an intellectual young woman whose life
ended tragically a decade after she met Joel Barlow. Her pitiful
story inspired a melodramatic novel illustrating the perils of seduc
tion and the faithlessness of men. Born in 1752 the great-grand
daughter of Solomon Stoddard (her father and Jonathan Edward
were cousins), Betsy Whitman came from an impeccable line o

New England divines. Her Puritan blueblood notwithstanding, by the time she entered Barlow's life, she already had become a sort of college widow. The family talent for rhyming had gone mostly to her cousin John Trumbull, and she was a poet of more aspiration than accomplishment. Betsy versified, however, with successive classes of Yale undergraduates and was one of the friends who encouraged Joel to run around Connecticut hunting a rich patron. She had been courted by two Yale tutors, Joseph Buckminster and Joseph Howe, but for some reason matrimony did not follow. Buckminster had moved to Portsmouth and Howe to Boston.

Ruth Baldwin is the heroine of this story, and a gay, loving, amiable lady she is. Robert Fulton, who sometimes squired her about when her husband was busy, affectionately named her "Ruthinda." Loyalty was perhaps her great trait, for she often sat like patience on a monument while her husband traipsed off to Paris, Algiers, or Poland on matters that did not include her. She frequently suffered poor health, and she bore no children, but survived her husband by six years. After twenty-nine years of marriage she advised her sister: "Precipitate yourself not into matrimony—few men are worthy the sacrifice of liberty, and all the evils they entrain upon us, poor women, so I think. Though I cannot complain for myself, having been more fortunate in my matrimony than most of my sex, yet *Love*, my sister, is a soft but delusive passion; trust it not. I have been its votary, and now know that it is not worth the pangs it costs." But she was hopelessly in love to the very end, and certainly would have married Joel again if she had lived her life over.

The Baldwin family provided its fair share of brains and talent for the American republic. Ruth's father, Michael Baldwin, was a blacksmith in Guilford, Connecticut, who believed in education and sent his boys to college. His son Abraham graduated from Yale in 1772, became a tutor, then a chaplain in Washington's army. After the war he left New England to practice law in Georgia, was instrumental in founding the state university, and later represented Georgia in both the Constitutional Convention and the Senate. Another of Michael's sons was Henry, who grew up to be an associate justice of the Supreme Court. Ruth was nineteen when her father moved his young second wife and family from Guilford to New Haven and settled on George Street opposite College Street.

After Joel Barlow graduated from Yale without family or influential friends, he moved his clothes and books from Connecticut Hall to board at Michael Baldwin's house. There, what probably had been a casual friendship with Ruth soon flamed into romance. Late in January, 1779, Joel wrote Noah Webster: "I move at present in as regular a sphere as if I was governed by Sir Isaac Newton's laws; my circuit is from New College to old [College?] and from old to Mr. Baldwin's, for study, school-keeping, and eating, all which movements are regularly pointed out by my inclinations, my poverty, and my appetite." He added, however, that there were eccentricities in his orbit: "I spend every evening in Ladies' company."

During the next week, however, his Newtonian movements stopped abruptly for reasons that can only be inferred. He carted his clothes back to the dormitory, moved in with Abraham Baldwin, and Ruth rode off for a visit in Guilford. Michael Baldwin may have banished his daughter and ordered the poor schoolmaster-poet out of his house. Certainly he disapproved heartily of Barlow as a prospective son-in-law. Apparently he aimed higher. But Ruth may have gone to visit friends because she was jealous of Betsy Whitman. Betsy, who now lived in Hartford, was making an extended visit to Betsy Stiles in New Haven. She also was making a stiff play for Joel. Whatever occurred, Joel wrote to Ruth on February eighth in the first of his letters to her that survive: "I have been informed that you are extremely happy at Guilford. This is more than I can say for myself. . . . My dear Ruthy, your generous nobleness of heart bids me impart my afflictions into the tender bosom of sympathy and tell you all my soul."

So far, an ingratiating, perhaps a penitent, letter, but then Ruth read on: "Betsy is gone. That dear assemblage of perfections, the joint partner with yourself of my tenderest love, was yesterday snatched from my heart, like the tender infant from the mother's arms." Joel may have thought he was being facetious, but the humor is labored and Ruth's reaction is not known. At any rate, she stayed in Guilford through April and let Joel ponder his situation. Soon he was writing: *"Do come home."*

At almost the same moment that Barlow was writing Ruth in Guilford, he also was writing Betsy in Hartford. His letters to Betsy do not exist, but her replies are extant. To his first letter she answered: "What shall I say to all the tender things it contains but that my heart beats in delightful unison to every tender sentiment." And her subsequent letters throughout the spring refer to "your last charming packet," "that benevolent heart of yours," and "so many soft things [we say] to each other." Joel, it seems, was wooing two girls at the same time. Ruthy, who was only ten miles away and a better psychologist, came back in April, took command of the field, and routed the opposition. She knew when to play hard to get, while Betsy Whitman, who already had lost two men, wrote one ardent letter after another.

Betsy Whitman wore her heart on her sleeve. "Dear Joel, I had like to have said jewel," she permitted herself in her first letter. In her second she declared: "O you are certainly the paragon of husbands. Were all married men like you, what a happy world for our sex!" This reference to her marriage to Joel startles one at first, but the allusion was part of an arcane joke: Joel and Betsy, poet and poetess, were partners at a party given by Betsy Stiles on Christmas Eve and during a parlor game were ordered to act for the rest of the evening as though they were married. They carried out the game with spirit, adopting the nine muses as their children. One can imagine how Ruth liked this! Betsy, for her part, tried to make the most of the trivial incident.

Barlow was genuinely attracted to the bright young lady who wrote poetry and praised his own verses, but Betsy's letters soon began to pall. Ten times she wrote him in the next three months, and every time she called him the best of husbands, referred to herself as the happiest of wives, or in some way carried on the stale jest. By June she was complaining of Joel's two months' silence, and after that the correspondence lags. At the end of the year Betsy's letters adopt the same friendly Platonic interest in Barlow's career that one finds in the letters of Wolcott or Webster.

Betsy Whitman's life for the next eight years after her affair with

Barlow may only be conjectured, but apparently she lived in Hartford with her mother and never married. Instead of remaining an
obscure spinster, however, she appeared once more briefly and
finally in New England annals. A strange woman calling herself
"Mrs. Walker" checked into the Bell Tavern in Danvers, Massachusetts, one day in late May or early June, 1788. She was large
with child and quite obviously alone in the world. Though she
claimed her husband would join her, he never appeared; and no one
but sentimental ladies who told this pitiful tale during the nineteenth century ever believed she actually was married. Late in July
Betsy Whitman gave birth to a stillborn child, contracted puerperal
fever, and died a week later, still alone and unidentified. Only a
notice in the public prints later established the connection between
Elizabeth Whitman and "Mrs. Walker."

Before Betsy Whitman died, she burned all her papers but one
letter addressed to her lover: "Must I die alone? . . . Why did you
leave me in such distress? . . . May God forgive in both what was
amiss." The story was not quite finished, for its melodrama was
made to order for fiction. Hannah Foster, a distant relative, who
was privy to the details, put Betsy Whitman, alias "Eliza Wharton,"
into *The Coquette* (1797), one of the earliest American novels.
Written in the tedious epistolary style of Samuel Richardson's
piously immoral romances, this tale offered a generation of readers
a titillating story of seduction and a Sunday-school tract on the
wages of sin.

In April, after Ruthy had been in Guilford two months, Joel was
ready to capitulate. His letters grew increasingly warm and impor-
tunate: "My lovely Ruthy: If you think of me as much as I do of
you, it will seem a little forever since my last letter. . . . I read your
letters and contemplate your perfections till I grow sick of myself
and despair of any merit myself unless it can be perceived from my
connection with you." By July when he passed through Hartford
and even was visiting the Whitmans, he wrote Ruthy: "I am as far
off as Hartford and cannot go a step farther without sending back
a piece of my soul."

His letters became ever more affectionate and intimate as the months passed. In November he wrote Ruth one Sunday morning while her brother Dudley, who had spent the night with him, lay in bed "snoring away the dregs of Sallyism." Joel got up early to "catch the unsullied inspiration of a few morning thoughts and transcribe them to my Ruthy." On another occasion, apparently after an evening with Ruth, he reported: "In pulling off my cloak last night, down dropt a little bright piece of love and sparkled along the moonshine on the floor, as if it would wake up all the family." The same letter ends with high optimism: "I feel like an emperor, happy and clever."

Barlow reached this euphoric plateau about the time the fog began lifting from his prospects. The date on which he and Ruth became engaged cannot be determined because there was no formal betrothal. Michael Baldwin did not want his daughter to marry Barlow, and since, theoretically, Connecticut law still made wooing a maid without her father's consent a misdemeanor, the courtship had to be conducted discreetly. In the same letter that Joel reported success in obtaining his chaplaincy he confidently linked his future with Ruth's: "Every moment that you lose of the present unenjoyed, or soured away with unavailing trouble, is so much lost out of life. . . . You know, my Ruthy, that my plans are large. I want yours to be projected upon the same scale and blended with my own." In the following months he wrote cheerful accounts of his army life and continued to plan for a future with Ruth.

As the military separation lengthened into weeks, however, a note of deepening anxiety crept into his letters. On one occasion, after Ruth had implied that Joel doubted her constancy, he wrote: "I know your heart and soul are mine. I would risk anything short of my eternal salvation upon your love." In another letter he raged at the double life their secret engagement necessitated: "Your present situation is groveling; it is abject; it is wretched. This afternoon I have opened all my soul to Abraham upon the subject." Michael Baldwin no doubt suspected the seriousness of his daughter's romance, but a simple blacksmith by trade, he was ill-equipped to cope with a grown daughter in love. If he was urging her to accept a suitor of his own choosing, he found he could not put her heart on his anvil and pound it as he pleased. Moreover, the old man's second wife, Theodora, just ten years older than Ruth, was still having babies, and Ruth perhaps found herself saddled with nursery chores in a hostile surrounding.

Joel's long talk with Ruth's brother convinced him that it was necessary to get Ruth away from home. Abraham promised to see that she was placed in an "eligible situation." If this cannot be accomplished, declared Joel, "I am determined on one of the three things which I mentioned to you." What these three things were he did not repeat, but he wanted her away from New Haven for longer than the winter, a year or two, because "the war and my own plans will keep me unsettled for some time." It is apparent that he did not plan marriage until he could appear before Michael Baldwin as an acceptable candidate.

When the army went into winter quarters in November and Joel returned to Connecticut, he thought Ruth's problem could be worked out satisfactorily. He wrote her for the last time from camp in a romantic outburst. She was virtuous, she was lovely, and he knew that she was wholly his: "When I speak to you I but speak to my own heart. What in me is wrong you can reclaim; what is lovely you can adorn; what is uncouth you can polish; what is fickle you can steady; what is trifling you can dignify; what is gloomy you can smile away." But there were shoals ahead for the lovers, as Joel found out when he reached New Haven. The plans hopefully talked out with Abraham in October went awry, and in December Joel left Ruth "in tears in the little chamber." As he departed to "pass a long winter at a frozen distance from the dearest object under heaven," he counseled: "Be resigned, my dear, to this necessary evil [separation?], and be assured that my attachment to you is inviolably increasing."

Details of the next four weeks are totally lacking, but the plain fact is a matter of record. In January, 1781, Ruth traveled to Kensington, near Hartford, to visit friends, the Reverend Benoni Upson and his family. Joel met her there and on the twenty-sixth their host married them. The newlyweds perhaps spent a few days together, but by February eleventh, they were separated once more, Joel in Hartford and Ruth in Kensington where she remained for the winter. Kensington, however, was only a few hours by horseback from Hartford, just far enough away to keep the marriage secret.

What began in deception and subterfuge ripened into an ideal marriage that lasted thirty-one years. Joel and Ruth took each other for richer and for poorer and lived both in poverty and in wealth. They clung to each other in sickness and in health and were a faithful, devoted couple till death parted them. They loved each other with as strong a passion at fifty-five as at twenty-seven and exchanged love letters till the day Joel died in southern Poland. The last thing Joel ever wrote was a letter to Ruth from Warsaw on December 17, 1812, reporting that tomorrow he would "fly back to the one that is more lovely & more divine, more every way endearing—who to me is all that was & is & is to come."

During the first spring and summer of the secret marriage Ruth was supremely happy. Her earliest surviving letter, written after Barlow recovered from a fever in camp, is testimony:

> *You dearest of men, how much* you endured whilst your thoughtless Ruthy, unconscious of your afflictions, was gallanted round, gaily taking her pleasure. . . . You are the tenderest & best of *Lovers*. Certainly I am a fortunate girl in getting so *good a sweetheart*, one that will make me forever happy. I know the Ladies all think so; they all love you. . . . Betsy Whitman, Chauncey & Polly say we must marry this commencement. . . . What do you think of it, my dear? . . . Perhaps I shall get a better husband than you would make, and perhaps you may suit yourself better!

An elopement against the wishes of Ruth's father was a desperate remedy for a situation that only seemed desperate. That a Connecticut clergyman would be a party to such an act is surprising, but nonetheless the Reverend Mr. Upson performed the rite and was enjoined to secrecy. For a year the wedding was successfully concealed. Not even brother Abraham was taken into the couple's confidence. When he heard of it the next January, he wrote his sister for confirmation, not without a trace of annoyance: "Do you think I could believe it?" But he concluded: "If you were suited it would ill become me to grumble at any thing which you supposed would be conducive to the happiness of so dear friends."

Two months later Joel had to defend before old Michael Baldwin his indefensible act.

Ruth, on whom the burden of deception weighed heavily, grew increasingly restive as the months passed. During the second winter of their marriage, while Joel lived with his brother in Redding and worked furiously on his poem, Ruth longed to join her husband. Joel was hard put to keep up her spirits: "You are a sweet girl to temper so much tenderness with so much resolution, which enables you to breathe such ardent raptures of impatience to leap into the arms of him you love. . . . Think not that he (Joel) is a stranger to the heart-rending conflict of *love* & *appearances* which necessity has imposed upon us." For Ruth, at least, the end of the subterfuge came as a welcome relief.

Between the time Abraham heard the news and Michael Baldwin was informed, Joel traveled to New Haven to prepare the ground for the inevitable recognition scene. He preached a sermon in the college chapel for which he received six dollars, then called on Ruth's father, though not to confess the elopement. "I had a very clever confab with the old Dadda," Joel wrote at midnight; "he feels well & I believe is proud of me." His son-in-law's analysis was correct, for old Michael had been favorably impressed the preceding September when Joel preached in the Yale chapel, read publicly another ambitious poem, and received his master's degree. He even had been elected a tutor, but the appointment had come a year too late when he no longer wanted or needed it.

A few days after this interview Joel found to his chagrin that the marriage was fast becoming common knowledge. He then was in Hartford and unable to confront his father-in-law in person. On March 9, 1782, he wrote Ruth to explain his action: "Our marriage is known here & at N. Haven by everybody, so that I knew it must get to the old gentleman's ears before I got home, & concluded it would be best for Dudley or Prom [Abraham] to tell him." The task was performed by Dudley, who reported that Michael was "much displeased"—no doubt a large understatement. However continued Joel, the old gentleman says that since "we acted without his knowledge or consent . . . we may go on as we have begun [and] he shall give himself no trouble about us."

Once Dudley had told Ruth's father, Joel postponed the unpleasant duty of calling on Michael immediately. He went directly back to Redding and wrote an explanation:

> From my first acquaintance with your daughter she appeared to me the only person that could make me happy; my situation in life, as it appeared to others, was then unpromising . . . and I was repeatedly told that the connection would be disagreeable to you. . . . To crowd himself into a family is what no Gentleman of my feelings ever will do; but to take a daughter from any family upon the principle of mutual affection is a right always given by the God of nature wherever he has given that affection . . . we have been married more than a year. My affairs are now in a good situation; I think they will enable me to maintain a family.

The old blacksmith realized that the deed had been done and submitted to it with good common sense. Though he was no match for Barlow's dialectic, he must have marveled at his clergyman son-in-law's ingenious apologia that defended the elopement on grounds of natural right and named God as co-conspirator.

Once the news was out, the Barlows finally could make plans to set up housekeeping. Joel began addressing his letters to "Mrs. Ruthy Barlow" and hunting for a house to rent for the next winter. Abraham, meantime, talked his father out of his injured feelings, assured the old man that Joel was properly contrite, and prepared the way for a reconciliation before Barlow left for camp. Prom wrote: " 'Well,' says the old gentleman, 'Repentance is the only cure for a fault.' " Joel then spent most of April and May in New Haven, after which he rejoined his brigade for the summer season. When the army went into winter quarters again, the Barlows would begin a five-year sojourn in Hartford.

While they waited to move to Hartford, Ruth became a summer camp follower. At the end of May, 1782, she rode with her husband as far as Ridgefield, which was about twenty-five miles from Joel's summer quarters on the east bank of the Hudson a little below West Point. At Ridgefield she unpacked for a long visit with the Bradleys, cousins of Joel's, and her husband went on to camp. During the summer she often saw Joel, who rode over to Colonel Bradley's after preaching his weekly sermon. In July she made a visit to camp and found her husband comfortably housed at Mr. Mandeville's, the same place in which he had convalesced after his illness the summer before.

Lack of military activity in camp that summer was offset by elaborate ceremonies designed to break the monotony of garrison life. Joel arrived at West Point just in time for the grand *"Dauphinade"* celebrating the birth of Louis XVI's son. The extravagant decorations for the event, wrote Barlow, "exceeded all description." A building nearly two hundred feet long supported by columns in the form of palm trees was built for the occasion. The saloon was surrounded by a peristyle of doric columns, and everywhere were garlands of cedar and yew and hanging medallions emblematic of the Franco-American alliance. With latent irony the entablature at either end of the pavillion bore inscriptions twenty-five feet long proclaiming: "LONG LIVE THE DAUPHIN OF FRANCE . . . INDEPENDENCE, PEACE, AND PERPETUAL ALLIANCE." Later in the season Ruth was in camp for the next festivity that punctuated the summer doldrums, the observance of the Fourth of July. While it was not so gala an occasion as the Dauphin's birthday party, it was nevertheless a good excuse to hoist innumerable toasts to Independence, France, Washington, Louis XVI, Lafayette, General Greene, and others.

Joel was in high good humor all that summer. He could enjoy the tender pleasures of his delayed honeymoon, in Ridgefield or under a shady tree outside Mandeville's house, without any twinge of conscience that he was neglecting his army duty. "Nothing is talked of here but a speedy peace which I am fully confident will take place," he wrote in August. He had seen the preliminary outline of terms proposed by Britain and had inhaled the general optimism pervading camp. So carefree was he that in July the loss of his sorrel mare scarcely disturbed him and he versified his notice of the horse's disappearance:

> Stray'd from West Point the Lord knows where
> A tall, bright-sorrel, bold fac'd mare;
> I say she's tall, although I fancy
> She's not much more than fifteen hands high,

With four white feet all shod at bottom,
And ne'er when spurr'd declines to trot 'em,
Unless in haste for bet or banter,
She'll sometimes run & sometimes canter;
But though a trotter & a racer,
She's no old puritanic pacer. . . .

Whether or not he got his horse back, the deponent sayeth not, but the pleasant summer lapsed gradually into fall without further incident.

When the army went into winter quarters for the last time, the Barlows began keeping house in Hartford. In preparation for this event, Joel rode to Philadelphia at the end of October to enlist support for the publication of his poem. A month later he headed north elated at his success. He wrote Ruth "to spare no necessary cost in furnishing" and authorized her to "run into debt as much as you please," to which he added: "If I cannot pay it, I will advertise you: 'Whereas my wife &c.'" This hopeful letter ended by reporting the recent birth of a friend's baby and suggesting to Ruth—"an example for some folks."

CHAPTER III

Poet, Lawyer, and Connecticut Wit

1: *Postwar Preparations*

In the 1780's Brissot de Warville, the French Revolutionary leader, called Hartford and environs the "Paradise of the United States." He reported that the approach to Hartford displayed a charming cultivated country, neat elegant houses, vast meadows covered with herds of cattle of enormous size, sheeps, hogs, geese, turkeys in great abundance. "There is here more equality, less misery, more of everything which constitutes republicanism," he discovered. The town itself was an overgrown country village where most of the inhabitants were supported by agriculture. To Brissot the Connecticut Valley above and below Hartford seemed more like a continuous village than a region punctuated by urban centers. The old paper mills and glass factories and the other newer industries did not disturb the rural appearance of the town. The first bridge across the Connecticut River would not be built for a generation.

When the Revolution ended, Hartford was not yet a city, but the Peace of Paris injected a new vigor into the town's blood stream. Hartford incorporated in 1784, and in the same year the new city council voted to have the streets named and the houses numbered. The population by then had reached about fifty-five hundred, though near-by Wethersfield, noted for its pretty girls

72

and onions, was almost as large. Manufactures were springing up, and a building boom advertised the community's general prosperity. The city stood on a navigable river that provided easy water transportation to Long Island Sound. But Hartford was not yet the insurance capital it later became, and it had to share the political capital with New Haven for almost another century.

The Revolution brought significant changes to the social mores of Hartford and other Connecticut cities. Oldsters who had grown up under the post-Puritan dispensation worried about youth and juvenile delinquency and shook their heads over what seemed flagrant disregard for the old laws. The younger generation went to sleep in meeting, took part in public lotteries, speculated in land, played billiards and cards, and went dancing. Although there was no regular theater in Hartford until 1794, strolling players and performers visited the city in the previous decade. When a Mr. Griffiths of New York opened the first dancing school in Hartford in 1787, he quickly drew ninety pupils eager to learn four kinds of minuets and the hornpipe. Mary Anne Wolcott wrote her brother at Yale the year before that she had been dancing all morning and planned to dance again all evening. Christmas was not yet celebrated as a holiday, but the Fourth of July and Election Day were occasions for lavish partying.

The social life in Hartford, Brissot reported, was the most agreeable in all Connecticut, and the girls throughout the state simply charmed him. "At their balls during the winter," he wrote, "it is not rare to see an hundred charming girls, adorned with those brilliant complexions seldom met with in journeying to the South, and dressed in elegant simplicity." The beauty of Connecticut belles dazzled the Frenchman, and the girls' lack of inhibitions with strangers, in contrast with heavily chaperoned French maidens, made him marvel. On the road he met good-looking Connecticut girls traveling alone on horseback "galloping boldly; with an elegant hat on the head, a white apron, and a calico gown. . . . You see them hazarding themselves alone, without protectors, in the public stages . . . a stranger takes them by the hand, and laughs with them, and they are not offended at it." The Barlows settled in Hartford because they liked the people there. It was Noah Webster's home town; Oliver Wolcott worked for the state government; John Trumbull, the poet, lived there; so did the Whitmans.

By New Year's Day, 1783, the Barlows were comfortably settled in the Connecticut capital, and Joel was hard at the business of revising, emending, polishing, and rewriting the *Vision of Columbus*. This poem already had been a major preoccupation for four years, ever since he had hit upon the idea of Columbus as the subject for an American epic poem. He had worked up the outline while an usher at Timothy Dwight's school in Northampton and written part of it, Book I, even before being commissioned a chaplain in the army. The plan for an epic, in time, had evolved into something a little different, a visionary poem in which Barlow could recount the deeds of Columbus, describe the growth of America, peer into the New World's future, and incorporate in the narrative a vein of philosophy.

Barlow was never dedicated to the ministry, as we have seen, for he regarded his chaplaincy only as a means to an end. He was not so much interested in saving souls as in saving money to finance his writing. There is no evidence that he ever preached another sermon after the army disbanded, though his relations with the Connecticut clergy remained cordial. Accordingly, he spent the leisure months of his military service deep in the throes of poetical composition. During the winter of 1780-1781 in Hartford he had written seven hundred lines, most of Book IX, but his greatest burst of creative energy came after marriage. During the succeeding winter when he had lived in Redding with his brother, he had poured out an enormous surge of verse. Between December and May he produced about four thousand lines, so that when he reached Hartford at the end of 1782 he had completed approximately four-fifths of the opus. From the beginning of 1783 until spring, 1784, he plugged steadily away at the poem and dreamed of fame. His army wages, which ended when the troops were dismissed, paid for nearly a year of additional literary activity.

Long before the poem was finished, Barlow had staged a preview for his friends. The occasion was the Yale graduation exercises of 1781, the first public commencement held in seven years, when

Barlow, Wolcott, Webster, and others had received their master's degrees. When Barlow was asked to recite a poem, he obliged by reading snippets from the long poem in progress. He warmed up with some flattering remarks about Yale, then plunged into a prophecy of America's postwar march towards the millennium. The brave new world, he forecast, was to be achieved through the shaping influence of a great new literature. His lines, which showed improvement over the commencement poem of 1778, were appropriate for an occasion that anticipated Cornwallis' defeat the next month and the early successful conclusion of hostilities.

Barlow, however, still was not receiving good criticism—only praise. In reporting the commencement exercises, Ezra Stiles made an unusual note of the poet's success by recording in his diary: "Mr. Barlow was clapped." The following April Stiles read in manuscript the eight books of the poem then completed and registered approval by copying half a dozen lines into his journal. Even more flattering were Barlow's contemporaries, especially David Humphreys, who poetized:

> Rous'd at the thought, by vast ideas fir'd,
> His breath enraptured, and his tongue inspir'd,
> Another bard, in conscious genius bold,
> Now sings the new world happier than the old.

In the face of vast uncritical enthusiasm Barlow's innate good sense alone kept him from becoming an insufferable egotist.

The primitive state of book publishing in eighteenth-century America provided impossible difficulties for an author. A poor young man with a manuscript had two undesirable alternatives: he could find a rich patron to pay his board, room, and printing bills; or he could secure mass patronage by means of the subscription list. In the absence of established publishers, royalty arrangements, copyright laws, and distribution channels, books were a precarious commodity. Newspaper editors who owned printing shops often doubled as book publishers, but they knew that the total reading public was small and that any successful book could be pirated safely. Barlow already had tried unsuccessfully to find a rich patron. He next fell back on the subscription list.

When his poem was four-fifths completed, Barlow set out to get subscribers. In September, 1782, Colonel Humphreys wrote General Greene, who commanded the army in the South, that the "great Poetical Work . . . is now nearly compleated, & will be ready for publication in the course of the Winter or Spring." He wrote "to solicit in the most earnest manner your patronage & protection of the Work." What Humphreys and Barlow hoped to obtain was Greene's help in passing around a subscription list in the South. But this hope was stillborn, for no more than a handful of Southerners ever ordered the poem. If the reading public in the North was small, in the South it was infinitesimal.

Barlow next visited Philadelphia to drum up interest in his poem. As the seat of the Continental Congress and nerve center of the war effort, Philadelphia seemed an obvious place to obtain subscriptions. Armed with letters of introduction, he set off on October 29, 1782, with General Benjamin Lincoln, the Secretary of War, and John Pierce, Paymaster General. Barlow, who always loved to travel, never had been south of New York or west of the army camps along the Hudson River, and the ride through New Jersey via Newark, New Brunswick, Princeton, and Trenton delighted him. The company of General Lincoln, with whom he held "very learned disputes," was equally enchanting. When he gazed across the Delaware River from King's Ferry, Philadelphia beckoned invitingly.

For a month Barlow promoted his poem and enjoyed the social life of Philadelphia. He used his fifteen letters of introduction to good advantage and reported to Ruth: "My reception here is quite as favorable as I ever expected. I am treated with civility by the great, with formality by the many, and with friendship by the few." He never had seen such a cosmopolitan place as Philadelphia, and he marveled at the night life: "They have a strange knack of turning day to night, and the contrary. It is common in splendid entertainments not to sit down to dinner till candlelighting." But even so, he felt that Philadelphia was not nearly so extravagant, haughty, or idle as folks back in Connecticut were inclined to think.

By November twelfth Barlow was sure his trip was succeeding magnificently. He now told Ruth that "my reception is flattering beyond our expectations." Not only the gentlemen to whom he had letters were showing interest in his project, but "many others of the first and greatest character, offer the matter the warmest encouragement, and think that they and their country will be more indebted to me than I to them." Three days later the visit came to a great climax when Barlow talked to the Chevalier de la Luzerne, the French minister to the United States. Barlow had hatched the notion of dedicating his poem to Louis XVI and wrote Ruth that night in high spirits: "I have this day finished my business with him according to my old romantic wishes which you used to laugh at. He promises to promote the subscription here; he has taken a paper to send to France & will procure permission for the Dedication." The French minister also offered to send Benjamin Franklin a subscription paper.

Not even Ruth's failure to write during Joel's first three weeks in Philadelphia dampened his spirits. He punished her by inventing a black-eyed Quaker girl with ten thousand pounds who had bewitched him enough "to cancel all former obligations." Then he added that he was sending a box by Charles Hopkins containing muff and tippet, four yards of satin, eight yards of lace, mitts, silk handkerchief, and three half joes (twenty-four dollars) sewed in a glove. Ruth, he concluded, might give Charles "one kiss for bringing your box." He expected to be home in early December determined to work like a sprite all winter getting the poem ready for publication.

Even Barlow's congenial optimism might have been shaken if he had known on his ride north from Philadelphia that his poem still was four years from publication. The book eventually appeared and was a financial as well as critical success, but not until 1787, and then the thousands of subscribers who seemed eager to buy the poem in 1782 had shrunk to less than eleven hundred. After two more winters of labor on the poem and the exhaustion of his army stipend, Barlow had to find a more practical way to support Ruth and himself.

On Monday morning, July 12, 1784, people in Hartford began reading a new weekly newspaper, *The American Mercury*. The proprietors of the paper, who had set up shop near the State House, promised in their prospectus to "furnish a useful and elegant entertainment for the different classes of their customers"; and in a later issue they further observed that the "circulation of printed papers is not only one of the greatest blessings of freedom, but it is among the principal means of preserving it." The paper would be a four-page sheet, printed from an "elegant new type," which would be delivered to subscribers at eight shillings the year, one half to be paid in advance. The paper would offer readers, besides news, public announcements, and future acts of the legislature, a serialization of Captain Cook's latest voyage, which could not be bought in book form for less than four dollars. The publishers of the new enterprise were Elisha Babcock, a Springfield printer, and Joel Barlow, ex-minister.

Not only did Barlow and Babcock plan to issue a weekly paper, but also they set up a partnership for printing and publishing, selling books, stationery, and groceries. Babcock, who was a journeyman printer, was to supply the mechanical skill for the firm; Barlow was to write for the paper, bring in business, and lend the enterprise the prestige of his Yale connections and poetic reputation. The venture was a success from the start, for nine weeks after the first issue the editors reported that despite continually increasing press runs, they could not keep up with demand. The initial success of the paper was chiefly due to the serialization of Captain Cook's voyage—a happy thought that was very likely Barlow's idea, for he was an inveterate reader of history and travel literature. By the twentieth of September the *Mercury* had to advertise for an apprentice to learn the printing business.

The *Mercury* provided Barlow with a place to publish his own writings. It was a training ground for his later political pamphleteering, and a place to get his poetical effusions out of his system. The essays and poems published in the *Mercury* while Barlow worked on it are not signed, but undoubtedly Barlow was responsible for most of the paper's contents, especially the verse, none of which is distinguished. He probably wrote, for instance, the poetical essay on a thunderstorm in which a Captain Israel Seymour was killed by lightning. In the same sort of turgid elegy that Barlow wrote on the death of Titus Hosmer, the Connecticut bigwig who once gave him moral support, he describes Captain Seymour's death:

> The winged bolt glides through thy inmost frame,
> Breathless thou fall'st, nor know'st from whence it came.

The *Mercury* was a well-edited paper by eighteenth-century standards and outlasted both of its founders.

Once the newspaper was safely launched, Barlow and Babcock turned to book publishing. In October they announced that *Bickerstaff's Genuine Almanack* for 1785 was ready for sale, and the following February they brought out part three of Noah Webster's *Grammatical Institute of the English Language*. The former was any bookseller's staple item, as Poor Richard had been for Franklin; the latter was one of Webster's schoolbooks containing rules of reading and speaking and an anthology of essays, dialogues, and poems. Prominently included were ample selections from Barlow's unpublished *Vision of Columbus*. The chief publication venture of the year, however, was a new edition of *Watts's Psalms*.

Barlow spent most of his spare time this winter making an up-to-date version of the Psalms for use in American churches. In this project he had official authorization from the ministerial association and help from another poet-friend, Dr. Lemuel Hopkins. There was a slight excuse for a new edition, because the English Watts occasionally had referred to the King and used monarchal terminology offensive to American republicans. But the essential changes were few, and Barlow went on to tinker a good bit with Watts' text and to add metrical versions of psalms Watts had omitted. When the project was completed, a special committee of ministers gave it their imprimatur, and the book was offered to the public.

Although Barlow's version of Watts went through two editions, it was not an unqualified critical success. Ezra Stiles confided to his diary that Barlow "corrected too much and unnecessarily mutilated the Book & sometimes hurt the poetry." He complained that Barlow had put his name on the title page and thus "mounted up at one Leap to all the Glory of Watts." This was a new way, he fumed, of elevating oneself to genius and honor. However, Stiles was fair enough to add that Barlow was an excellent poet even if "he cannot retouch Watts to advantage." Another critic, Oliver Arnold, cousin of Benedict, who was noted for impromptu rhymes, met Barlow in a bookseller's shop in New Haven. When Barlow asked him for a sample of his wit, he is supposed to have replied sourly:

> "You've proved yourself a sinful cre'tur;
> You've murdered Watts, and spoilt the meter;
> You've tried the Word of God to alter,
> And for your pains deserve a halter."

Although Hartford was growing and prospering, the printing and publishing business of Barlow and Babcock was unable to support two families. Barlow, who could neither set type nor operate the press, was the expendable member of the firm. He withdrew from the partnership in November, 1785, sixteen months after the *Mercury* had issued its first number, and the notice informing the public of the fact appeared in the paper soon after. The partnership was dissolved by mutual consent and the assets divided, Babcock keeping the paper and printing business, Barlow taking the stock of books and groceries. Barlow and Babcock remained friends, and the *Mercury* occasionally published contributions from the ex-partner.

2: *New Directions and Old Fruitions*

During the succeeding five months Barlow prepared for the next phase of his already varied career. While he kept store in a house owned by Dr. Jepson near the South Meeting House, he dug into Blackstone's *Commentaries* to prepare himself to practice law. The edition of *Watts's Psalms* sold briskly, probably better than the rum, sugar, molasses, tea, and other items that he also stocked, so that he was able to pay his bills and read law. Evidence of the new direction in his career appeared in March when he was elected to membership on the Common Council of Hartford, and in April he was admitted to the bar. Law was a career that several of his best friends, particularly John Trumbull and Oliver Wolcott, already were riding to security and prominence.

Barlow's bar examination was accompanied by a legal dissertation that he read to the assembled lawyers. If the examiners knew their candidate only as a visionary poet, they must have been surprised at the clear and vigorous logic displayed in the essay. They could not have foreseen it, but Barlow already was slipping away from the granite conservatism of Connecticut towards the liberal republicanism of his next decade. He developed a cogently argued brief for an evolutionary concept of law, a theory that allowed for growth and change as social organisms matured and developed. He disputed the contention that the laws of nature are simple and God-made while the laws of society are complex and man-made. The laws of nature and the laws of man are inseparable, he argued; for as soon as two men band together society has begun, though in terms of civilization or culture the pair may still live in a state of nature.

Once the listener accepted Barlow's premise, he was caught by an inexorable line of reasoning. If the laws of nature and the laws of society are inseparable, they both must be God-given. No one, theist or deist, would contend that the great Newtonian universe was not ordered by divine intelligence, be it God or the Great First Cause. Thus, if nature and man are governed by laws emanating from the same source, there must be divine sanction for social and legal change. Because "man is the most changeable of all animals & capable of greater improvements in the various stages of his social nature, very few of the laws of his nature therefore . . . can remain in full force through all the variety of changes that society is capable of producing in his nature."

Hammering home his points with specific examples, Barlow demonstrated the validity of this argument. Common law originally was common sense. Roman civil law and the feudal system once provided a workable, sensible way to govern society. The feudal system worked well in a simple military state, but it did not work in a modern commercial society. For instance, imprisonment for debt, which was still practiced, was defensible in an earlier age when property was small, permanent, and not subject to fluctuations of

commercial society. Then insolvency was properly a serious offense, but in 1786 imprisonment for debt was a cruel, inhumane,
obsolete punishment. And so his dissertation went. Throughout
Barlow's argument runs less concern for tradition and precedent in
the law than for change to meet new conditions. He was laying
the foundation for his humanitarianism and his faith in the early
idealism of the French Revolution. This was the theory, at least,
that eventually would lead to the twentieth century and the New
Deal.

Barlow was a member of the Connecticut bar for two years, but
during this time he practiced very little in the courts. One of his
associates observed that as a lawyer his "manners and address were
not popular; his eloquence was embarrassed; and he was thought
deficient in that *happy impudence* which is so essential to the success of an advocate." But this judgment is only partly true, for
Barlow had debated ably in college, recited his poetry in public,
preached for three years; and in 1787 he was invited to deliver the
Fourth of July oration before the Connecticut Society of the Cincinnati. The facts of his law practice are less picturesque. He soon
cast his lot with the organizers of the Ohio Land Company and
sold shares in the company's grant in the Northwest Territory. He
was so successful in this enterprise that it led to the next great adventure in his career, the event that changed his life, the mission
to Paris. Before he embarked for Europe, however, his poetical
avocation continued to consume much time and energy.

Connecticut was painfully grappling with problems of self-gov-
ernment three years after the Peace of Paris, but the stubborn
realities of freedom were hard to manage. As Barlow put it the
next year in his Fourth of July oration: "The Revolution is but half
completed. *Independence* and *Government* were the two objects
contended for, and but one is yet obtained." Into the ferment of
these times the postboy dropped the October twenty-sixth issue of
the *New Haven Gazette*. Under the heading "American Antiquities," readers of the paper discovered a minor sensation in satiric
verse. Twelve times afterwards in the next sixteen months further
installments of this feature appeared. Regardless of politics, no one
could be indifferent to these anonymous contributions. Both needle-

like barbs and meat-cleaver blows attacked the feebleness of Confederation, mob-rule democracy in Massachusetts, problems of state
debt, and the issuance of paper money in Rhode Island. Nor did
the assault ignore important public characters, who appeared in the
paper's columns in transparent disguise.

A headnote to the initial number of "American Antiquities" concocted a provenance for the satire. A recent archeological expedition to the banks of the Muskingum River in Ohio had discovered
ancient ruins of a buried civilization. Among other things found
was the manuscript of an epic poem in twenty-four books: *The
Anarchiad—A Poem on the Restoration of Chaos and Substantial
Night.* The authors of "American Antiquities" proposed to submit
from time to time samples of this epic, and as they made good their
promise, the public interest in the satire steadily mounted. *The
Anarchiad* provoked hot debate in the taverns and coffeehouses,
elicited counter-satire in the public prints, and was widely copied.
Launched at the same time as Shays's Rebellion, the satire's opening
lines set the theme of the whole series. The verse conjures up a
vision of Massachusetts ruled by Chaos and Daniel Shays, whose
insurrection has closed the courts. Then

> The stocks, the gallows lose th' expected prize,
> See the jails open and the thieves arise.
> Thy constitution, Chaos, is restor'd;
> Law sinks before thy uncreating word;
> Thy hand unbars th' unfathom'd gulph of fate,
> And deep in darkness whelms the new-born state.

A little later when Rhode Island was dumping paper money into
the economy, *The Anarchiad* proclaimed that people with any
sense would "like Lot from Sodom, from Rhode Island run."

The authors of *The Anarchiad* were the little group of friends in
Hartford who promptly were named the "wicked wits." Exactly
who wrote what and exactly how the poem was created are matters
for conjecture. Humphreys wrote Washington the month after the
first number appeared that he, Trumbull, and Barlow were the authors. To this trio must also be added Dr. Hopkins, Barlow's close
friend and, later, the leading physician in Connecticut. The project

was no doubt a genuine collaboration in which verses passed among the poets for additions and alterations until enough lines were ready for a new installment. There are marks of Trumbull's wartime political satire, *M'Fingal;* there are echoes of Barlow's and Humphreys' serious poetry; there are lines with a well-honed edge that Hopkins no doubt supplied. Hopkins' caustic wit had previously produced these lines in "An Epitaph on a Patient Who Died of a Pimple in the Hands of an Infallible Doctor":

> Here lies a fool flat on his back
> The victim of a Cancer Quack—
> . . . .
> Go, readers, gentle, eke and simple,
> If you have wart, or corn, or pimple;
> To quack infallible apply;
> Here's room enough for you to lie.
> His skill triumphant still prevails,
> For *Death's* a cure that never fails.

The inspiration for the satire was endemic in the political verse of the eighteenth century. For decades English poets and their American imitators had pumped out satirical couplets like a player piano grinding out mechanical tunes. Pope's *Dunciad* supplied some of the ideas, but the immediate model was *The Rolliad*, a contemporary satire in serial that had appeared in an English newspaper. There were in addition borrowings from epic machinery used by Homer and Milton and direct quotations from several poets. The vision apparatus probably came from as close a source as Barlow's *Vision of Columbus*, though Barlow, of course, had not invented that device. The entire performance was in a literal sense what the authors called it—a "hotchpot."

The wicked wits, however, were more successful in literature than in reforming society, despite the intense public interest. For instance, they aimed many of their blows at Judge William Williams, the Will Wimble of the satire, but the judge confounded them by winning his next election by a thumping margin. They cudgeled other public figures also without success and discovered to their chagrin that when the Constitutional Convention took place,

ιe of their supposed enemies, as delegates, voted for federation.
even if the wits did not accomplish much and tilted with wind-
ls, they enlivened the political scene for nearly two years and
ιulated a second generation of wits to carry on the political satin the turmoil of the 1790's.

ιfter eight years of planning and scheming, issuing prospectuses
corralling subscribers, the great poem appeared in May, 1787.
January the *Connecticut Courant* carried an announcement that
work finally was in press. It would be published by Hudson
Goodwin in "one Volume, Octavo, and delivered to Subscrib-
at the price of ONE DOLLAR and a THIRD." The advertise-
ιt added that this price was "not higher than imported Books
this size have commonly borne in America." A month later
ιe obliging friend of the author contributed a newspaper essay
'ing everyone to buy the *Vision* and see for themselves whether
ιot "the writings of the Poets now living in Connecticut, are not
ιal to any which the present age can produce." Barlow's poem,
essayist added, gave the reader of discernment "an exalted idea
American genius and refinement."

Vith all this fanfare the poem was a financial success. The sub-
ιption list, printed as an appendix, is a curious document. Louis
I, in gracious response to the dedication, bought twenty-five
ιies; George Washington took twenty; Lafayette ten; Benjamin
nklin six. All the important names, like Hamilton, Livingston,
ιr, Pickering, Paine, appear on the list. Among the additional
ιscribers were twelve generals, three major generals, thirty-three
ιonels, seventeen majors, and fifty-two captains. The Revolution-
' army subscribers averaged nearly three copies apiece, buying
ιll more than one fourth of the edition. An eminent scholar ob-
ves: "It was their greatest exhibition of patriotism since the siege
Yorktown." Barlow grossed over fifteen hundred dollars on the
ιlication and probably more, because the publisher undoubtedly
nted extra copies for non-subscribers. Five months later a second,
ιller edition was needed to satisfy the demand. All things con-
ered, the poem was in a modest way the first American best

seller after the Revolution, and Barlow probably was the first Am
ican writer anywhere to receive fair pay for a book.

In view of Barlow's hard work and eventual triumph one ha
to introduce a discordant note. But the fact remains that the *Vis*
of Columbus is a dinosaur in the clay pits of literary history. Sor
how Barlow and his fellow versifiers like Timothy Dwight, Jc
Trumbull, and David Humphreys never realized that literature l
to be alive to endure. They wrapped their poetic mantles ab
them, retired to their ivory towers, and spun out attenuated ve
suitable only for wall hangings in museum attics. They never m
aged to establish the link between literature and life. When Barl
turned his hand to writing political pamphlets or letters to
Ruthy, his prose breathed life and vitality. It is more than lik
that the *Vision of Columbus* was more admired than read. Geo
Washington, for one, never managed to read the poem, as he c;
didly admitted in notes he sent with presentation copies.

Readers who did stagger through the endless parade of her
couplets found a poem dealing with the history of America, p;
present, and future. After a prose summary of the life of Columb
the first book opens with the hero soliloquizing in prison on
cruel fate that has overtaken him. An angel appears and takes C
lumbus to the Mount of Vision to cheer him with a glimpse of
great future of America. At this point, readers must have be
reminded that Michael does much the same for Adam in the l
two books of *Paradise Lost*. Then the poem goes on to describe
considerable detail the geography and the natives of the Americ
continents.

Somewhere along the tortuous path of composition Barlow c
covered the history of the Inca empire and the story of its legend;
founder, Manco Capac. The tale of empire-building in prehisto
Peru fascinated Barlow, who could not resist a long flashback chrc
icling the rise of this civilization. His colorless couplets, howev
turn the red meat of his source material into a bland sausage. M
interesting than the poetry is a fifteen-page prose essay "On
Genius and Institutions of Manco Capac" that he inserts midway
the poem. From Peru the poet turns to post-Columbian histc
and ends Book IV with an account of the seventeenth-centu

olonization of North America. Books V and VI then carry the arrative from the French and Indian wars through the Revolution. s the patriot army closes in at Yorktown, Columbus glimpses the efeated Cornwallis:

> Shells rain before him, rock the shores around,
> And craggs and balls o'erturn the tented ground;
> From post to post, the driven ranks retire,
> The earth in crimson and the skies on fire.

his is a good example of Barlow's narrative style, but one doubts the war veterans who bought the poem relived the old campaigns s they read.

In Book VII, after beginning with a spirited hymn to peace, arlow shows Columbus the glories of American progress in the rts and sciences. "Bold Franklin" with his lightning rod "curbs e fierce blaze and holds the imprison'd fire," Benjamin West boldly bursts the former bounds of Art," and the tuneful tribe of onnecticut poets sing their "deathless strain." Then the vision uspends for a book of philosophizing which inquires into the relaionship between God and man, the errors of extreme passion and eason, and the happy union of these forces in the discovery of ruth. In the final book the poet takes off into the wild blue yonder, he vision resumed and extended over the entire earth. Columbus ees great progress in science and technology culminating in a fuure of universal peace and happiness. The last view, prophetically, onjures up an assembly of united nations, which can give to each ealm its "limit and its laws" and

> Bid the last breath of dire contention cease,
> And bind all regions in the leagues of peace.

The concept here is noble, the subject fit for epic poetry; but Barow was not Milton, and this matter had best be treated succinctly.

One of Barlow's difficulties lay in the ambivalent nature of the oem. He never really decided whether he was writing an epic or philosophic poem. The subject matter he wished to treat could ot be written in pure narrative, but the models he had at hand were narrative epics like those of Homer, Virgil, and Milton. Then, too,

his major interest lay in the narrative sections of the poem, such
the Inca interlude and the scenes of the Revolution which occu
the bulk of the lines, and for these sections he used works li
Robertson's *History of America* that imposed narrative treatme
on the material. Yet the vision structure and the desire to celebra
and explain the glories of America demanded commentary a
philosophy. In the final amalgam the philosophical passages a
slighter than the narrative and somewhat diffuse, but the ideas Ba
low expounds are of importance in tracing the growth of his min

The intellectual content of the poem represents an end of Ba
low's youth rather than a beginning of his mature career. In t
four years that lay between the poem's writing and publication
was questioning his original assumptions. His legal dissertati
points the new direction; the *Vision of Columbus* sums up the o
beliefs. There is nothing objectionably unorthodox in the poe
all of Barlow's friends, including those keepers of Connecticut co
servatism, Timothy Dwight and Noah Webster, had read the wo
in manuscript and approved it. An easy faith in the inevitabili
of progress, a belief in the immutability of human nature, an a
firmation of divine revelation—all of these traditional articles
New England thought—flow smoothly in couplets from the mou
of Barlow's angel into the receptive ear of Columbus. False religi
results from an excess of passion over reason, but reason carried
excess also leads to error and cannot alone "reach with immor
hope the blest abode." In summation, man's hope and man's fa
lie in "the attracting force of universal love," the great truth e
bodied in Christian theology.

The critical reception of the *Vision of Columbus*, if not ecstat
was at least favorable. A British edition promptly appeared in Lo
don, and later another edition, in English, was brought out in Par
The *Critical Review* (London) for January, 1788, thought the lin
had "no great pretensions to originality" and wondered if Was
ington would not smile "at seeing himself represented as mowi
down whole armies like an Amadis or Orlando." But on the who
this notice concluded that so daring a muse as Barlow's "must som
times be expected in her sublime flight to veil her head in the clou
. . . Mr. Barlow thinks with freedom and expresses himself wi

irit." Many American readers forgave the poet for his sins be-
ɩuse they rejoiced in the production of an authentic American
ɔem. The demand for a national literature already was insistent,
ough not so agonized as it later became when Sydney Smith
ɩsed American hackles with his impertinent question, "Who reads
ɩ American book?" Richard Alsop summed up the case for the
ɩtionalists when he wrote:

> And in Virgilian Barlow's tuneful lines
> With added splendour great Columbus shines.

CHAPTER IV

An American in Paris

1: *Prelude*

On the first day of March, 1786, a group of ex-Revolutionary ar⟨my⟩ officers gathered at the Bunch of Grapes Tavern in Boston. Th⟨eir⟩ purpose was to set up a company to sell land in the wilderness ⟨of⟩ the Northwest Territory. They were motivated both by pub⟨lic⟩ and private motives: public because they envisioned new towns a⟨nd⟩ cities mushrooming with their help on the frontier as the course ⟨of⟩ empire took its way westward; private because they had been p⟨aid⟩ for their military service in practically worthless Continental c⟨ur⟩rency and hoped to cash it in for land that anybody could ⟨see⟩ would someday be valuable. The gentlemen assembled chose G⟨en⟩eral Rufus Putnam of Massachusetts chairman of the meeting, Ma⟨jor⟩ Winthrop Sargent clerk; and the Ohio Company formally beg⟨an⟩ operations that soon were to open up a vast tract of southeast Oh⟨io.⟩

Congress at the close of the Revolution had abundant liabili⟨ties⟩ but little power to meet its obligations. One thing it had, howev⟨er,⟩ was land—millions of acres. The land was full of Indians, to ⟨be⟩ sure, and unsurveyed, and the separate states claimed various pa⟨rts⟩ of the wilderness, but the real estate was there and represente⟨d a⟩ great potential source of revenue. The needs of the governm⟨ent⟩ and the desires of the Ohio Company inevitably merged. Congr⟨ess⟩

anted to pay its debts in a hurry and did not care to involve itself
selling off the land in farmlots to individuals. The Ohio Com-
ny was willing to take on the job of developing the public lands
Congress would make a profitable arrangement. The chief diffi-
lty in working out an accommodation between the two interests
as that General Putnam and his friends were small and not very
fluent petitioners. When the company found it needed a go-be-
veen to deal with Congress, a suave, shrewd financial manipulator
imed Duer entered the picture.

The annals of American finance contain no character more fas-
nating than William Duer. This bold speculator began life in
ngland in 1747 as the son of an aristocrat and died in a New York
ebtors' prison. After studying at Eton, Duer served as ensign
ider Lord Clive in India, then turned up in America a few years
efore the Revolution. A financial wizard, he prospered hand-
imely before, during, and after the war, first selling masts and
ars to the British navy, then outfitting the American army. He
iarried Lord Stirling's daughter, who was brilliantly connected
ith the De Peysters, Livingstons, and Schuylers, and at the time
ie Ohio Company was formed he occupied a key position as Sec-
etary of the Treasury Board. In 1787 no one yet had invented the
onflict-of-interests law, and Duer saw in the Ohio Company a
eautiful chance to use his official position to make a fortune. He
oncocted a plan to extract a million dollars from the public—all
i a perfectly legitimate way.

The Ohio Company sent one of its ablest men, Manasseh Cutler
f Ipswich, to New York to buy a million acres of land from Con-
ress. Displaying a real talent for lobbying, this lawyer-clergyman
xerted a significant influence on the text of the Northwest Or-
inance, which provided orderly procedures for carving new states
ut of the Territory; but he was totally unable to persuade Con-
ress to sell land to the company. At this point, Duer approached
utler with the offer of his services and a startling proposition: he
vould help the Ohio Company obtain from Congress rights to buy
ot one million but five million acres at a dollar an acre. The com-
any would contract with the Treasury Board to purchase one and

a half million acres; he and his friends (the Scioto Associates) wou
dispose of the additional three and a half million acres. Both tra
would lie adjacent to each other, north of the Ohio and east of t
Scioto rivers. Duer, the financier and Secretary of the Treasu
Board, would lend the company one hundred thousand dollars f
part of the down payment to the Treasury on its million and a h
acres.

Cutler, dazzled by this proposition, accepted Duer's offer, a
miraculously the Congressional resistance to the Ohio Compa
vanished. How Duer manipulated Congress is anyone's guess, b
it is likely that his wealth, his official position, the sheer magnitu
of the project, and perhaps the secret offer of shares in the spec
lation accomplished the deed. Once Congress had granted the pr
emption rights, no matter how the approval had been engineere
there was nothing illegal about the business. Cutler did confi
naïvely to his diary that Duer had asked him to keep the Scio
contract a "profound secret," but he also boasted that "many
the principal characters of America" were involved in the ventu

Cutler and his fellow ex-officers, it seems, were pawns for t
crafty Duer. The Ohio Company contracted to pay for its lar
at stated intervals and in stated amounts. The Scioto Associat
undertook only to peddle their option to buy three and a half m
lion acres. The Ohio Company soon made its down payment ar
General Putnam led a band of New Englanders to found Mariett
Ohio. The Scioto Associates, who paid no money, acquired righ
to buy more than twice as much land under an arrangement whic
if it failed, would leave Congress holding the sack. It was the o
tion, or pre-emption rights, that they planned to sell. They wou
make a quick dollar and get out without having to develop t
land.

Another pawn in the game was Joel Barlow, who was studyir
for his admission to the bar at the time the Ohio Company w
formed at the Bunch of Grapes Tavern. Many of the organize
of the company were his old comrades in arms and fellow membe
of the Cincinnati. Barlow, too, had his bounty rights as a veter
and no doubt a drawer full of depreciated paper money. He join
the company as agent for one hundred and forty of its one thousar

shares and traveled about Connecticut selling the land. As author of the *Vision of Columbus* he commanded a good bit of public notice, and as land salesman he managed to dispose of one hundred and thirteen shares in less than four months. He no doubt was pleased with his success, though surely he realized his Ohio real estate was a great bargain. Each share cost one thousand dollars in Continental paper and ten dollars in gold or silver and was redeemable, after Congress had been paid, for one thousand acres. Barlow himself was able to buy three shares.

While Putnam, Cutler, and Barlow promoted the legitimate ends of the Ohio Company, Duer and the Scioto Associates schemed of ways to cash in on their pre-emption rights. The obvious place to tap a reservoir of wealth was in Europe, but the speculators' early long-distance efforts to unload on foreign bankers yielded no golden results. They would have to send a special agent abroad for this purpose. Duer picked one of his associates, Royal Flint, who promptly took sick and had to cancel his plans to go. Then in February, 1788, Manasseh Cutler wrote Richard Platt, one of Duer's associates: "Mr. *Barlow* is the only man . . . that can be obtained, to whom I should feel myself willing to entrust our business." Duer was at first skeptical when Barlow was proposed to him, but he allowed himself to be persuaded.

Barlow was not averse to taking the assignment, for it offered a chance to see the world and make his fortune at the same time. He knew there was no shortcut to wealth via his Hartford law practice, whereas the glittering names of William Duer, Andrew Craigie, and all the Scioto Associates blinded him, as they had others. The "principal characters of America," as Cutler told him, backed this venture. Barlow thought he was being sent to Europe to sell land and help populate the United States, a project that would benefit humanity as well as himself. Understandably, land and pre-emption rights seemed to him pretty much the same thing. Duer, the shadowy, off-stage manipulator, perhaps thought the author of a vision poem might be the right person to sell land that he and his associates did not own. But regardless of aims and motives, both men anticipated success.

The United States clearly was entering an era of abundant possibilities. While the new Constitution was in the process of ratification, increasing numbers of emigrants were crossing the mountains and floating down the Ohio and sending back enthusiastic reports of the alluvial bottom land in the Ohio Valley. New Englanders tired of coaxing crops from their flinty hillsides were joining the chorus and the westward trek. Europeans, too, seemed hungry for land, impatient to swell the movement, and affluent enough to buy the land. Peace following the years of war furnished the proper context for settlement and expansion. Congress wanted the western lands sold, and the Scioto contract was drawn in favorable terms dictated by Duer himself.

All these thoughts were in Barlow's mind in mid-May, 1788, when he kissed Ruthy goodby at Brother Dudley's in Greenfield and took the stage for New York. His confidence ran high as he waited eight days in New York for favorable winds to allow his ship to leave the harbor. On the twenty-fifth passengers were summoned aboard, sails set, cables cast off, and the French packet on which Barlow had booked passage stood out for the lower bay and Sandy Hook. As he looked back, the ship slowly moved away from Manhattan, temporary capital of the infant republic, and Brooklyn Heights, scene of the military debacle in August, 1776. Behind him was one career; ahead was another. He would not pass through the Narrows again for seventeen years.

2: *Allegretto*

Tourists crossing the Atlantic today on luxury liners two blocks long have no idea of the rigors of sea travel in the eighteenth century. Barlow's ship, a former sixteen-gun English frigate captured by the French during the American Revolution, had been converted into a packet to carry mail and passengers between New York and France. Small and ill-equipped for such service, the vessel crossed the Atlantic in one month if the weather was good—two months if not. Moreover, the hazards of storms, contrary winds, and cramped quarters were only part of the ordeal, for the captain, too, was ill-

94

suited for his job, being "extremely parsimonious in his provisions and barbarously inattentive to his passengers." Time after time during the voyage Barlow regretted that his restless ambition had driven him from Connecticut to embark on the high seas of European adventure.

Living conditions aboard the ship were primitive and filthy. Barlow's cabin was a wretched little dark hole, six and a half feet long, three wide, and five high, lined with grimy, tattered calico. Passengers had to supply their own bedding, as the stingy captain explained after passage had been bought, because it would ill become him to offer a gentleman mattress and sheets that had been used by others. This necessity perhaps was fortunate, for the dirty little staterooms were infested with fleas and bedbugs. After one night Barlow remarked ironically to a fellow passenger that the Count de Buffon must be right in his theory that living creatures degenerate in the New World. The ship's insect population, being French or English, had attained remarkable size and voracity; in fact, Barlow observed, the Count must have evolved his notion of American fauna by studying Old World vermin. "The European flea," he noted in his journal, "is at least heavier by one third of a grain than that of America."

The food served on the packet equaled the quality of the accommodations. The captain served ham so hard and dry and cheese so mouldy and unpalatable that the passengers went hungry. As the dining-room steward lugged out the same ham and cheese at least forty times during the voyage, the captain praised his food, while the passengers cracked their teeth on hardtack or picked at stewed mutton swimming in grease and garlic. Fortunately for the passengers, some of them inspected the larder before sailing, discovered deficiencies, and brought on board their own stock of tea, coffee, and sugar, none of which the captain provided. Daily, in fair weather or foul, the table was set at ten and at four, and the captain had no idea that any person, sick or well, could eat at any other time, or fail to eat at those hours.

Barlow, however, was relatively unconcerned with problems of shipboard cuisine. The vessel barely cleared Sandy Hook before he took to his bed with acute seasickness. For virtually the entire month he suffered the tortures of the damned, while the rest of the passengers enjoyed mostly brisk breezes and pleasant weather. "The mouth of the Hudson received the first sacrifice of the contents of my stomach," he wrote; "that of the Seine was honored with the last; & I hope that the palate of his Oceanic Godship was sufficiently sweetened with the copious libations of bile it received from my gallbladder." For the first two weeks of the voyage he literally could keep nothing on his stomach; then during a six-day calm he discovered in the ship's galley a small quantity of rice that he was able to digest. As the vessel approached the English Channel, however, a violent five-day storm tossed the packet "from heaven to hell" and brought the voyage to a nauseous end at Le Havre on June twenty-fourth. Barlow crawled ashore and into a bed at the Hotel de l'Aigle d'Or, and six days later recorded in his journal that he still could scarcely write. "The house & everything about me appears as much in motion as a ship in a storm, & it is with difficulty [that] I can stand upon the floor, especially in the morning, without steadying myself." In time, however, solid land and a returning appetite cured the ills of his body, and he focused his attention on Europe.

Throughout Europe in 1788 outward tranquility belied seething currents boiling up from beneath the surface. The pressures of a new industrial and commercial society, new political ideas and old economic infirmities were about to change Europe beyond all recognition. The older generation, raised in the shadow of absolute despotism, was ill prepared for the events of the coming decades. The reigning monarchs held Europe together with frayed cordage in a system of ententes that threatened to rip apart at any moment. Russia, Austria, and France grouped themselves, chiefly by dynastic alliance, against England, Prussia, and Holland. But Austria and France were traditional enemies and despite the efforts of an enlightened despot, Joseph II of Austria, and the marriage of Louis XVI to the Austrian Marie Antoinette, the alignment was unstable and unpopular. The great day of the Hapsburg Empire simply was over; and France, for its part, though it had looked sound enough in helping humble England in the American Revolution, was a cancerous wreck inside. French economic and political institutions, as the world soon would learn, were in a state of advanced decay. On the other hand, England had suffered a severe blow in the loss of her colonies, and Prussia since the death of Frederick the Great two years before was really a decrepit power. Elsewhere in Europe, Sweden and Russia were at war, and Poland was awaiting its partitioning. Thomas Jefferson was prophetic when he wrote from Paris on July eighteenth: "There is great probability that the war kindled in the east, will spread from nation to nation, and in the long run, become general."

On the first of July Barlow set off for Paris with two Swedish businessmen he had met in Le Havre and twelve-year-old George Washington Greene, son of General Greene. Barlow had brought the boy with him from New York, having agreed to deliver him in Paris to Lafayette, who was going to supervise his education. Barlow's first trip across France was memorable, for he traveled with every pore open to new sights and sounds. Modes of European transportation interested him enormously at first, and he noted in his journal that traveling in France really was a science. One could journey by public diligence, horseback, or, as his party did, private carriage, the traveler supplying the vehicle but renting the King's horses and postillions every few miles. With a courier riding ahead to arrange for horses, the traveler could average eight miles an hour day and night for a week if he wished. Travel was fast; the roads were smooth. There was time to see sights along the way and still get to Paris on July third.

Despite his lingering seasickness, Barlow managed to inspect Le Havre before setting off inland. Unlike Mark Twain's innocents eighty years later, Barlow compared public buildings in Europe to things at home to the latters' disadvantage. New York's City Hall and perhaps even the State House in Philadelphia were not so fine as the *hôtel de ville* at Le Havre. His superlatives flowed unstintingly when he reached Rouen the next day and visited his first Gothic cathedral. It was so totally unlike anything he ever had seen in America that the ex-plowboy from Redding stood with mouth open. The amplitude, solemnity, and magnificence overwhelmed him. He tramped all over the building, even climbed the belfry where the guide told him the bell was the largest in Europe and weighed forty thousand pounds. Yankee empiricist that he was, Barlow measured the bell so that he could calculate its weight later for himself. Just before leaving Rouen he met two Mr. Appletons from Boston, fellow businessmen who expected to make their fortunes in France with a new way of processing whale oil.

Arriving in Paris on the third, Barlow immediately put up at a hotel with young Greene and sent his letter of introduction around to Jefferson's house. The next day he and the boy celebrated the Fourth of July with the American minister and two days later dined with him to discuss plans for the lad's education. Barlow also lost no time in renewing a wartime acquaintance with Lafayette and handing over his young charge. George Washington had written Lafayette:

> Notwithstanding you are acquainted with Mr. Barlow . . . I thought I would just write you a line by him, in order to recommend him the more particularly to your civilities. Mr. Barlow is considered by those who are good Judges to be a genius of the first magnitude; and to be one of the Bards who hold the keys of the gate by which Patriots, Sages and Heroes are admitted to immortality.

Despite the General's hyperbole, Lafayette, who *had* read the *Vision of Columbus*, greeted Barlow cordially, and the two remained friends for life. Meanwhile Jefferson, to whom Barlow had sent a copy of his poem, was equally warm in his reception. Barlow never had met Jefferson but instantly was attracted to him; a lasting friendship rooted in personal attachment and political sympathy grew from this meeting. Barlow's first visit to Paris, however, lasted only nine days, after which he set off for London with Daniel Parker, American businessman, who was to help with the Scioto speculation.

The trip non-stop by post-chaise to London took only three days, and though Barlow felt a little self-conscious visiting the country he recently had rebelled against, he immediately went sightseeing. The Tower of London, Hyde Park, Kensington Gardens, and Vauxhall impressed him greatly, and as he moved about, he met a good many agreeable people. On separate occasions he dined with Tom Paine, who was in England to promote his iron bridge, and John Trumbull, the American painter. He also met Sir Joseph Banks, president of the Royal Society and visited the Marquis of Landsdowne, the King's minister who had made peace with America. He tramped out to Windsor Palace, went to the Haymarket Theater, and attended church in the King's private chapel. George III, he noted, was an active-looking man with light sandy hair and a stammer in his speech; the Queen was not handsome but amiable looking; the princesses were surprising beauties.

Because he was a poet of heroic couplets, he made an early pilgrimage to Twickenham, the famous estate of Alexander Pope. The current owner, also a Pope venerator, showed him about the gardens and grotto, the most delightful spot he thought he ever had seen. He found a dozen acres of carefully planned wilderness and artfully contrived thickets laid out by the master. The whole effect, Barlow observed, "is in the truest English style of gardening, rather more solemn and gloomy than what is common, but perfectly in harmony with the turn of mind that most distinguished the planter." The owner had not changed a thing since Pope had lived there, and Barlow felt "silent veneration" as he walked about. "There is as much real taste discovered here as in any of his writings," he recorded in his journal. In addition to the gardens, Pope's grotto exceeded all description. The subterranean passage from the Thames to the gardens which passed under the house and under the public road excited and astonished him.

3: *Andante Moderato*

Barlow spent eight weeks in England having a wonderful time, then returned with Parker to the Continent. He relied on his experienced companion to steer the Scioto speculation into a safe harbor; in fact, Duer's instructions had been for him to work closely with Parker. Therefore in London Barlow indulged his curiosity with no twinges of conscience. The Ohio lands were not yet fully surveyed, Europe was prosperous, and before long some banking house or group of rich men would snap up the Scioto tract. Barlow was oblivious of the sort of men Duer and his associates were—devious, complex speculators in everything: state debts, Pickering Notes, new emission money, Treasury warrants, loan office certificates, notes of hand, stock margins, Continental certificates, claims of persons against the United States and vice versa. After seven weeks in England Barlow naïvely recorded in his diary: "I dine abroad at least six days in the week; this, to a man of business, would be a bad economy of time, but for me it is the best way of collecting information, and does not interfere with other business."

During September and October Barlow and Parker made two business trips to the Low Countries to see the Dutch banking firm of Van Staphorst, who expressed some interest in the Scioto lands. Barlow's optimism never flagged, and his journal during this going and coming, visits to Calais, Antwerp, Ostend, Brussels, Dunkirk, and adjacent cities, never mentions the slow progress of the business. He was busy observing and learning about people and places. After seeing all the Channel ports from Le Havre to Flushing, he concluded that "there is none to be compared with that of New Haven, which is only the second in that state [Connecticut] where we reckon no harbors at all," and after they had ridden three days with an unchaperoned young Englishwoman, he recorded that her "sprightliness & discretion . . . rendered the separation, to me at least, a real subject of regret."

By winter Barlow was comfortably settled in Paris and busy cultivating his new friends, learning French, going to the opera, and studying French politics under the tutelage of Mr. Jefferson. Meanwhile, Lafayette, whom he saw frequently, had placed General Greene's son in school at the Pension Lemoyne across the street from Jefferson's house. Daniel Parker, however, soon decided that the Scioto business was wasting his time and dropped his efforts to promote the speculation. But this development did not ruffle Barlow, who continued unsuccessfully trying to interest investors in his pre-emption rights. His expense money advanced by Duer and the Associates held out nicely, and there was no end of things in Paris to absorb a curious, alert American. Thus the winter and spring passed quickly and not unpleasantly. After Barlow had been abroad more than a year, Poet John Trumbull in Hartford wrote Oliver Wolcott: "I cannot conceive what Barlow is doing . . . you tell me he has got so far as to *see favorable prospects*. If he should not effect something soon, I would advise him to write 'The Vision of Barlow,' as a sequel to those of Columbus and M'Fingal."

There was not world enough and time for the Scioto venture, however, and a year after Barlow first saw Paris he began to realize the fact. The Parisian mob stormed the Bastille on July fourteenth to begin the memorable epoch of the French Revolution. Soon after, the cold, hostile Gouverneur Morris replaced the friendly Jefferson as American minister in Paris. Simultaneously in America the new Constitution was turning a shaky confederation into a stable union. This event, happy for Americans, was unwelcome to speculators who had counted on paying for land in severely depreciated government paper. The stronger the United States grew, the worse bargain the Scioto contract became. All this time the shrewd Duer, who never committed his speculations to written communication if he could help it, left Barlow to his own devices in Paris.

Yet in July, 1789, the cloud on the horizon over Scioto was no bigger than a man's hand. The storming of the Bastille dwarfed everything else that summer; Barlow, an eyewitness to the momentous event, thrilled at his ringside seat on history. "The sudden and glorious revolution," he wrote Ruth, "has prevented my completing the business"; but his letter immediately dismissed the land speculation to give a report on recent days in Paris. "You will get ten thousand lies and a great deal of truth . . . in the American papers," he wrote, but "all the true things . . . have passed under my eye." It was a matter of tremendous gratification, he added, to have "seen two complete revolutions in favor of liberty" in one lifetime. At the moment of his writing everything was quiet in Paris, but he reflected: "I look upon the affairs of this nation to be on the point of being settled on the most rational and lasting foundation." The only thing that compensated him for the long separation from "my adorable Ruthy" was the "contemplation of the infinite happiness that I am sure will result" from the Revolution. The irony of this early optimism came home to him later as he watched his friends fall under the guillotine during the Terror.

Even before the Bastille fell, the unfriendly Morris assessed correctly the problem Barlow was beginning to comprehend: "Barlow has no Title but a Right of Preemption from the Treasury Board, who are to make Title if the Payments be made within a certain Term. Not having Title he cannot give Title, and therefore the [European] Adventurers will not advance their Money." Morris, it might be added, made this analysis with a measure of satisfaction. He, too, had come to Europe to sell land, not only to represent the United States, and before sailing had been rebuffed when he tried to ally himself with Duer. If Barlow had a rival land salesman in Morris, he also had other competitors among other expatriated Americans in Europe. Because many of these land agents could show title, they greatly reduced the market for the Scioto Associates' mere option.

A year after Daniel Parker abandoned the Scioto business, Barlow began to feel at home in France and able to handle the complexities of transatlantic business. His French was becoming fluent and his circle of friends had expanded well beyond the limits of the American community. As agent for the Scioto Associates, he never doubted that his mission was to sell land, even though the land was not yet paid for. The distinction between option and title really seemed academic. Reviewing the situation in the fall of 1789, Barlow saw a chance to turn the Revolution into an advantage. If the situation were properly exploited, would not the *émigrés* from the *ancien régime* be good prospects for Scioto lands? At the end of the summer Barlow had taken into partnership a smooth-talking, ironically named Englishman, William Playfair, and six Frenchmen, and organized in Paris La Compagnie du Scioto. Its purpose was to sell shares in France in somewhat the same manner that the Ohio Company had marketed shares in New England.

By the end of the year the French Scioto Company threatened to turn the speculation into a legitimate project for developing the land. Brochures appeared in Paris advertising the Ohio land as an earthly paradise where the soil was rich, the crops unbelievably huge, the climate excellent, and the government beneficent. Investors were promised a rapid increase in the value of their land, as the territory quickly filled up, and were urged to buy now. Barlow wrote at the end of November that the business was going well. He even was negotiating with the royal treasury to barter land for depreciated American bonds held by the French government. He expected to wind up the business in a year with more than a million-dollar profit for the company. Ten days later his optimism soared even higher. Business was better "than I ever expected." Some of the land already had been sold to individuals who were on their way to America.

The success of the venture now depended on settling immigrants on the Scioto land. If the Associates could not realize their option one way, Barlow reasoned, they would surely wish to do so another. His original instructions from Duer gave him carte blanche to dispose of the pre-emption rights as best he could, but the Scioto speculators never in the world intended to sponsor colonization. They were dismayed to learn that Barlow was selling land, which they did not own, in small lots and recruiting settlers; but by the time they found out, the first immigrants already were on their way. In December the settlers began collecting at Le Havre preparatory to sailing for America, and in January the first shipload departed. Barlow wrote Duer that everything depended on the expeditious treatment of the first group. Thousands of Frenchmen were interested in emigrating but hung back waiting to see how the first settlers fared. To the leader of the first shipload Barlow wrote: "My heart goes with them—I consider them as the fathers & founders of a nation."

Barlow was certain in January that his desperate gamble was succeeding. He wrote Duer by the first group of immigrants that he hoped in a few days to have funds to pay the United States Treasury for half a million acres. Several weeks later he authorized Duer to draw on him for one hundred thousand livres (about eighteen thousand dollars) and another one hundred thousand at ninety days' sight, if need be. "The affair goes extremely well," he reported, though he had to admit in the next breath that he did not have the money in hand. But the payments, he assured Duer, surely would be made, and he added that if favorable reports came from the immigrants then at sea, he would be able to sell twenty million acres within the next two years.

Simultaneously, however, notes of reproach and urgency slipped into the same communication: "I have not received any letter nor any necessary information since I left you. It is not my personal feelings alone which are affected. . . . The business has required that I should know the situation & intentions of the concern, the progress of the surveys, the disposition of the savages & a thousand other things." He was beginning to feel abandoned after twenty months without instructions from Duer. He admitted there was a risk in sending the immigrants, but the risk was necessary, he emphasized, to success in disposing of the land. A month later he added frantically: "Don't, for God's sake, fail to raise money enough to put the people in possession. Make any sacrifice rather than fail in this essential object. If it fails, we are ruined; all our fortunes & my character are buried under the ruins."

4: *Intermezzo*

Barlow missed his wife dreadfully as the days of his European junket lengthened into months. He had set off blithely expecting the mission to last a year or less, but one complication had led to another until he lost sight of a terminal date for the business. A year after he reached Europe, he began urging Ruth to join him in Paris, but Ruth, who never had been farther from home than West Point, regarded a trip to Europe as far too great an undertaking. She ignored the first suggestions that she make the voyage, then in December, 1789, gently said no. But the entreaties increased in urgency, and early in January she gave in. By this time Barlow had organized the French company, sent off the first group of settlers, and planned activities that would keep him in France at least another year.

As he importuned Ruth to come, he wrote: "I shall . . . point out to you every inch of the road. . . . Many wives have done the same thing . . . the difficulties have been principally in imagination . . .

104

there is no more difficulty in it than in going from Hartford to N. Haven." On New Year's Day he wrote by the first shipload of immigrants that the year 1790 was sure to be a better year than '89 because they would spend the greater part of it together. "While my careless & insensible associates at home conceive me to be rioting in the luxuries of Europe, I should be infinitely more happy to be locked in a prison in America, where I might hear the cheering voice of my Ruthy through the grate."

In March he sent detailed instructions for the journey. She was to engage passage for England with one of four captains Barlow knew personally, all of whom were good fellows and "much used to carrying passengers and ladies." She was to talk with Mrs. John Adams and her daughter in New York to find out just what to take and how to prepare for the voyage. She was also to hire a good maid to travel with her and to lay in a private stock of provisions: oat meal, Indian meal, rice, chocolate, peppermint oil, some stomach medicine—rhubarb or salts. Further, Ruth should give the captain a good price, even double fare, to insure that he would take good care of her. Then Joel sent the address of Mrs. Rogers, 18 King Street, London, where Ruth was to lodge and he would meet her. These directions she received in time to set sail in May to join her husband.

Ruth's ordeal did not begin until she landed in Europe. Though her crossing took thirty-seven days, she was seasick only a fortnight and liked the trip better and better as the weeks went by. Captain Woolsey was a stalwart Yankee, Mrs. Timothy Dwight's brother, and took care of her like a sister. "I was half in love with him," Ruth wrote Mary Dwight; "had I been young and disengaged, my heart would have been irretrievably lost. I should not recommend a young lady to him unless she possessed charms capable of winning his heart, for she must lose hers." But when Ruth reached England and Mrs. Rogers' house in King Street, she received a letter from Joel saying he could not possibly leave Paris for eight or ten days.

For nearly a month Ruth languished in London waiting for Joel to meet her. The continued separation with only the Channel between them was agony for both. Ruth felt unwell the entire time and could not understand what kept Joel from leaving Paris. He wrote impassioned letters every few days to justify his delay but kept putting off his departure a little longer. He sent Colonel Blackden's wife, a Connecticut woman, to London to keep Ruth company until he could get there, and two weeks later wrote: "My charming Ruthy, you must not, shall not, blame me. . . . I know your patience is exhausted." Overleaf he added a postscript for Mrs. Blackden: "I suppose you sleep together. Tell her I have not slept with anybody but God since I slept with her." On the nineteenth the situation approached a crisis as Barlow wrote: "My heart is torn assunder on seeing by Mrs. Blackden's letter to her husband of the 13th that my charming Ruthy is too unhappy to eat or sleep, that her health is very bad, & I conclude she is too unhappy to write."

A few days later Barlow managed to set off for London, and the tearful reunion finally took place. There is no doubt that the land business required Barlow's presence in Paris during the first three weeks of July, 1790. The affairs of the French Scioto Company were deteriorating rapidly, but at the same time Joel was not so distressed over his business affairs and separation from his wife that he could not dabble in French politics. He joined eleven other Americans in a congratulatory address to the French National Assembly on July tenth and wrote Ruth pining in London: "Yesterday we made our wonderful address to the National Assembly— such thunderclaps of applause never were heard. The president made a most excellent speech in reply. The Assembly ordered both to be printed."

Ruth's introduction to Europe was so unsatisfactory that one wonders how she ever came to enjoy living abroad. When Joel finally met her in London and escorted her to Paris, Ruth found herself amid the alien corn, unable to speak any French, and very homesick. The deterioration of Joel's business and the cruel wait in London tincture this letter to Mary Dwight:

> No person can have an idea of extravagance & luxury, folly, wickedness & wretchedness without coming to Europe. . . . O! it is altogether disagreeable to me. . . . I have not an hour I can call

my own but when I sleep, must at all times be dressed & see company, which, my dear Madam, you know is not to my taste. We are pent up in a narrow dirty street surrounded with high houses, can scarcely see the light of the sun. The noise, folly & bustle with which I am surrounded almost distract me. We have no Sabbath. It is looked upon as a day to amusement entirely. . . . . O! how ardently do I wish to return to America & my dear friends there, to Greenfield, that dear delightful village where I have passed so many pleasant hours.

But despite the strangeness and vexations, Paris was Paris, and Ruth was a woman. She concluded her letter by observing to Mary that this season the "ladies wear very small caps, hats, & bonnets."

5: *Presto e Furioso*

Ruth Barlow arrived in Paris in time to witness the decline and fall of the Scioto speculation. She soon had to stop feeling sorry for herself and become the matriarchal rock on which her husband could cling. The story which unfolds during the six months after Ruth reached Europe is one of punctured optimism, unfulfilled commitments, and bad faith. Joel's practical education in commerce and finance was progressing rapidly but not fast enough to solve the multitude of problems thrown at him. The bottom dropped out of his career about January, 1791.

Trouble began late in the summer when Duer, who never bothered to write his agent, did trouble to cash a bill drawn on Paris. In an evil moment Barlow had told Duer to draw on him for one hundred thousand livres. He had expected the trickle of money already collected to swell to a torrent, but funds to meet the demand did not come in and he had to refuse acceptance of the obligation. Nothing could have damaged the land sales more than the whisper of insolvency, and to compound Barlow's troubles his financial embarrassments ramified. Other land salesmen were dismayed when the news got out that Barlow had refused payment of a bill. Gouverneur Morris was furious, for Barlow was ruining the game for everyone. Morris wrote a friend in Philadelphia that if he did not manage to sell his own land, "you may place it to the Account of this same Company [Scioto], against whose Deceptions the Cry is general here." Though Duer did not write Barlow, Andrew Craigie warned him in May that various bills had been drawn on him. Craigie hoped that Barlow had been cautious because a "demur would ruin the whole business." By the time Barlow received Craigie's warning, however, the damage had been done.

Trouble had come in a steady procession during 1790. Soon after the first shipload of immigrants sailed, two of the principal men of the French Scioto company had to flee France. One was the comptroller-general of the royal treasury, whose departure resulted from "his politics or delinquency in public office"—Barlow did not know which. After that, payments for shares in the company stopped coming in, and Barlow realized that the venture had collapsed. For six months he stewed over the situation, kept quiet about the company's failure, and tried to sell land himself. But he was unable to meet Duer's drafts and could only wait for the blow to fall. During the frantic month that Ruth had been waiting in London, Barlow was concocting a last desperate remedy: a contract with a new firm, DeBarth, Coquet, and Company, who advanced a little money and took over the land sales. The second contract, as Barlow later explained, "arose from a train of indescribable events which filled my mind with horror," and the arrangement with DeBarth was "conceived in caution and brought forth in a state of anxiety and vexation which borders on despair."

Though Barlow pumped manfully, the ship was sinking slowly and inevitably. The second contract was highly unfavorable for the original Scioto speculators. It offered them a tiny profit and called for payments only after the land had been sold. This agreement required the speculators to buy the land from Congress, get their money back after the land had been sold in France, and then split the proceeds with the French firm. This was such a bad arrangement for Duer and his associates that Rufus Putnam accused Barlow of being "a consummate villain or greatly wanting in sagacity not to see the fatal consequences of such an arrangement." Duer, meantime, was deserting the sinking ship and planning a new speculation in Maine land, on which he would make a quick three-hundred-per-cent profit.

General Putnam could afford some righteous indignation over the contract negotiated four thousand miles away. He was on the ground in Marietta dealing with a colony of dissident Frenchmen who had discovered that southern Ohio was not the Garden of Eden. Barlow had bestowed his blessing on the immigrants and shipped them as far as Philadelphia and Alexandria. Duer, who kept his own counsel and stayed as usual in the background, pretty well managed to avoid any responsibility for settling the French on the Ohio land. It remained for other Scioto associates and the Ohio Company to take charge of the six hundred excitable Frenchmen who landed in America with deeds to land that Congress still owned.

The French colonists followed a trail of delay, frustration, and disillusionment from the East Coast to the town they founded at Gallipolis. William Duer had a chance to be a statesman and empire-builder, but he lacked the vision and enthusiasm of Barlow and sank to the depths of petty procrastination and evasion. His contract with Congress was immensely valuable, and the land was as fertile as the French brochures had claimed. A rich man with all the right connections, he could have backed the French colony and opened the way for an extensive development of the three and a half million Ohio acres. But Duer shoved off the task of getting the French to Ohio on Andrew Craigie, whose record in this business is only fair. Craigie delayed and equivocated but in the end had enough decency to take a little responsibility for the settlers. The ultimate task of leading the immigrants to their land, however, devolved on subordinates who got precious little direction from either Craigie or Duer. Craigie was guilty of gross misrepresentation when he wrote Barlow in May: "Every exertion has been made to realize in the fullest manner the expectations of the Settlers and they are generally as happy as can be."

The fact is that they were intensely unhappy and were months getting to Ohio. When they reached America, of course, something had to be done with them. Since Duer did not own any land, he had to find some, and he arranged to buy a tract, which he never paid for, from the Ohio Company. All the while, he kept out of sight so that no one would know the Scioto Associates were in any way concerned. He was, however, forced into financing the overland trek. The French eventually were settled on the Ohio at Gallipolis in time for an Indian uprising that drove the surveyors into the settlements and terrified the settlers. Then the French faced the hardships of rooting themselves in the new country and carving out homesteads from the wilderness while facing possible eviction because they really did not own their land. To make matters impossible, the immigrants were a heterogeneous bunch, mostly illprepared to be pioneers anyway. When Constantin Volney visited Gallipolis in 1796, he found only about eighty sallow, thin, sickly remnants of the original six hundred French; the rest had drifted elsewhere in discouragement or never had reached Ohio at all.

One can imagine the horrendous accounts of America that traveled back to France by letter. While Barlow waited in Paris for glowing reports to revive the collapsing business, relatives heard that their loved ones were about to starve or be scalped by the savages. Barlow was threatened with assassination and feared that he would be attacked at his hotel. In December he was called to a friend's house and warned to get out of town immediately. This friend expected a mob, Barlow wrote, and was sure that neither the civil nor military police would dare to interfere. Barlow brazened out the clamor, however, and nothing happened. But by this time he was out of money, in debt, and under a cloud both at home and among the Americans in Paris.

When the Scioto speculation reached a hopeless tangle, Duer and his associates sent a special agent to investigate Barlow's activities. In December Colonel Benjamin Walker reached Paris with three commissions: he could supplant Barlow as agent; he could act with Barlow as joint agent; he could audit the accounts. Walker arrived in the same month that Barlow was threatened with assassination, and the unhappy young man was never so glad to see anyone in all his life. Walker calmly examined the books, reviewed the transactions from the beginning, and cleared Barlow of any charge of dishonesty. As he described the business, however, it was "so miserably entangled and in the hands of such a set of rascals" that he was ashamed to have anything to do with it. "Our friend Barlow," he explained, "has from a concurrence of untoward circumstances, and some weakness on his part, ruined the Company and rendered himself wretched."

Walker stayed several months in France determining that nothing could be salvaged from the fiasco, then returned to America leaving Barlow, in his words, "in a most ineligible situation and undecided what to do." Barlow presently cut himself loose from the Scioto adventure and with a little self-pity wrote an apologia to his old classmate Oliver Wolcott, who by this time was Comptroller of the Treasury: "I . . . shall probably return to my dear country without any other advantage than having seen & heard much, & experienced as many disappointments in the turn of three years as are in the common course of things crowded into the life of any one man." Barlow's private summary of his disaster was reasonably correct. He had dealt with "perfidious men, who have deceived me," but he added that the true cause of the failure was the "eternal delays of my associates in America, & the unaccountable silence that they have always kept towards me."

So far as he was able to assess the situation, he was accurate, and he might have added that the dishonesty of William Playfair, who seems to have embezzled some of the funds from the land sales, was another factor. But his greatest shortcoming was inexperience. Duer and his associates sent a boy to do a man's job, and though the boy grew up trying to do the job, the mission was an expensive failure. Barlow trusted people he should not have trusted; he persisted in optimism when he should have remained profoundly skeptical. He accepted promises and poor collateral and spent what little money he collected to send off the immigrants. But the blame finally belongs on the shoulders of William Duer, who stood in the wings to take applause if there was any and to get away quick if the show failed. Barlow never realized until too late that Duer preferred to abandon the project rather than convert it into a legitimate business.

There is nice irony, however, in the epilogue to this sorry affair. Barlow learned about men and business from this experience and after a subsequent interlude of heavy politicking in France and England succeeded in making his fortune in commerce. William Duer, the canny manipulator, speculated once too often, and when the government sued him over two unbalanced accounts he went bankrupt. Though he had been Hamilton's Assistant Secretary of the Treasury, he was arrested for debt in 1792 and spent the last seven years of his life in prison. His smash was so resounding that it caused the first financial panic in New York history. One of the contributing factors in Duer's downfall was the Scioto speculation, which through the presumption of Joel Barlow involved him willy-nilly in the settlement of the West.

CHAPTER V

Politician of the World

1: *Mission Discovered*

Grass turned green in the public gardens and birds came back to the *bois*, but the Barlows took little pleasure in the arrival of spring. They were down and nearly out in Paris. Almost three years before, Joel had set out for Europe to make a fortune and (somewhat incidentally) to help populate the Ohio Valley; but he had succeeded in neither objective. If he returned to America now, he must regard himself a failure. If he remained in Europe, what was he going to do? While the horns of this dilemma pricked him hard, his brother-in-law Abraham Baldwin, now a United States Senator, wrote him an unembellished sermon on the ignominy of the mercenary motive. Baldwin included his sister in the blunt reproach: "Because Scioto did not clear you seventy thousand dollars for an independent fortune to be lazy upon the rest of your days, you are quite vexed and think yourselves ill used. There have been so many fools and goose heads making three times that sum since you have been gone, by speculating on the proceedings of some of us big fools that I almost feel myself more happy and am no doubt in better credit in my poverty. . . . In fact I began to fear your anxiety for money getting would make you less useful and less pleasing to your friends."

During this spring of stocktaking the Barlows lived frugally on the top floor of the Palais Royal Hotel. To get to their rooms a visitor had to climb three flights of stairs and knock on the locked door of a gambling casino. When the porter opened the door, the visitor, announcing himself as a guest of the Barlows, was passed through the barrier and up another flight of stairs to the fourth floor of the building. Among the Americans in Paris, the Boston businessman James Swan and his wife and the Blackdens remained friendly with the Barlows and often climbed the four flights for an evening of conversation or a game of loo. Colonel Blackden, who was in Paris selling rival Kentucky land, even had tried to help Barlow make a go of the Scioto speculation.

The immediate necessity was making a living. After Colonel Walker returned from Paris, Andrew Craigie, feeling some measure of responsibility for the Barlows' predicament, sent them a draft for one hundred guineas—presumably to return home on. But before that remittance arrived, Joel turned to the literary byways to seek support. In April Brissot de Warville, now a prominent Girondist and leader of the Revolution, published his *Nouveau Voyage*, an account of his travels in the United States in 1788. The book was, Barlow believed, the most judicious and candid glimpse of America written by any recent European traveler and, furthermore, it was the work of a great friend of republican principles and the United States. Barlow translated the *Travels* into English, sent off one copy of the manuscript to America, and soon took another to London.

More than wounded *amour propre* and reluctance to face his critics at home kept Barlow in Europe. The French Revolution exerted a growing fascination that held him like a moth to a candle. The prospects of making a living seemed as good in Europe as in America, or so he convinced himself. An American with an intimate knowledge of France could find business opportunities in the burgeoning commercial society around him. In addition, a man with even a modest literary reputation could support himself, precariously to be sure, as a writer in London or Paris. Soon after the middle of July, 1791, the Barlows left France for England. They traveled by way of Lille, where Joel planned to transact some un-specified business, and reached London about the first of August.

For several months Barlow's plans were in a state of flux, and during this period he would have welcomed a steady job. Before crossing to England, he had heard rumors that James Madison was to be the American minister to England and wrote Baldwin that· he would like very much to be secretary of the legation, if Baldwin could get the post for him. In October he wrote Wolcott that he would come home the next spring if his friends could find him a suitable position. He had been informed that Secretary of the Treasury Hamilton planned to open a land office in Philadelphia, and he wanted to know if there was any chance of his being ap-pointed to run it.

Gradually, however, Barlow found his immediate vocation in political journalism. This, he discovered, was the career he had been looking for. Here was a chance to lose himself in the cause of freedom. He still hoped to make a name, but the matter of earning a living would have to take care of itself. For the next two years he worked tirelessly and idealistically for the principles of liberty, equality, and fraternity. In the course of his exertions he attacked institutionalized tyranny both in England and on the Con-tinent. He had left the ministry in America, not feeling a sufficient call to do battle with the devil in Connecticut, where indeed it might be said the devil, if he existed, was in that happy state a benign fellow. Three years abroad had toughened Barlow and con-vinced him that sin existed. Once he had rid himself of the albatross of speculation, he was free to confront a European Satan disguised as the Old World Tyrant.

Events of the spring before Barlow left Paris were impelling him to active involvement in the French Revolution. In his early en-thusiasm over the fall of the Bastille he thought that great, irre-pressible forces of human destiny were carrying the principles of liberty to Europe. The freedom that flamed in men's breasts in 1776 was moving eastward, first to France, then to other Old World countries. But it soon became apparent that the old order would not give up easily; "tyranny like hell," Paine had written during

Washington's retreat across New Jersey, "is not easily conquered
. . . what we obtain too cheap, we esteem too lightly."

The canny Leopold of Austria, working with all the considerable
diplomatic skill he possessed, was alerting the crowned heads of
Europe to rally around the beleaguered Louis XVI and Marie Antoinette. When the shrewd Mirabeau died in April, 1791, Louis
lost the one advisor who might have steered France into a constitutional monarchy. Irritated beyond endurance at their palace imprisonment, the King and Queen fled Paris, only to be caught
immediately and returned as real prisoners. From this time forward
none of the European monarchs could overlook the threat France
posed for royal institutions. The French people, too, could not
overlook the Bourbon opposition to economic and political house-
cleaning. During the summer, Leopold issued manifestoes and called
conferences to mobilize the power of France's neighbors, and in
September Louis was forced to swallow an unpalatable new constitution. During Barlow's first few months in London these occur-
rences, like star shells bursting overhead, illuminated the site of the
coming battle. In England, meantime, when the Barlows took lodging in Great Litchfield Street, a vigorous debate was in progress.

In London during 1791 the French Revolution was an object of
intense interest, but so long as the French Assembly sparred with
the King over domestic issues, the Pitt ministry was inclined to remain a spectator. Not so, many Englishmen, who hurled pamphlets at each other in fervent argument. The topic might have been
stated: Resolved that the French Revolution is a blessing to mankind. For the affirmative stood Richard Price, Thomas Paine, Mary
Wollstonecraft, Joseph Priestley, James Mackintosh, and others;
for the negative towered the giant Edmund Burke over a group of
mostly anonymous coattail riders.

The debate had begun several months after the fall of the Bastille when Price eulogized the French Revolution on the anniversary
of England's own Glorious (but bloodless) Revolution. Burke,
who once had championed the American revolutionists, now took
alarm at events in France. When the mob broke into the palace at
Versailles, it seemed to him that "the age of chivalry is gone . . .

116

the glory of Europe is extinguished forever." Late in 1790 Burke issued his famous manifesto, *Reflections on the Revolution in France*, a savage attack on Price and a powerful challenge to the legion of articulate liberals who saw in France a new day dawning for all of Europe. The gauntlet flung down by a writer of Burke's eloquence was immediately picked up; within a year dozens of replies attacking Burke cascaded from the presses in thousands of copies. The *Reflections*, meantime, went through twelve editions in a few months.

The chief adversary was Paine, who abandoned his iron bridge project and sat down to the task he had performed so well during the American Revolution. His reply to Burke, the equally famous *Rights of Man*, appeared three months later. Its success was as great as Burke's (seven editions by the end of the year), and both sides of the controversy now had champions of major stature. When Paine suggests that hereditary mathematicians are as logical as hereditary legislators, or answers Burke's lament for the demise of chivalry with the retort that Burke "pities the plumage, but forgets the dying bird," one does not wonder that the *Rights of Man* seemed a dangerous book. When the great debate reached a noisy fortissimo, Joel and Ruth Barlow appeared in England.

Although he had planned some sort of unspecified business relationship with Henry Bromfield, ship and cargo broker, Barlow landed almost at once with both feet in the political arena. He carried with him the translation of Brissot's *Travels*, which he hoped to find a publisher for, but he did not expect writing to be more than a profitable avocation. As he prepared to leave Paris, he described himself as a "luckless wight, who once in vain/ Strove to unlock the Muses' hallowed fane" and, as he put it, had been

> Doom'd for his fault through endless miles to roam,
> Each clime his country and each cave his home.

Before he knew what had happened, however, he was associating daily with the leading English friends of the French Revolution. Paine's publisher, J. S. Jordan, soon brought out an edition of the *Travels* and also was interested in issuing John Trumbull's pro-republican political satire, *M'Fingal*, with Barlow's introduction and notes. Mary Wollstonecraft's publisher, Joseph Johnson, was eager to publish whatever Barlow cared to contribute to the great debate.

Barlow crossed the Channel already knowing, personally and by correspondence, several prominent English liberals. He had struck up a friendship with Dr. John Warner, who had gone to Paris as chaplain to the British ambassador and had imbibed revolutionary ideas. He had spent a couple of days with Paine in 1788 during his first visit to London and no doubt had seen Paine more recently in Paris. He had dined with Horne Tooke in London. He long had felt a strong intellectual kinship with Richard Price, who once read and praised the *Vision of Columbus* in manuscript, and when he first visited England he had carried a letter of introduction to Price from Jefferson. This nucleus of Warner, Paine, Tooke, and Price quickly expanded to include all the prominent liberals and radicals: Mary Wollstonecraft, later wife of William Godwin and mother of Mary Shelley, who became an intimate friend of both Ruth and Joel and whom Barlow described as "a woman of great original genius"; Godwin, her husband, who was a novelist, philosopher, author of the important *Political Justice* and "an amiable benevolent man"; Joseph Priestley, who was scientist and liberal clergyman; James Mackintosh, later Sir James but then "poor as a rat"; William Hayley, the poet; Thomas Holcroft, Thomas Hardy, John Thelwall—all important names in the history of English radicalism.

By autumn Barlow was deeply involved in his own reply to Burke's *Reflections*. This would be, he candidly wrote his brother-in-law, an atonement for and a counterbalance to the Scioto smash. To accomplish it he would have "to chin up to the level of the politics of Europe." He explained further that he was meditating an attack to be announced in a manifesto something like this: "The Renovation of Society, or An Essay on the Necessity & Propriety of a Revolution in the Governments of Europe."

> I have such a flood of indignation & such a store of argument accumulated in my guts on this subject, that I can hold in no longer;

& I think the nurslings of abuses may be stung more to the quick than they have yet been by all the discussions to which the French Revolution has given occasion. Taking it for granted that a similar change through all Europe is inevitable, I propose to examine how far it is desirable, and what will be its consequences.

2: *Pamphleteer*

Indignation at Burke's assault on Dr. Price, excitement over the French Revolution, absolute faith in republican principles, and naked ambition produced Barlow's most important and lasting work. From October, 1791, till January, 1792, he labored over his manuscript. On February fourth, a few days before part two of Paine's *Rights of Man* appeared, Joseph Johnson offered the public Barlow's work: *Advice to the Privileged Orders in the Several States of Europe Resulting from the Necessity and Propriety of a General Revolution in the Principle of Government.* The book sold for one shilling, sixpence, and soon went through three editions. It never had the wide circulation that both Burke and Paine achieved, but next to the *Rights of Man*, Barlow's *Advice* was the work considered most seditious by the British government. When Thomas Hardy later was tried for sedition, the crown prosecutor declared, as he brandished a copy of the *Advice* in court: "Barlow's book you will find is in the plainest and most unequivocal language, as I understand it, an exhortation to all people to get rid of kingly government." The prosecution, however, was not able to show that Hardy's approval of the *Advice* and his activity as Secretary of the London Corresponding Society were more than peaceful efforts to bring about parliamentary reform. The defendant was acquitted and then drawn through the streets of London in a carriage by a host of well-wishers.

The *Rights of Man* and *Advice to the Privileged Orders* were complementary works. Paine, the brilliant journalist who could reduce complex arguments to language any literate butcher could grasp, was the more dangerous fellow. His book, a downright inflammatory document, was proscribed the next year and Paine himself convicted *in absentia* of seditious libel. Barlow, who had enjoyed more education and was more reflective, produced a better reasoned, more philosophical, but less subversive pamphlet. The *Advice* never was banned, nor was Johnson ever indicted for printing it, as Jordan was for publishing *Rights of Man*. The *St. James Chronicle*, reviewing the *Advice*, noted that while Paine had been sparing in his treatment of law and religion, these omissions were corrected by Barlow. The paper discovered that the ex-lawyer and ex-clergyman was particularly lucid on these two topics in which he had had the most experience. Such was Barlow's design, for he intended his pamphlet to round out Paine's work. He was sure that his book would find no reader "who will not have read the *Rights of Man*." Paine, he wrote, is "a luminary of the age, and one of the greatest benefactors of mankind."

Advice to the Privileged Orders, despite its condescending title, addresses itself to the rational, educated minds of Europe's upper classes. Barlow assumes that any intelligent person will agree that eighteenth-century Enlightenment has ushered in a new era. He feels it his mission, so the introduction states, "to induce the men who now govern the world" to adopt the principles on which the American and French Revolutions are based. The political reformers have two powerful weapons, he writes, the force of reason and the force of numbers, but it is their sacred duty "to wield with dexterity this mild and beneficent weapon [reason], before recurring to the use of the other."

In this appeal to man's intelligence and in this faith in his reasonableness there is a mixture of idealism and naïve optimism that makes the political philosophy of the eighteenth century particularly attractive in an age of disillusioned uncertainty. Given Barlow's premise that government of, by, and for the people was an accomplished fact, given his faith in the rightness of republican principles, the *Advice* is a cleverly argued and penetrating, though sometimes inconsistent, brief. Sometimes he is carried away by his rhetoric, but the tone is usually moderate and calm.

The pamphlet begins with a chapter on the feudal system that traces the evil effects of lingering medieval institutions. Barlow

120

strikes hard at primogeniture and entailment, devices which per-
petuate inequality and tyranny. Political freedom cannot take root
where the laws of property continually re-enforce ideas of special
privilege. In the second chapter the attack shifts from legal institutions to the church, another means historically conceived and
employed to maintain despotism. Barlow makes a clear distinction
between the state church as an ally of authoritarian government and
plain religion. He argues that the wedding of church and state is
a great evil and points to the blessings enjoyed by the United States
without a state church. As a result, he asserts, "in no country are
the people more religious."

Chapter Three deals with the military system. To Barlow, as to
other philosophers of the Enlightenment, the standing army is the
cause of war, and if the armies of reigning princes can be abolished,
the great obstacle to freedom and to a constantly rising standard of
living will be removed. All modern wars are caused by the am-
bitions of greedy kings whose whims or pique can thrust war on
unwilling subjects. This attitude, of course, makes good sense in
the era before the rise of modern nationalistic states. As an expatriate from a fast-growing commercial and republican society,
Barlow sees clearly the need for peace to protect a nation's economic
development and its democratic institutions.

Barlow's essay on the administration of justice, Chapter Four, is
perhaps the most effective part of his pamphlet. The *St. James
Chronicle* praised his "endeavors to prove . . . that the formalities,
delays, and expensiveness of the English jurisprudence, are unnecessary, burdensome, and grievous; since the same ends are obtained
in America with one hundredth part of the trouble and expense."
As a lawyer who recently had practiced in Hartford and now was
observing the law's delay in Europe, Barlow argued ably for legal
reform. He believed that English civil courts obstructed rather
than aided justice by making the legal machinery grind exceedingly
slow and too expensively for a poor man. His attack on criminal
law is less detailed but characteristically humane and is influenced
by the "compassionate little treatise" of Beccaria, *Of Crimes and
Punishments*, a book Barlow once had for sale in his Hartford shop.

Advice to the Privileged Orders appeared in 1792 in four chap-ters, though eight were promised in the introduction. Barlow planned a second part, but Paine's *Rights of Man*, Part II, a treatise on government, went on sale in the same month and covered much of the ground he had intended to travel. Accordingly, he waited until late in the year, then wrote only one more chapter, which was not published in England for three years. By the end of 1792, as the French Revolution threatened to spread, the English government panicked, put agents on the trail of leading radicals, and began preparing information for indictments. When Johnson lost his nerve and refused to publish Barlow's final chapter, it was brought out in Paris the following year.

Chapter Five, "Revenue and Expenditure" is hardly a seditious work, though it contains an intemperate attack on Burke. Most of the essay is a cogent brief against indirect taxes. Barlow argues that corrupt governments use hidden levies to obtain revenue for needless and harmful activities. Political reform must be accompanied by tax reform, and the people must know when they are paying taxes if the government is to be kept honest. The great secret in the modern science of finance, Barlow explains, is to keep the taxpayer ignorant of the precise source of the government's income. To illustrate, he quotes Cardinal de Richelieu's principle: "The people must be hoodwinked . . . if you would have them tame and patient drudges."

Before finishing the *Advice*, Barlow could not resist blistering the chief spokesman for the status quo. Though all the enemies of the French Revolution had revealed in their tedious arguments the "deformities" of unrepresentative government, Burke was the most shameless: "Mr. Burke, in a frenzy of passion, has drawn away the veil; and aristocracy, like a decayed prostitute, whom painting and patching will no longer embellish, throws off her covering, to get a livelihood by displaying her ugliness." Later Barlow returned to the attack and traced all opposition to the Revolution to Burke's *Reflections*. By then the wars of the French Revolution had begun, and with magnificent oversimplification he declared: "The present war, with all its train of calamities, must be attributed almost exclusively to the pen of Mr. Burke." It was Burke's war, and the Englishman's motives were evil.

Barlow wrote the *Advice to the Privileged Orders* for an audience on both sides of the Atlantic. Two days before the pamphlet was entered in Stationers' Register, he tied up a bundle of copies and sent them to Oliver Wolcott to be handed to Abraham Baldwin, Mr. Jefferson, and Jeremiah Wadsworth, Hartford's representative in Congress. The pamphlet promptly was reprinted in the United States, and Jefferson in an appreciative note of thanks wrote: "Be assured that your endeavors to bring the trans-Atlantic world into the road of reason, are not without their effect here."

Jefferson certainly agreed with many of the ideas in the *Advice*, for the sources of Barlow's pamphlet were often the same sources that formed Jefferson's own mind. Barlow had mastered Blackstone, Locke, Montesquieu before going to Europe. In France he had drunk from the springs of the *philosophes;* in England he had profited by reading and talking with Price, Priestley, and Paine. The warp and woof of his work, in the final analysis, came out of the context of eighteenth-century liberal thought.

Barlow's answer to Burke, in effect, admitted him to the full fellowship of English radicals. On March ninth Horne Tooke, one of the twelve men to be acquitted in the famous sedition trials of 1794, nominated him for membership, along with James Mackintosh, in the Society for Constitutional Information. He was elected a week later, and for the next nine months, whenever in London, he attended the weekly meetings of the society at the Crown and Anchor Tavern. As time went on, he took an increasingly prominent part in the society's activities until finally his name reached debate in Parliament. Burke complained on the floor of the House of Commons in December that he was "pursued and reviled," whenever the subject of France came up, by "assailants of eminence," one of whom he named as the Prophet Joel, "who threatened to lay our capital and constitution in . . . ruin."

Like all governments frustrated by an inability to control unfriendly external events, the British ministry took an hysterical view of the revolutionary societies then flourishing in England. The Constitution Society that Barlow joined, Thomas Hardy's Corresponding Society, and the Revolution Society (formed expressly to commemorate England's own Glorious Revolution) existed

123

chiefly to cheer the French Revolution from the sidelines and to urge badly needed English parliamentary reform. The clubs were hardly subversive unless articulate criticism of the government and support for constitutional monarchy in France were subversive. Paine and a few firebrands did advocate republican government for England, but Barlow's club, which was typical, contained mostly solid citizens: Sir John Carter, Major Cartwright, the Earls of Derby and Effingham, Lord Edward Fitzgerald, Richard Price, Richard Brinsley Sheridan, and others. When France and England went to war the next year and the Terror convulsed France, members of these societies recoiled from the excesses of the Revolution and hugged English institutions to their bosoms. Then Pitt's government began its sedition trials.

In March, 1792, however, the dawn of the brave new world was coming up like thunder from across the Channel, and Barlow went on pamphleteering. He soon published a heavy-handed verse satire, *The Conspiracy of Kings*, which he called a "little mad poem." In it he laid about in all directions, hurled insults at Burke, "degenerate slave" who fought to restore the "scourge to tyrants, and to man his chains," and warned kings to beware for "the hour is come":

> From western heav'ns th' inverted orient springs,
> The morn of man, the dreadful night of kings.

Barlow noted when he sent a copy of his satire to Jefferson that "though one of my kings died while the poem was in the press, it was not my fault." He added: "If this had been the case with all of them, I should have been willing to have suppressed the publication for so good a cause."

The king who died was Leopold of Austria, Marie Antoinette's brother and Louis' ablest ally. His death was a blow to monarchist hopes in France, but it did not weaken the coalition of powers opposing the French Revolution. Hardly had Joseph Johnson begun hawking *The Conspiracy of Kings* than hostilities broke out on the Continent. After Leopold's death on March first Gustavus III of Sweden, another of Louis' allies, was shot on the way to a masked ball. The Girondists then came to power in Paris, and France declared war on Austria. On the eve of the outbreak Barlow left London for France on a mysterious business mission.

The precise nature of the trip, unfortunately, can only be inferred. Barlow's letters from the Continent allude rather cryptically to his business, because English authorities were opening the mail of known radicals. This much is clear, however: A few days before his departure Barlow received a letter from S (James Swan?) in Belgium summoning him to cross the Channel. He was to transact business that required him to visit France. Two days after he landed war broke out, and when he reached Ghent, his friend had gone but left word for him to follow on to Coblenz. Barlow did this and after reaching the German city, the two men laid plans "to render the most essential service to France."

Barlow next was to make his way to Lafayette's headquarters near Metz where the French army was facing the Austrian invaders. On May fourth Barlow got within one mile of the frontier, was stopped by Austrian soldiers and sent back to Luxembourg. He then turned west and traveled towards the Channel, trying several times to get into France, but each time he was turned back till he reached Ostend and embarked on a Dutch ship. He rocked and rolled in a Channel storm for three days and nights before landing at Dunkirk about May twentieth. He proceeded through France to Lafayette's camp and was immediately sent back to Paris by the Marquis to negotiate S's proposition with the appropriate minister.

Whatever the mission was, an evil fate pursued Barlow. When he reached Dunkirk he wrote Ruth: "O my Carissima, had I set out one fortnight sooner . . . everything would have been done to my wish. . . . Had I arrived at Luxembourg three days sooner, I might have got, without difficulty, into France. Had I sailed a tide sooner from Ostend, it would have saved me four days." The original mission, which was to have lasted ten days, dragged on and on, and though Barlow did not succeed in rendering his "essential service to France," he watched history in the making and did not regret his presence in the beleaguered country. Being in the cockpit of action seemed even a bigger thrill than taking part in the great debate in England, and besides, he wrote Ruth, "I make them pay my expenses."

Buried in the archives of the French revolutionary government is a probable explanation of this mission. One cannot be sure, but at precisely the moment that Barlow was trying to get to Lafayette's headquarters, James Swan and a French partner were petitioning the Minister of the Interior to subsidize a tannery and leather-processing business at Longéac. They proposed to prepare hides in the English manner, which many French experts regarded as the best way, both for the enrichment of themselves and for the benefit of the French economy. Lafayette had agreed to sponsor the project, and officials of the Department of Haute Loire had enthusiastically urged the government in Paris to approve the plan. But despite Lafayette's prestige and the promptings of provincial officials, the Minister of the Interior called in his own experts who turned down the proposal. Swan realized that a new effort was needed if the plan was to see light, and he may have called in Barlow, who was acquiring a reputation in France for his writings and knew Lafayette well. Nevertheless, Barlow's trip to Lafayette's headquarters at Metz and his visit to government offices in Paris had no effect on Swan's enterprise, and the proposal died unborn.

Joel, meantime, remained in Paris observing the Revolution. When the mob broke into the Tuileries on June twentieth, and though this event snapped the final link between the King and the people, Joel reported reassuringly: "You will hear frightful stories about the riots . . . believe but little. There was no violence committed. This visit to the king by armed citizens was undoubtedly contrary to law, but the existence of a king is contrary to another law of a higher origin." Before the invasion of the Tuileries he had informed his wife: "Through all France one breathes only liberty, firmness, resolution immovable to establish the cause at any price."

During the ten-day trip that stretched to ten weeks, Ruth Barlow remained patiently in London awaiting her husband. She contented herself with Mary Wollstonecraft's growing friendship and Joel's frequent letters filled with tender sentiments. These epistles are wholly characteristic of all his correspondence with his wife, but Mary Wollstonecraft, who was shown the letters, read them with a good bit of impatience. While Ruth was delighted by Joel's eloquent terms of endearment, Mary, the ardent feminist, wrote her sister: "I was almost disgusted with the *tender* passages which afforded her so much satisfaction, because they were turned so prettily that they looked more like the cold ingenuity of the head than the warm overflowings of the heart." Mary concluded, somewhat ungenerously, that while Ruth had a very benevolent, affectionate heart, she was a "little warped by romance."

Mary Wollstonecraft, though temperamentally impatient with sentiment, had her own reasons for wanting Barlow back in England. He had talked of returning to America soon and taking with him Mary's younger brother Charles. When such plans were made tentatively in February, Mary had written her sister enthusiastically about her new friend. She confided that Barlow had taken a great liking to Charles and would keep him in his family. "Such a situation would be a more desirable one, for he [Barlow] has a sound understanding with great mildness of temper . . . rather a regulated temper than natural good humour." Mary further reported that recently Barlow had clapped Charles on the knee and said that "as his wife and he could never contrive to make any boys they must try what they could do with one ready brought up to their hands." When Barlow's fascination with politics kept delaying his departure for home, Mary grew impatient and finally sent the boy to America to seek his fortune alone. He carried with him cordial letters of introduction from Barlow, but Mary, with considerable pique, wrote her sister that while Barlow was a worthy man, he was devoured by ambition. His thoughts were turned towards France, she said, and till the present commotions were over, he no doubt would find some excuse every month to make to himself for staying in Europe.

3: *Citizen Barlow*

By the first of July, 1792, Barlow was back in London where excitement was running high over recent events on the Continent. Mary Wollstonecraft was correct in her notion that he would keep postponing indefinitely his departure for home. Within a few months he was more deeply committed to the Revolution than ever, and by the next spring he would be writing friends in America: "I shall not now fix any time when I shall see you." In August the leaders of the Revolution suspended Louis XVI from his office and took over the Tuileries. In September the notorious prison massacres of political victims foreshadowed the coming blood bath of the Terror. In the same month the defenders of France stopped the invading armies in the Argonne, and the National Convention declared France a republic. By the end of the autumn the French Revolutionary armies, victorious everywhere, occupied Belgium and the Rhineland, and the revolutionary fervor reached an absolute peak on November nineteenth when the French Convention proclaimed itself ready to bring freedom to all Europe.

Barlow's enthusiasm and reputation mounted steadily during the fall. When news reached London that France might soon become a republic, he sat down to address the National Convention on measures that should be adopted in drafting a new constitution. Between the middle of September and the end of the month, he wrote *A Letter to the National Convention* and sent it to Paine to deliver in Paris. He declared when he posted a copy to Jefferson that France now was taking steps to "establish a glorious republic" and his pamphlet stood "a chance to do some good." Even before the *Letter* had been delivered to the Convention, however, Brissot's newspaper suggested that Barlow be made a French citizen for writing the *Advice*, a book described by the paper as "almost equal in merit to the work on the Rights of Man by Mr. Paine." Barlow's *Letter* subsequently insured his election to French citizenship. When he became Citizen Barlow, he joined the select company of Washington, Hamilton, Madison, and Paine, who already had been honored similarly.

A Letter to the National Convention is a statesmanlike document making specific proposals for the new constitution. In broad outline Barlow's ideas derive from the experience of the United States in establishing republican government. He argues that experiments with limited monarchy have failed in France, for experience has shown "*that kings can do no good.*" Any people, whether wise or vicious, he asserts, are better able to govern themselves than the wisest of hereditary legislators. "A republic of beavers or of monkeys, I believe, could not be benefited by receiving their laws from men, any more than men could be in being governed by them." The sure and only characteristic of a good law is that it be the perfect expression of the will of the nation. To insure the popular voice in government, he goes on to urge, representation in the government must be based on population, not property; the voting base must be broadened, the age of majority lowered, elections held frequently. The *Letter* is full of practical measures clearly expounded: he is against large salaries for officials, imprisonment for debt, capital punishment, colonization, and standing armies. He also urges the separation of church and state and ridicules the idea that the people of France must learn the proper mode of worshiping God from the decrees of the Council of Trent. It would be just as absurd, he argues, "to appeal to such a council to learn how to breathe."

Barlow's *Letter* boosted his standing in France and prepared the way for the next phase of his political career. On November seventh Paine, who was a member of the National Convention, presented the pamphlet to the assembly and paid tribute to his friend's republican principles. Henri Grégoire in the chair accepted the gift and had it sent to the Constitutional Committee. He also ordered it translated and made part of the minutes of the Convention. Finally he proposed that Barlow's name be added to the list of foreigners to whom the title and rights of citizenship previously had been extended. This nomination was referred immediately to the Diplomatic Committee.

How much Barlow's ideas influenced the Constitutional Committee is a moot point. Some of his proposals are embodied in the new constitution while others are not, but none of his suggestions was original. Nevertheless, when Guyton Morreau, reporting favorably on Barlow's proposed French citizenship, spoke to the Convention on February seventeenth, he declared that Barlow's *Letter* had exerted a significant influence on the new constitution. Before Barlow wrote, he said, there was a universal prejudice that a country as large as France could not be governed as a republic, but "Barlow reversed this prejudice by the logic of his argument."

129

Whatever the truth of this matter may be, Barlow gave articulate voice to notions then current and perhaps helped precipitate a few ideas in the deliberations of the Constitutional Committee. His pamphlet was immediately circulated in French and made available to members of the Convention. Dr. Warner, then visiting Paris, wrote that the *Letter* would "do great credit to the writer." Barlow should come over to France, he begged, to exult with him "at the glorious successes of the infant republic." William Hayley, in response to a gift of the pamphlet, wrote: "Dear Politician of the New World . . . Many thanks for your new publication, which, though I am not yet a Republican, I have read with great pleasure."

Barlow also sent copies of the *Letter* to the various revolutionary societies in England. To one of them he wrote in his accompanying note: "Although the observations . . . are more particularly applicable to the French nation . . . yet, as the true principles of society are everywhere the same, their examination cannot be unseasonable in any nation or at any time. . . . It is the duty of every individual to assist . . . in removing the obstructions that are found in the way of this revolution." The Constitution Society, which read the *Letter* at its October twelfth meeting, voted Barlow thanks for "so valuable a present . . . [which] by exhibiting the most important political truths . . . is . . . happily calculated to inform the inquiring mind, and to inspire an ardent and enlightened zeal for the freedom and happiness of mankind."

These letters of transmittal and resolutions of thanks alarmed the government, which later used them as evidence in its sedition trials, and though Barlow never was indicted, his departure for France in November may have forestalled legal action. As Pitt's government tightened its security measures, Barlow prepared to cross the Channel to carry a congratulatory address from the Constitution Society to the French Convention. He hardly needed Dr. Warner's invitation to come to France, for he was promptly put on a committee to prepare the greeting, which he wrote himself. The society approved the address and delegated Barlow and John Frost to deliver it in person. Soon after the middle of November the two men slipped out of London, and by the twenty-second Barlow was lodged in Paris waiting to present the address at the bar of the Convention. With high spirit he wrote Ruth in Italian soon after arriving: "I am lodged in the house of a widowed citizeness with her family. This lady shares her table with me but not her bed."

Two days later Barlow's great moment came on the floor of the Convention. He stood before the assembled leaders of the Revolution, Grégoire presiding, and read his message to the universal applause of the deputies. When he finished, Joel reported: "The president gave us the kiss of fraternity . . . which we returned in behalf of our society. The scene . . . drew tears from a crowded assembly. It gave rise to reflections, which can scarcely be conceived." To a man whose previous efforts to sell land in France had ended in disaster, the thunderclaps of approval must have been sweet sounds that fortified the ego and erased the anguished memories of Scioto. Barlow still was a poor man, but he was rapidly becoming famous, or from another point of view, notorious. The address was so alarming to the British government that some observers said it touched off the state trials of 1794.

As he read his message, he saw the shackles falling from oppressed peoples everywhere. "Benefactors of mankind," began the address, "we rejoice that your revolution has arrived at . . . perfection." Then he went on to assure the French that people in all countries were behind them and only waited to be delivered by their arms from the dreaded necessity of fighting against them. "Go on, legislators, in the work of human happiness," he rhapsodized; "the benefits will in part be ours, but the glory shall be all your own." And finally after five hundred words of florid prose he concluded that the glories of the Revolution would dispel all despotism and create a new character in man: "For nations, rising from their lethargy, will reclaim the rights of man, with a voice which man cannot resist."

Barlow's enthusiasm for the French Revolution was shared by his countrymen in America. Even New England Federalists approved at first of events in France, and Barlow's old friends began to hear of his new prominence. Ezra Stiles, for example, wrote warmly: "I congratulate you upon the celebrity & fame which your *poetical* & *political* writings have justly merited & acquired to you." And he went on at length to praise the work of the French National

Convention, "one of the most important & illustrious assemblies that ever sat on this terraqueous globe." More tangible approval was offered by James Watson, Yale friend and New York businessman: "Should fortune have enrolled you in the list of worthies too dignified with intellectual riches, to possess those of a humbler nature, I beg you to draw on me for one thousand dollars at a short sight." Barlow did not accept the money but was delighted by the gesture. Stiles died within two years, before Barlow became anathema to Federalists, but Watson, if he remembered, later regretted his support of Barlow's republicanism.

While Barlow kept his finger on the revolutionary pulse of France, the King called Parliament into special session to meet a crisis in England. The government mobilized the militia, and the Crown asked for extraordinary powers to deal with the revolutionary societies that allegedly were propagating seditious doctrines. Charles James Fox, who had broken with Burke two years before, opposed the King's minister. He denounced the proposals for special powers as a "new scheme of tyranny" by which "we are not to judge of the conduct of men by their overt acts." "We are to arraign" men for their "secret thoughts," he charged, and to punish them "because we choose to believe" them guilty. The Whig fight to preserve hard-won English liberties, however, was a rear-guard action, for in January the French executed their king and in February declared war on England. The great debate in England came to a close as former friends of France turned against the Revolution. Prime Minister Pitt found it necessary to suspend the writ of habeas corpus, and if the sedition trials of the next year had been successful, he might have gone down in history as a witch-hunter. Fortunately, the government lost its cases, and the hysteria under which hundreds of other indictments had been prepared eventually subsided.

Meantime, Ruth Barlow, left behind in England, faced alone the changing climate of opinion. She had to see and hear her husband denounced as a dangerous radical, and she wrote him in early January: "I am obliged to avoid company not to hear you abused." A week later: "You are very obnoxious here and it is thought you cannot return with safety. . . . Mr. Burke said, 'The members of the Constitutional Society held open correspondence with certain societies in France, for the express purpose of altering the constitution of this country.'" Shortly before war broke out, Ruth wondered what was to become of her and believed that she would have to go home alone. "My heart revolts at the idea, but it must be." And she added that "my feelings have been much wounded . . . to see & hear my beloved . . . thus scandalized as he has been here, when I know so well the goodness, the rectitude of his heart & intentions." On the day war was declared she continued in despair: "Heaven only knows when we can meet again. . . . Our fortune is hard, but . . . I have more philosophy than you imagine. Pray take care of your life & health that we may one day meet again. You will see that some tears blot my paper. This tribute you must allow to my weakness."

Joel received the tear-stained letter a long way from the strenuous events of Paris or London. When Louis XVI was guillotined, Barlow was off in Savoy running for election to the National Convention. One of the first persons he saw in Paris in November was Brissot, who promised that there should be things for him to do, and almost before the applause died away from his address, he joined Henri Grégoire, Bishop of Blois, and other commissioners chosen to organize the newly annexed Department of Mont Blanc (now Savoie and Haute Savoie). He wrote Ruth in haste before leaving that the commissioners intend "a certain friend of yours" shall be chosen one of the new deputies to the Convention from Mont Blanc. He added that he was not counting on this event too much, but he was delighted at the chance to see southern France and the Alps "at the expense of the republic." In his expectations he was not disappointed, for the Savoyards he found "a people, vigorous and hardy, just born to liberty." They long had struggled under terrible tyranny "without being broken down in their spirits or debased in their morals." Their character, he observed, strongly resembled the mountains that gave them birth. The commissioners reported to the Convention that they had arrived in Chambéry "in the midst of a crowd of citizens, the noise of the town's bells, and a salute of eighty-four cannon [one for each department]. . . . Everyone has come to tell us how happy he is to be part of France."

On Christmas Day Barlow wrote from a Chambéry inn that he was hard at work on another pamphlet, "a little work on the political situation of Piedmont." If the Department of Mont Blanc had been peacefully added to France, he reasoned, why could not the adjacent province of Piedmont also be annexed bloodlessly? The French Revolution at the end of 1792 was at high tide, and everything seemed possible. In ten days of inspired composition Barlow wrote *A Letter Addressed to the People of Piedmont*, just as he had written his *Letter to the National Convention* three months before. In the second letter he explained the advantages of the French Revolution and the necessity of adopting its principles in Piedmont. The language of the letter was clear, vigorous, compelling, the work of a skillful writer convinced that France had "conquered liberty for all men, and laid the foundation for universal public felicity." Carefully he refuted the lies circulated about France by the republic's enemies and explained the principles of the Revolution as he understood them. The cause of France was the cause of reason and of God. Liberty would not capitulate to the monster despotism which must be driven beyond the sea. "Italy must be free; she cannot wear her chains much longer. . . . Italy is destined to form one great republic."

Barlow's hope and idealism never reached higher than this eloquent appeal to Italians to throw off the yoke of the King of Sardinia. The pamphlet was rushed into print, in French at Grenoble, in Italian at Nice. So dangerous was the letter to the status quo in Piedmont, so thorough was its suppression by the authorities, that no copy of the Italian edition is now known to exist. Barlow hoped that during the winter, while snow blocked the Alpine passes, the Piedmontese would read his pamphlet. He hoped that the message would foment an irresistable desire for freedom and that soldiers of the Revolution would be welcomed triumphantly in Piedmont in the spring. By the time the snow melted on the mountains, however, the bright promise of the Revolution also was receding before the coalition of powers against France and the dwindling fortunes of the Girondists.

Nevertheless, January was a month of idyllic interlude between the pamphleteering immediately past and the Terror immediately ahead. On the twenty-sixth, his twelfth wedding anniversary, he composed ardent verses in praise of Ruth's attractions:

> Those charms that still, with ever new delight,
> Assuage & feed the flame of young desire,
> Whose magic powers can temper & unite
> The husband's friendship with the lover's fire.

Simultaneously, though reports of imminent war filtered down to Savoy, he wrote Ruth enthusiastically: "With you and a little farm among these romantic mountains and valleys I could be happy." The wooded slopes and snow-covered upland meadows reminded him of Connecticut, and for a moment he was overcome with longing for Redding, Hartford, and New Haven, which he had not seen for nearly five years. When he sat down to an unexpected dish of New England hasty pudding in the Chambéry inn, his homesickness was complete. These promptings to memory had a remarkable effect, and for the first time in his life he really became a poet. From sheer joy in his surroundings and nostalgic stirrings he wrote his best poem, a delightful mock epic in praise of corn-meal mush. This work, *The Hasty Pudding,** is worth a dozen Visions of Columbus or Columbiads, though Barlow never realized his accomplishment. Readers since the poem's first publication in 1796, however, have enjoyed it and never have let it go out of print. It has been published in numerous separate editions and anthologized many times.

As if to apologize for his *jeu d'esprit* on such a trivial topic, Barlow prefaced his poem with a solemn letter addressed to Mrs. George Washington. "The example of your domestic virtues has doubtless a great effect among your countrywomen," he wrote sententiously and then went on to praise simplicity in diet. But when he swung into the poem, his verse was spontaneous, natural, witty:

* Reprinted in Appendix.

Dear Hasty-Pudding, what unpromised joy
Expands my heart, to meet thee in Savoy! . . .
My soul is soothed, my cares have found an end;
I greet my long-lost, unforgotten friend.

For thee through Paris, that corrupted town,
How long in vain I wandered up and down, . . .
London is lost in smoke and steeped in tea;
No Yankee there can lisp the name of thee . . .

After recording his delight in finding his favorite dish in the Alps,
Barlow's memory takes fire. He traces extravagantly the recipe for
hasty pudding, beginning with corn planting in the spring and ending with advice on spoons, bowls, and table manners. There is an
amusing apostrophe to the cow: "Blest cow . . . Great source of
health . . . Mother of Egypt's God," and the verses abound in Connecticut local color: memories of husking, courting, milking, eating, plowing, harvesting. So evocative of New England farm life
is the poem that the anonymous editor of a New Haven edition was
pleased to observe "the warmth of affection which he [Barlow]
appears to retain for his native country." The same editor astutely
recognized the work as "one of the Writer's best performances."

After two months of bracing mountain air and leisurely politicking, the pleasures of Savoy came to an end. Barlow's bid for election to the National Convention failed, and he immediately returned
to Paris. He wrote Ruth several days before the voting that he did
not expect to win, and if he did not, he promised, they would sail
for home promptly. He probably was lucky in not becoming a
member of the Convention, for he was close to Brissot and other
Girondists who died during the Terror. He might well have suffered at least the same evil fortune of imprisonment that struck
Paine a few months later. In any event, he wasted no regrets over
his defeat in Savoy because another proposal immediately materialized to occupy him.

A few days after returning to Paris he announced to Ruth the
prospect of a new adventure. Though he could not explain the
nature of the plan by letter, he wrote: "It will suit you, my love,
much better and me too because it will carry us both home upon

a good mission." The project was an abortive scheme to detach Louisiana from Spain and to give the colony liberty under French protection. Citizen Genêt, French minister to the United States, already had been sent to America with instructions to dispatch agents to Louisiana to lead the expedition. Barlow, with dual French-American citizenship and noteworthy service as propagandist, was a logical choice to serve under Genêt in the enterprise. A document in the archives of the French foreign ministry dated March, 1793, describes Barlow as "a real friend of liberty, a philosopher . . . who merits all sorts of confidence . . . to whom one might entrust the general direction [of the plan] under Genêt and the handling of groundwork." Tentative arrangements were made to send Barlow and three others to Philadelphia.

In mid-March Barlow sent Ruth a passport to come to France so that they could sail together. He addressed his letter to "Mrs. Brownlow," Great Litchfield Street, London, because Ruth had written that all letters with "Barlow" on them were being opened. He did not dare to cross the Channel to escort her in person and begged forgiveness once more for involving her in all the labor of packing. "But it cannot be avoided," he concluded. Four days after he sent the passport, however, disasters began overtaking France. The French army was decisively defeated at Neerwinden, Holland, on the nineteenth, and the hero of the previous autumn's campaigns, Dumouriez, deserted to the Austrians on April fifth. From this time forward, the French were forced on the defensive, and ambitious plans like the Louisiana expedition went into automatic discard.

Yet in late March Barlow still planned to meet Ruth in Boulogne to begin the return journey to America. He wrote her frequent letters of instruction, many of which she did not receive. In one of them, entrusted to the sister of John Paul Jones, he reported that he had been to Boulogne on the twenty-fifth, but communications with England were absolutely cut off. Colonel Hichborn, a friend who had set out for London with letters for Ruth, had been stopped at Calais. "I returned [to Paris] almost in despair," Joel wrote. He added that if communications did not reopen soon, they would have to "submit to the cruel necessity of going in different ships."

But they did not depart, either together or separately, and by mid-April Barlow was embracing still another project, this one non-political, that would keep him in Europe. Ruth in London, nerves frayed and patience exhausted, came close to leaving her husband and going home alone, but in the end she remained in England. Yet when travel eventually became possible again, she refused for two months to join her husband in Paris.

Her reluctance to return to France was fully justified. The execution of the King and the declaration of war during January and February began the chain of events leading directly to the Terror. When all Europe united against France, the leaders of the Revolution gave up the luxury of democratic government, formed the Committee of Public Safety, and became a frightened oligarchy. In the struggle for power within the Convention Robespierre's extreme party of the Mountain overthrew the moderate Girondists. The Revolutionary Tribunal soon was searching every department of France for enemies of the state. At the end of the year the tumbrels were creaking daily to the guillotine, and by the middle of 1794, before the blood bath ended, nearly two hundred persons a week were sacrificed to the hysteria of the hour. When Joel wrote plaintively in May, "I meddle with no politics," Ruth waited another month, then crossed the Channel.

By this time Joel was beginning a business venture with Colonel Hichborn and watching with increasing dismay the tarnishment of his hopes for France. In August he admitted that "the affairs of this country . . . looked discouraging to the friends of liberty," but his congenital optimism refused to project the real course that France was following. "The people will recover their dignity," he asserted, "& their cause must be triumphant." By the end of the year, however, there were few excuses left, and Barlow's letters stopped mentioning the internal affairs of France. In October he was horrified at the slaughter of the Girondist leaders and later in a moving eyewitness account described the terrible event: Brissot sang the Marseillaise on his way to the place of execution; no one showed the least sign of cowardice when the carts stopped before the "engine of death." The report goes on: "Brissot preserved a fixed silence, looked distinctly at every one of his colleagues, submitted his head to the guillotine." Others shouted "*Vive la République*" as the blade fell, and "the whole of this shocking ceremony took up no more than thirty-seven minutes." The leaders of the Gironde, Barlow sadly summed up, "were . . . men of rare talents, profound learning."

The daily executions during the Reign of Terror sickened the Barlows, who had to stand idly by while their friends were hauled off to the guillotine. Joel wrote years later that he had lived in daily fear of his own life during this period. But despite the pressure to flee or remain silent he did what little he could to help victims of the purge. When the South American patriot, General Francisco de Miranda, was tried by the Revolutionary Tribunal, Barlow appeared as a witness and gave a deposition in his favor. Though he knew the general only by reputation, he bravely stood up to be counted on behalf of a man who had fought in both the American and French revolutions. If there was some satisfaction in seeing Miranda escape execution, it was soon offset by a great shock that occurred as the year 1793 ended.

Shortly before noon three days after Christmas there came a knock on Barlow's door at the Hotel Great Britain. Outside stood Tom Paine in the custody of two government agents. He had been arrested at three a.m. while he slept in temporary lodgings in the city. After hours of questioning he had been brought to Barlow's hotel in the Rue Jacob where he said his papers were. When the agents arrived with him, they discovered that Paine had fooled them. He wanted his lawyer-friend's help and had led them to the Hotel Great Britain instead of his real residence. The stratagem worked, however, and Barlow was allowed to accompany the agents to Paine's house and to go through his papers with them. As a result, he was able to convince the officers, before they took Paine off to the Luxembourg prison, that the papers contained nothing incriminating. Left with Barlow to be published the next year was the first part of *The Age of Reason*, which Paine had finished only six hours before the arrest.

Paine and Barlow must have expected the arrest, for on Christmas night the former had been denounced on the floor of the Convention and expelled. Ever since Paine had opposed the execution of

Louis XVI, he had been growing more and more unpopular with the revolutionary government. Still he remained in Paris trying to help friends flee the country and writing *The Age of Reason,* by which he vainly hoped to curb the spread of atheism in France. During the summer and autumn he had lived on the outskirts of the city in a house once occupied by Madame de Pompadour where he had a pleasant garden and orchard. The Barlows often visited him, watched the neighbor children play marbles and hopscotch, and ate his greengage plums. Always lurking undiscussed in the back of their minds was the question: when will the blow fall?

After Paine was taken to prison, Barlow did what he could to obtain his friend's release. He circulated a petition among the American residents of Paris and collected eighteen signatures protesting Paine's imprisonment, but conspicuously absent was the name of Gouverneur Morris, the American minister. The president of the Convention promised to consider the petition, but nothing came of the appeal, and Paine remained in prison for more than ten months. The story of his narrow escape from the guillotine through the carelessness of a guard belongs in his biography rather than Barlow's, and it is enough to say here that Robespierre finally fell, the Terror came to an end, and James Monroe, who replaced Morris, rescued Paine from prison. The paths of Barlow and Paine crossed often in the next few years until Paine returned to America in 1802. Thereafter no record of further meetings exists, though the two friends seem to have corresponded occasionally.

While Paine returned to America to be harassed and reviled in his old age, Barlow prospered in reputation and material possessions. Paine's friend and early biographer Rickman later accused Barlow of ingratitude and littleness in not writing Paine into the *Columbiad* as "the principal founder of the American republic." But the charge is unjust and Barlow valued correctly the contribution Paine had made. He explained in a letter the year Paine died that his friend was "one of the most benevolent and disinterested of mankind, endowed with the clearest perception, an uncommon share of original genius, and the greatest breadth of thought." Unfortunately, Paine could not endure the slanders of a public that called him atheist and forgot his service to American independence. "From that moment he gave himself very much to drink, and, consequently, to companions less worthy of his better days." Yet he had been "one of the most instructive men I have ever known. He had a surprising memory and a brilliant fancy . . . he was full of lively anecdote and ingenious, original, pertinent remarks upon almost every subject." To another correspondent Barlow declared that in the history of the United States he was then writing (but did not live to finish) Paine would find his proper place and justice would be done him.

CHAPTER VI

Commercial Interlude

When the infant French republic collapsed during the Reign of Terror, Barlow found himself once again in need of new employment. As deputy midwife, he had helped deliver the new French democracy, and as nurse he had ministered to it; but the suspension of the constitution in autumn, 1793, clearly ended his services. Thus he was grateful when Colonel Benjamin Hichborn of Massachusetts offered him a chance to go into business as shipping broker and agent. His Scioto speculation was far enough in the past to provide sinews of experience without inhibiting memories. Two years of intense political activity, a wide circle of friends, and considerable linguistic proficiency had turned him into a sophisticated cosmopolite. It is safe to say that he had become one of the most prominent Americans in Europe. All he needed now was a fortune to secure his position in the world, for the eighteenth century, like the twentieth, set great store by the size of a man's bank balance.

The general state of war in Europe brought economic distress to many people and a chance to make money to a few. British merchants lost Continental markets, and French *émigrés* lost their estates, but United States businessmen in Paris and elsewhere profited by the chance to trade that American neutrality gave them. The dislocations of normal commerce also created a demand for all kinds of goods, and the bold American agent who slipped his cargoes into France through the British blockade profited handsomely. During the wars of the French Revolution and the later Napoleonic campaigns, American shipping to Europe expanded furiously. Despite the impressment of American seamen and depredations of both England and France against American cargoes, trade went on, fortunes were made. Economic considerations became increasingly important in shaping American foreign policy during the next two decades.

Barlow was caught between two desires as he charted his immediate future. The French Revolution had run wild and fallen into the evil grasp of men no better than other Old World tyrants. One ought to oppose the subversion of liberty, equality, and fraternity. But on the other hand, France was surrounded by despots whose aim was to restore the monarchy and to bring back the Bourbons. The lesser of two evils was to continue supporting the United States' traditional ally in hopes that the butchers of France soon would fall and that the country would return to the principles of 1792. Thus Barlow rationalized his predicament and reconciled his liberal political views with the opportunities for trade in Terror-ridden France.

On a more theoretical plane he also could justify the chance to make money during the wars of the French Revolution. He saw a "convenient correspondence between . . . the natural rights of man and the natural rights of the business man," one economic historian explains. All men, Barlow believed, have an inalienable right to life, liberty, and the pursuit of happiness. American ships running the British blockade were carrying food that men had a natural right to and supplying goods that nourished the resistance of France to her enemies. If the coalition of hostile powers could not defeat France, it eventually would have to make peace. Freedom then would return to France and also might spread to her discredited, unsuccessful opponents. If economic warfare failed at sea, land armies alone could not impose the will of large countries on small ones. A free exchange of goods between nations, therefore, offered the surest formula for obtaining popular, responsive government. By helping to keep the supplies flowing to France, Barlow was striking a blow for freedom. If an American businessman could aid these worth-while objectives and also make a profit, why should he not do it?

Unlike Barlow, most of the Americans in Paris had no strong convictions about anything but the desirability of making money. They were complete opportunists who turned a quick dollar wherever they saw a chance, and it made little difference to them whether France were governed by Robespierre or a Bourbon king. When Monroe replaced Morris in France in 1794, after Barlow had left Paris, the new minister found that his commercial countrymen were "a set of New Englanders connected with Britain . . . who on British capital were trading with France." They were hostile to the principles of the French Revolution but perfectly willing to trade on American good will.

As businessman and friend, Barlow watched with mounting indignation while England tried to subdue France by harassing American shipping. He understood perfectly well the the vital relationship between commerce and history and tried to aid France by proposing economic retaliation. In a long letter to Jefferson in December, 1793, he outlined a plan to boycott British and Irish manufactures in the United States. This, he thought, would bring the English Cabinet to its senses by threatening national bankruptcy. The war between England and France, he said, already had caused distress in England's manufacturing towns, and further economic pressure from the United States would be very effective. Jefferson, however, had been unable to block pro-English sentiment among the Federalists and had resigned as Secretary of State before he got Barlow's letter; but he was sympathetic to the idea of peaceful economic pressure and later tried embargo during his own presidency.

Meanwhile, Barlow concocted still another plan for helping France relieve the external pressure. This project, in addition, promised a tidy profit for its promoters. Incredible as it seems today, Barlow and his friend Mark Leavenworth proposed a private revival of the abandoned Louisiana scheme. They suggested a filibustering venture that would cost France nothing but would cause plenty of trouble for Spain. Barlow and Leavenworth offered to liberate Louisiana from Spanish despotism as an act of humanity and as an example for other colonies in Spanish America. They petitioned the Committee of Public Safety to let them arm and equip at their own expense a force of two thousand men. They proposed then to take over Louisiana from the feeble Spanish garrison in the name of France. Barlow and Leavenworth wanted in return for their services all the confiscated property of the Spanish government in Louisiana. This remarkable program, if it had been carried out, certainly would have produced sensational repercussions. It was probably fortunate for Barlow and Leavenworth that their proposal was filed away in the foreign ministry archives and never acted upon. The Louisiana scheme, however, was only a brief interlude in Barlow's prospering business relationship with Colonel Hichborn.

The colonel's business was shipping. He had proposed to Barlow that they join with Daniel Parker and Mark Leavenworth to charter an English vessel for trade with the Continent. Hichborn went to London in the late spring of 1793 to find a suitable ship. While he was there, he also explained to Ruth Barlow that her husband was getting out of politics and into commerce. The colonel brought back a contract with Henry Bromfield, London merchant, leasing the *Cumberland* to the four Americans for one hundred and fifty pounds per month. Hichborn and his associates then loaded the vessel with flour and rice for Spain, but the *Cumberland*, supposedly bound for Bilbao, never landed there. Like scores of other ships carrying cargoes consigned to Spain, the chartered ship turned up at Bordeaux. Hence the flour and rice carried by an English bottom no doubt ended up in the messkits of French soldiers fighting Great Britain and her allies.

Barlow was a useful man for Colonel Hichborn to take into his business. He had participated in the Revolution but had managed to survive the purge of the Girondists. Hence he had entrees to government offices denied most of the expatriate Americans in Paris. Except for Paine, who was soon to be imprisoned, Barlow was the only other American in Europe who was also a French citizen. Certainly Hichborn, in proposing a commercial partnership, counted on Barlow's contacts with the government. When Robespierre's regime set up a three-man purchasing commission late in 1793, Barlow dealt directly with the commissioners. He obtained in December, the same month Paine was arrested, permission to import any goods not specifically prohibited and to export items not salable in France.

By January he was deep in another transaction, apparently not with Hichborn, but this time involving trade with Scandinavia. During that month he sold the French government four thousand quintals of potash, an entire shipload that had reached port successfully at Le Havre. Though the purchasing commission complained that the price was too high, it bought the cargo for about eighty-eight thousand dollars. Because of the risks involved and France's need, Barlow and his associates certainly realized a handsome profit on the sale. One of Barlow's partners in this and similar ventures was Gilbert Imlay, American lover of Mary Wollstonecraft and father of her child.

Barlow negotiated with the purchasing agents in Paris while Imlay handled the incoming shipments at Le Havre. The two Americans in turn worked with an energetic Swedish merchant, Elias Backman, who made his headquarters in Gothenburg. This pattern of trade, from Scandinavia to France, was fairly typical during the ascendancy of Robespierre and the later Directory. Backman carried on a large shipping business with England, France, and Spain and dealt in grain, steel, wood, naval stores, as well as potash. Despite Barlow's skill in dealing with the Commission des Substances, war conditions made every shipment a gamble. Mary Wollstonecraft wrote Ruth Barlow from Le Havre that Imlay was continually harassed by hindrances and mismanagement and "the constant embarrassments occasioned by those shipping embargoes, that slip off and on, before you know where you are."

By spring Joel and Ruth were weary of the French capital and eager to get away from the sickening proximity of the guillotine. When an unexpected opportunity came to do some business in Hamburg, they left France for more than a year. Once again Barlow expected to wind up his affairs in a few months and then go home, but as usual one transaction led to another. Business opportunities in Hamburg—and adjacent Altona—turned out to be even more promising than in Paris. In Germany fortunes could be made from the nominal two and one-half per cent agents' commissions (which usually amounted to eight or ten per cent) for handling cargoes in transit. As the middleman, he could collect his fee without the responsibility or risk of owning goods. Also he could look after his own part-cargoes, like a dispatcher in a control tower, from a strategic port of reshipment. He performed in both rôles while he was in Hamburg and Altona. He forwarded exports from France as agent for James Swan, the chief American merchant in Paris (called "a corrupt unprincipled rascal" by Monroe), and received incoming goods from American and Scandinavian merchants. By the time he went back to Paris fifteen months later he was a comparatively rich man. As Abraham Baldwin later commented: "Mammon has always been more propitious to you than to me."

The busy port of Hamburg in 1794 and its adjacent little sister Altona (as close as Cambridge to Boston) were, in the phrase of the American consul, "the Emporium of the North." Two thousand ships a year, hundreds of them American, dropped anchor in the Elbe River opposite the wharfs of these cities. Having the best natural harbor on the North Sea, Hamburg was the chief port of the North German plain and, with New York and London, one of the great ports of the world. Hamburgers had a way of prospering even during wartime, and when General Pichegru's French army late in 1794 drove the English out of Holland, literally skating across the country during one of the coldest winters on record, Hamburg doubled its business. Mary Wollstonecraft reported disparagingly of the city that conversation was "ever flowing in the muddy channel of business," and "the interests of nations are bartered by speculating merchants." The more she saw of the city, the more deleterious she thought the effect of speculations on human nature.

Hamburg had thrived since the old medieval days of the Hanseatic League when it joined with Lübeck, Bremen, and other North German cities for the greater glory of trade. It had continued to prosper during the Thirty Years War when much of northern Europe exhausted itself in bloody religious conflict. Though Lutheranism was the state religion till 1860, in Barlow's time the city was full of refugees of all religious persuasions who were allowed to worship freely. By keeping religion and politics damped down, Hamburgers stoked the fires of commerce, and their city became a cosmopolitan center. It built the first German coffeehouse, published an imitation of Addison and Steele's *Spectator*, established the first Masonic lodge in Germany, and governed itself in a middle-class, democratic fashion.

Near-by Altona, where the Barlows lived during their German stay, was part of Denmark. Originally it was a fishing village on the Elbe; Danish kings had given it customs privileges and exemptions to lure away some of Hamburg's business. In time it became a formidable rival, though its warehouses always held goods of Hamburg merchants and its traders did business on the Hamburg exchange. As a place to live, however, it surpassed the larger city, being higher and healthier, and was built on spacious squares and wide, tree-lined streets. One stately avenue, ending on a terrace a hundred feet above the Elbe, commanded a fine view of the river stretching northward towards the sea eighty miles away. From his lodgings in Altona Barlow could walk into Hamburg in a few minutes.

Though Hamburg appeared to Mary Wollstonecraft as an "ill, close-built town swarming with inhabitants," it had for most travelers a comfortable solidity that advertised the prosperity of its many hard-working, well-upholstered burghers. There were always several large ships anchored in the river, while the inner port next to the customhouse swarmed with small craft. Some of the most prominent merchants lived in imposing houses overlooking the river, but even the smaller fry, who fronted on squares away from the Elbe, owned sturdy, four-and-five-story, timber-and-stucco houses with gabled roofs and upper floors that overhung the street. The lower parts of the city, near the confluence of the Elbe and Alster rivers, had the appearance of a Dutch city, being bisected by canals crossed at intervals by bridges. Along the course of the smaller Alster River was a lake bordered by shady promenades. When Barlow later visited Barcelona, an avenue beside the sea reminded him of Jungfrau Strasse in Hamburg, "except that it is not

148

shaded by trees and the sea is not tranquil like the beautiful lake of Alster."

Joel and Ruth Barlow caught their first glimpse of the Elbe River in early April, about the time the Terror reached its climax in Paris with the execution of Danton and Desmoulins. As their ship approached Cuxhaven, still seventy-five miles from Hamburg, the pilot boat came out to meet them. They took on a river pilot and sailed up the broad Elbe, tacking back and forth endlessly against contrary winds, until they dropped anchor opposite Hamburg two or three days later. The Barlows engaged lodgings with a German merchant in Altona and settled down for the spring and summer. They found life pleasant enough in the Danish town and German city; plenty of society and creature comforts were available, and more than two dozen Americans lived there. Joel, however, missed the intellectual stimulus of Paris or London—"wise friends with whom to discuss questions of morals, which is my happiness." Only rarely, he complained, did he entertain well-informed people (*"gens éclairés"*). But Joel and Ruth were together in a peaceful commercial city after years of anguished separations, hard times, and political upheavals, and that was happiness enough.

Barlow's business flourished as shipping of all nations, particularly the United States, crowded into Hamburg. As the French armies bounded back from their defeats of early 1793, they recaptured Belgium and drove into Holland. Merchants in the Low Countries shifted their operations to the German port and eagerly engaged the services of neutral American ships and agents. In one late summer month of 1793 seventy American ships were loaded at Hamburg with wheat for "Lisbon," carrying their cargoes at twice the normal freight rate; and a year later twice as many American ships had called at Hamburg by the end of August as had arrived in all of 1793. This trend continued. When Gouverneur Morris visited Hamburg two years afterwards, he reported that most of the shipping in the Elbe was American. As agent for part of this trade, Barlow, therefore, was a busy man during the first eight months he lived in Hamburg-Altona. Mary Wollstonecraft may have had

Joel in mind when she observed: "Mushroom fortunes have started up during the war."

In Paris, meantime, the affairs of France had taken a turn for the better. Barlow wrote with obvious satisfaction when news reached Hamburg that Robespierre was losing his grip on the Convention. Before the end of the summer, the extremists of the Mountain Party fell from power and the Terror ended. Because Barlow was genuinely committed to the principles of the Revolution, he took hope from this event and permitted himself once more a cautious optimism. He now wrote that the Revolution would in the long run offer even the United States a useful example. He was thinking of the disturbing reports he had heard from America of monarchical sentiment. The Revolution, he believed, had spread sound principles for "the general diffusion of information, the preservation & improvement of morals, & the encouragement of such a degree of equality in the condition of men as tends to their dignity & happiness." At the suggestion of Wolcott and others he went so far as to project a history of the French Revolution, but other activities and other interests eventually derailed this plan.

When winter, 1794-1795, came, the Barlows went into hibernation. The bitterest cold in many years closed all the northern ports. Though the weather enabled the French to capture the ice-bound Dutch fleet, it also stopped shipping on the Elbe from the end of November until the eleventh of March. During the winter the river froze hard, and hundreds of people gathered on the ice for winter sports and barbecues. Public places of amusement were closed by official order when the temperatures dropped below freezing and remained there. During this prolonged cold snap many of the city's ill-housed and ill-clothed poor froze to death; but some of the real distress that winter occurred among the French *émigrés*, many of whom had fled from France with little more than the clothes they wore.

Barlow, as a prominent republican, did not associate with the shabby array of displaced French aristocrats who crowded the city. But he was accustomed to seeing them on the streets, sometimes with the Cross of St. Louis glittering from beneath threadbare garments. Women who had commanded a dozen liveried servants had to undertake menial housework. Madame Lafayette, whose husband was in an Austrian prison, lived up two flights of stairs with her daughters and no servants. Other refugees were General Dumouriez, who was writing his memoirs in Altona, and Madame de Genlis, whose husband had been guillotined and who later became a prominent figure in Napoleon's court. When Morris visited Hamburg-Altona, he spent his time with various *émigrés* whom he had known in Paris: Madame de Flauhaud, illegitimate daughter of Louis XV and traveling companion of Louis-Philippe; Princess de Vaudemont, a lady Louis XVI had been fond of and whose death is supposed to have made Talleyrand cry for the first time; Comte de Choiseul, who later died in exile in Russia. He returned their former hospitality by spending some of his own money to relieve their privations.

The Barlows cultivated quite a different circle of friends, which included political exiles from England and German intellectuals. One of the former was Joseph Gales, who once had published a radical newspaper in Sheffield. He had left England for Altona with his wife and children. He later emigrated to the United States and ultimately crossed paths again with the Barlows in Washington. Another close friend of this period was a German professor of history and Greek at the Hamburg gymnasium, Cristoph Ebeling, who also was an enthusiastic collector of Americana. Barlow spent many evenings with Ebeling answering questions about American geography. He also brought Ebeling and Ezra Stiles into correspondence so that Ebeling could obtain books needed for his lifework, a seven-volume geography and history of America. A month after the Barlows left Hamburg, Ebeling wrote wistfully: "How much do I feel your absence and the want of your instructive conversation!"

Both Joel and Ruth devoted the cold winter nights to the study of the German language and literature. They not only learned to read the language, but they also managed to "speak tolerably." Joel wrote Stiles, after immersing himself in this program, that Americans ought to study German. He had discovered that German literary productions "are more numerous, and perhaps more excellent than those of any other modern nation." Barlow wrote

151

that he had gotten to know the Hamburg poet Klopstock "whom the Germans think as much superior to Milton, as we think Milton superior to him." The charming old poet "mounts a horseback like a young man, and makes odes with as much fire as Collins." Barlow attended the poet's eightieth birthday party, which was celebrated by the ringing of bells and the firing of guns. He observed approvingly that the old man was greatly venerated in Hamburg: "His immediate neighbors, indeed all Germans, looked up to him as a superior being."

When the ice went out of the Elbe in March, 1795, and shipping resumed, Barlow again turned to business. There was still great demand for American ships and services, but two distant events cast long shadows ahead: the Jay Treaty just negotiated between the United States and England and a recent truce between Portugal and Algiers. The former would restore good American relations with England at the expense of France and the flourishing trade through Hamburg, and the latter, which had uncorked the Straits of Gibraltar to let out the Barbary pirates, would involve Barlow personally. Joel wound up his German affairs in four months and returned to Paris. Ruth wrote her brother on June twenty-ninth: "We leave this country in about a fortnight for France. Mr. B. has some affairs to settle there, and should they not detain him too long, we intend sailing [for home] in September, but France always [has] something fascinating to the dear Man, and I much fear he will stay until the season shall be too far advanced to make the passage." Joel finally had both money and reputation, but Ruth's premonition was only too correct. The Barlows returned to Paris just long enough for Joel to prepare for a brand-new adventure—this one a worrisome two-year diplomatic mission to Algiers.

CHAPTER VII

Daniel in the Lion's Den

1: Preparations for Barbary

The Barlows returned to a Paris that had passed through its time of stress and storm. After three years of war, France had re-entered the community of nations and broken up the coalition formed against her independence. The Treaties of Basle, which brought peace, were being negotiated in Switzerland; the one with Prussia already had been signed. The Party of the Mountain, after conducting fourteen months of terror while also waging victorious war, ceased to exist, and the government of France passed into the hands of able, moderate leaders. Barlow was sure now that the Revolution, despite its awful internal convulsions, had survived and triumphed. He came back to Paris planning to write the history of France during the revolutionary years he had observed and taken part in.

Arriving happy and prosperous, he was at once eager to pick up old threads, meet new friends, and renew old acquaintances. One of his first acts was to call on Jefferson's young protégé, James Monroe, the new American minister. He had not met Monroe before, but the two men began a friendship that culminated in Barlow's own mission to France under Monroe as Secretary of State. At the same time, Barlow saw once more his unfortunate friend

153

Paine, who was living in Monroe's home and convalescing slowly from an illness contracted in prison. But the great surprise of Barlow's return to Paris was the discovery that his old comrade and fellow Connecticut wit, Colonel Humphreys, was in town.

Humphreys had arrived several weeks before in pursuit of a tough diplomatic mission. As minister to Portugal, he was charged with obtaining treaties from the Barbary states: Algiers, Tripoli, and Tunis. He needed the good offices of France in dealing with Barbary, and he needed an able man to send to Algiers to supervise on the spot the ticklish negotiations. Colonel Hichborn had seemed the most likely American in France when Humphreys reached Paris, but two or three weeks later Joel Barlow unexpectedly appeared. When Hichborn begged off on grounds of ill health, Barlow was asked to go. Humphreys had no trouble persuading Joel to take the assignment, for he loved to travel, particularly at someone else's expense, and the prospect of a few weeks in North Africa enchanted him.

Barlow was eminently qualified for any diplomatic appointment Washington's administration might have given him. Forty-one years old, thoroughly at home in European society, proficient in German, French, and Italian, rich enough to afford diplomacy, a citizen of both France and the United States, he was a fair match for the international gangsters who inhabited the Barbary coast. Monroe, in reporting that Barlow had agreed to go, wrote: "No person can be found willing to accept that trust, in whom it can be so happily vested." President Washington wrote Secretary of State Pickering: "It has ever been my opinion from the little I have seen, and from what I have heard of Mr. Barlow, that his abilities are adequate to any employment; & improved as they must have been by travel, & the political career he has run, there can be little doubt of his fitness, as a negotiator."

Pickering, that hard-headed Yankee, was more specific and practical in his evaluation of Barlow's qualities: Since Congress only allowed two thousand dollars a year for the consul at Algiers, he said, and since few Americans knew Spanish or Italian, Barlow was a happy selection. Moreover, his going to Algiers under the patronage of the French government, Pickering declared, "might be very useful in obviating present, and preventing future difficulties." This last qualification was most important, for the United States then was working both sides of the diplomatic street. Barlow's mission began about the time news reached France of the Jay Treaty with England in which the United States, for various considerations, accepted British domination of the seas. Republicans in America and everyone in France denounced the treaty as a dirty Federalist assault on traditional Franco-American friendship, and from that time on, France and America moved towards the undeclared naval war of John Adams' administration. Monroe, the Republican, who had been sent to France to offset the effect of the Federalist Jay's mission to England, was greatly embarrassed at having to ask for French assistance with Barbary at this juncture, but the French foreign office generously agreed to help, and at the end of August Barlow's instructions were prepared.

Though Barlow's directions were brief and explicit, he was being sent on no boy's errand. He was to obtain a peace treaty with the three Barbary states, secure the release of American prisoners in Algiers, and pay as little as possible to reach these objectives. The infant American republic had been trying to achieve these ends for years without success. The United States' previous relations with Barbary had been one long frustration and humiliation, beginning with the capture of two American ships clear back in 1785. Shocking as it may seem, American seamen from these vessels had been slaves in Algiers for ten years. They had been joined from time to time by other prisoners until the number reached one hundred and nineteen the year before Barlow set out for Algiers. In addition to this indignity to American citizens, the Barbary pirates for years had been hijacking American cargoes without hindrance.

As a weak nation without a navy, the United States could deal Barlow no trump cards in the game he was about to play. Even the good offices of France did not mean much, for both England and France really wanted the Barbary pirates to continue in business. Their prepotent navies could have shut down this licensed racket any time they wished, but the corsairs served them well by preying on weak nations—Sweden, Denmark, Portugal, Holland, and others—one at a time. These small countries, though they had little naval power, possessed merchant fleets that competed vigorously with England and France. But piracy added greatly to their costs of doing business. When a peace was concluded with nation A, the pirates found a pretext to begin hostilities with nation B. All countries paid tribute to the Barbary states to obtain peace, including England and France, for whom the price was a bargain. But a treaty, Barlow found when he reached Algiers, was good only as long as the Dey wanted it, and when one diplomat negotiated a peace, someone else's treaty was torn up. Barlow wrote Pickering a month after landing in Africa: "Louis XIV said, if there was no Algiers he would build one; as it would be the cheapest way of depriving the Italian States of their natural right to navigate their own seas." This policy, he concluded, is "only fit for a king."

By the time Barlow went to Algiers, the United States finally had swallowed its pride and appropriated what was then a huge sum, eight hundred thousand dollars, to buy the treaty and ransom the American prisoners. Previously, in 1792 President Washington had asked and received from Congress permission to spend fifty thousand dollars to buy peace and the freedom of the captives. Jefferson wanted to build a navy and fight it out, but John Adams argued that paying tribute would be cheaper. The latter view prevailed, and John Paul Jones was commissioned to conduct the negotiations; but Jones died before he could carry out the mission. Then Humphreys was appointed; but by the time he reached Gibraltar, Portugal and Algiers had concluded a treaty engineered by England. This sly deal opened the straits to the pirates, who promptly seized eleven more American ships in the Atlantic. The Dey, finding that crime paid handsomely, refused to receive an American representative and said he wanted no treaty at all. By then, too, the money authorized by Congress was entirely inadequate to accomplish its purpose, and Humphreys had to go back home to begin his project over again.

When Humphreys returned to Europe, he went to Paris and sent a subordinate directly to Algiers. This was Joseph Donaldson, who was to look over the situation and start the treaty negotiations if he could. Though Donaldson had only mediocre talents as a diplomat, he landed in Africa just when England had annoyed the

Dey. Donaldson proposed a treaty, which the Dey, to spite England and to amaze everyone, immediately accepted. Barlow barely had started preparing for his mission as Donaldson's superior when Captain O'Brien, the first of the prisoners to be released, brought news of the treaty. For a moment it seemed as if Barlow could stay in Paris and write his history after all, but a sober second thought told Humphreys and Monroe that they should continue as planned. Putting a treaty into effect was far more difficult than signing one. As matters turned out, Donaldson proved to be an honest but not an adroit agent, and before Barlow could get to Algiers, Donaldson fell out of favor with the capricious Dey.

Prior to leaving, Barlow had to arrange his affairs. His newly made fortune had to be invested, and since Algiers was no place to take a wife, Ruth's living arrangements in Paris had to be taken care of. He disposed of the former matter by investing in a new issue of French government securities. He bought thirty-four thousand dollars' worth and held them for several years until French prosperity doubled their value. Part of his remaining capital of about fifty thousand dollars he invested in two parcels of Paris real estate; the rest he left liquid in case he encountered any choice investment opportunities in Algiers. Then he settled Ruth in rooms on the rue du Bac, where she was surrounded by congenial Americans, and asked the Monroes to look after her.

Next Barlow turned to official preparations, which consisted chiefly of buying presents for the Dey and his henchmen. Although Monroe had to work three weeks raising money for the expensive outlay, both he and Barlow were determined to carry off the mission with as lavish a hand as any Old World diplomat. As a friendly gesture, the French government listed for them the presents that pleased the Dey most when France had last made a consular gift. Then Barlow went Christmas shopping in Paris for the Moslem Dey and during November and December strained the skill and resources of French artisans and shops. He bought jeweled snuffboxes, diamond rings, pistols inlaid with precious stones, brocaded robes of state, linen, damask, carpets, and every sort of bauble that might please the childish fancy of the barbaric tyrant who ruled Algiers. When he supplemented his purchases in France with more

157

gifts bought later in Africa, the total bill came to twenty-seven thousand dollars—twice the usual consular present. By Christmas Day the gifts had been delivered, and Barlow set off for Algiers.

He traveled southward by private carriage with one companion, a Mr. Andrews, and the fortune in jewels packed around him. Except for forty-eight hours in Lyon, which he reached on New Year's Day, he pushed on without stopping. At Lyon he hired a mail boat to take his *voiture* down the Rhone as far as Avignon, and there he disembarked for the last lap of the journey overland to Marseilles. As his boat drifted into Avignon, Barlow passed under the old Roman bridge and studied it carefully. Later the same day on land he visited Roman ruins, marveled at the old walled city, and inspected the ancient Papal palace. While the post horses pulled him briskly over smooth roads through Provence, Barlow peeled off his greatcoat and cocked an appreciative eye at the fine vineyards and olive groves. He arrived in Marseilles on January fifth and put up near the home of the American consul.

In Marseilles Barlow had to wait three weeks for a ship to take him across the Mediterranean, but he took in the sights of the old port and did some homework for the Algerian mission. He found the city a pleasant commercial town, monarchical in sentiment but not very politically minded. As long as cargoes keep coming and going, he wrote Ruth, people here will give allegiance to whatever constitution exists and never take the trouble to read it. At least twice during his stay in Marseilles he dined with a group of Algerians and Tunisians. He managed to talk to them in their own language, which was mostly a melange of bad Italian and Spanish, but the generous sprinkling of Arabic words mixed him up. He got along well enough, however, that the Algerians in Marseilles gave him letters of introduction to their friends at home.

Even before he sailed, he began to miss Ruth fearfully and wished he had brought her with him. He knew, of course, that in Algiers, which was visited by the plague at frequent intervals, living conditions would be primitive and civilized companionship perhaps non-existent. When none of Ruth's letters reached him for more than two weeks after his departure, he wrote plaintively: *"Où es tu? Que fais tu, ma charmante? Que pense tu? Que sens tu? Je donnerais les deux doigts que tiennent la plume pour une réponse à ces questions.*" Then continuing in French, the language in which he wrote Ruth during most of his Algerian mission, he went on in characteristic fashion to preach to her about taking daily exercise and not playing cards too much.

Ruth had been writing her husband, though she never was as good a correspondent as he, and eventually her letters caught up with him. She had spent New Year's Day with the Monroes and was seeing a good bit of Grégoire, Lanthénas (a particular friend of Paine), and old Dr. Gun. The last, she wrote, "visits me often and talks of philosophy and love, the former to amuse himself, the latter to amuse me." She was walking almost every day in the public gardens and studying her French diligently. Soon she began writing in French whenever she would take the time for it. She missed Joel as much as he missed her. In one letter she directed her husband to tell her everything he did: "Even if you get a sweetheart, tell me." And a little later she wrote: "I am poor in everything but love & tenderness; in those you cannot outdo me, & with absence my love seems to increase. How I long to fly to you this moment."

On January 23, 1796, Barlow embarked on an American ship for Algiers by way of Alicante, Spain, and immediately sailed into a furious storm. After being buffeted about for two days, the vessel put into the Bay of Roses, Spain, for safety. Barlow's stomach could not take any more rough weather; so he devised new plans. He rode into Figueres on a mule and arranged for land transportation down the coast of Spain as far as he could go. For a man who loved to travel as much as Barlow, this overland trip was a windfall. Besides, it would take him three hundred and fifty miles closer to Algiers with only the inconvenience of bumpy roads and cantankerous mules.

The first night in a Spanish inn at Figueres was a portent of things to come. It was not too bad, he wrote Ruth with massive understatement: "Though the pigs inside disputed my right to enter, there was enough room for all. They let me climb to a little open room where I could enjoy the odor of the pigs, the kitchen, and the stable." It was in that chamber that Barlow met his first

Spanish flea: "She was beautiful, active, and extremely affectionate, but a bit of a coquette. For after her advances, not wishing to show myself insensible to such kindness, I extended my hand to feel her and to know what stuff she was made of; and she escaped me." But, he continued, he had his revenge in bed that night, for he slaughtered scores of her relatives and perhaps even her.

The journey from Figueres to Alicante stretched for thirteen incomparable days along the slender plain of Spain's east coast. Barlow and Andrews rode in a two-seated *calèche* drawn by mules led by a driver. The roads were so bad and the mule driver so reluctant to hurry his beasts that they could make only twenty-one miles a day at first. But the weather was lovely: it was balmy as spring, the almond trees were in bloom, and the orange groves were loaded with the same golden fruit "that Hercules went to look for in the gardens of Hesperides." The travelers passed through Barcelona on the third day, Valencia on the eleventh, and continued along the coast forty-eight hours longer to Alicante where they arrived ahead of their overdue ship from Marseilles.

The ship, battered and wracked, beat its way into port five days later, but Barlow remained in the Spanish town three weeks awaiting news from Humphreys in Lisbon. He found on his arrival that the capricious Dey was getting impatient for the money the United States had promised in the treaty. The Dey had released another American prisoner and sent him via Alicante to Humphreys with a strong note demanding that the United States quit stalling. Barlow explained his delay to Monroe: "I was well convinced that for any more of us to appear in Algiers without the means of fulfilling the contract and without anything new to say on the subject would only serve to irritate the Dey." After Barlow postponed his sailing, his decision was supported by similar instructions from Humphreys.

The troubles that the United States had in paying for the treaty would make a book in itself. In an era of Marshall Plans and ECA's one can hardly believe that the American government strained every muscle and taxed the ingenuity of all its representatives to raise eight hundred thousand dollars in Europe and get it to Algiers. The State Department first planned to sell United States Bank stock in London, convert the proceeds into bullion, and ship it to Algiers. To sell this much stock quickly necessitated discounting it fifteen per cent immediately, but even so, there would have been enough to buy the peace and ransom the seamen, both of which were to total six hundred and forty-two thousand dollars. The United States' London bankers, however, could not obtain specie because England's war with France had seriously depleted the country's gold supply. When Captain O'Brien sailed from Lisbon to London to get the money, he had to return with only a letter of credit. Further unsuccessful efforts then were made to raise the money in Hamburg. There was simply one delay after another: ships sailing wintry seas took forty days to go four hundred miles, wars and rumors of wars harassed international banking, and the miserable affair dragged on and on.

Barlow, meanwhile, amused himself in Alicante while he awaited developments. He went to the theater and watched a traveling troupe like those found in *Gil Blas*. It was hard to imagine how people could enjoy acting that was so gauche and mean, but there was no other amusement in town. He wrote Ruth: "The theater therefore is filled, noble, rich, great, and small. The governor of the canton has the first box, and after the first number, he amuses himself by calling the subsequent tunes and dances, each one of which is more repulsive than the last." Barlow also filled his days with side trips back up to Valencia and down the coast to Cartegena. He studied his Spanish and reported a week after reaching Alicante that he could read it as well as French. Finally at the end of February he heard alarming news from Algiers that the situation there was deteriorating rapidly. Money or no money, he concluded that he should be off, and on March 1, 1796, his ship weighed anchor and plunged once more into the stormy Mediterranean.

2: *Sufficient unto the Dey . . .*

As the ship ran a southeasterly course before a fresh offshore wind, Barlow pondered the problems he faced in Algiers. His immediate reason for leaving Alicante without further instructions was the Dey's mounting choler at not getting the promised American gold. On February sixth Hassan Bashaw, the Dey, had given the United States one month to pay him, or else the whole treaty would be canceled. Barlow heard this news before Humphreys and decided he must act at once, a conclusion that the minister in Lisbon also reached when the intelligence was relayed to him. Before sailing, Barlow wrote Humphreys: "I shall not hesitate to make use of all the means in my power to keep the treaty in suspense till we are furnished with the funds to fulfill it."

The fair wind for Africa lasted only a few hours before another gale overtook the ship, and though Algiers was only two hundred and twenty-five miles from Alicante, the voyage lasted five days. The tempest carried away one of the masts and some sails, and even after reaching port, the captain could not land his passengers for another twenty-four hours. Meantime, Barlow suffered from seasickness as violently as during his first voyage in 1788. But when he dragged himself ashore two days after the Dey's supposed deadline, he found that the treaty had not yet been scrapped. Hassan Bashaw was extremely irritated; yet Barlow felt he had an even chance to put off the Dey until the money arrived. He wrote Ruth: "You can say to Monroe that I have more hope now than when I wrote to him from Alicante the last time."

During the next week, however, Barlow regretted his cautious optimism. The Dey's ugly disposition grew more violent, and when Barlow sent word that he was ready to give the consular present, the Dey struck the messenger in the face and returned a "menacing and insulting answer." The messenger was at the same time delivering a letter from Humphreys, but the raging despot grabbed the letter and "threw it out the door with great fury, uttering many execrations and threats." When he heard of the rantings and received the letter back unopened, Barlow wished he had stayed a while longer in Alicante; but for the moment Hassan Bashaw was only sound and fury. The tantrum suddenly subsided, and Joel wrote Ruth on the fourteenth: "The affair sleeps . . . if I can make it sleep for some weeks, I hope that all will go well." For the rest of March he had time to look around.

If the Dey was an exasperating creature, the city of Algiers itself was equally unpleasant in 1796. "With the exception of the climate, the fruit, and the natural beauty of the vicinity," Joel reported, "it is doubtless, in all respects, the most detestable place one can imagine." His bill of particulars was extensive: dark little zigzag alleys for streets; heaps of bare, badly built houses thrown together without order; no transportation except by ass or mule (assuming that one could keep from getting lost in the labyrinth); an alien way of life that seemed unnatural and squalid even among rich residents; a mean, undernourished, hostile people that he called "the last debasement of the human hope." Algiers, he summed up, was "the haunt of pirates, this sewer of all vices, of all impurities that imagination can conceive or monsters practice."

In addition to all this, Barlow was appalled by the status of women in Moslem society. He informed Ruth that a woman in Algiers could not, under penalty of a severe beating, show her face to any man except her husband. "If a Turk or Moor enters the house of a friend, he must stop at the gate . . . and be announced, so that the woman of the house may be concealed." Furthermore, Barlow was told, the Algerians executed Mohammedan women taken in adultery by sewing them up in sacks filled with stones and casting them into the sea. The men in such cases, unless the woman belonged to somebody important, got off with only a beating. Barlow pursued his study of Moslem women by asking questions of James Cathcart, one of the American prisoners who had become the Dey's Christian secretary. "Is it the real opinion of a Mohometan that women have no souls, or is the degraded state in which they are held the effect of habitual jealousy?" The latter must be the real reason, he recorded in his notebook without indicating Cathcart's opinion on the matter. Then he jotted down reflectively a description of the thick, ankle-length muslin drawers worn by Algerian women and added: "It is here that, in a literal though not a figurative sense, women wear the breeches."

The curious mind of the ex-farm boy and Connecticut minister was equally fascinated by its first contact with Islam. As he picked his way about the narrow streets, Barlow noted that the mosques in Algiers seemed infinite in number, and while they were hardly decorated at all inside, they were spacious and well lighted after dark. The illumination, he supposed, was because the Moslems had to pray five times every twenty-four hours, including twice during the night. Though a Christian could peer in the door of a mosque, Barlow was warned never to set foot inside. "The penalty," he wrote Ruth, "is to become a Mohammedan, or to be hanged, or burned alive, according as one is a Christian or a Jew." He hastened to reassure his wife: "If it happens to me, through intoxication or some other accident, to commit this offense, I shall become a Mohammedan on the spot, for I have not enough religion of any kind to make me a martyr."

In addition to the social and religious life of North Africa, Barlow also studied the political system of the Barbary states. In a twenty-five-page letter to the Secretary of State ten days after arriving, he summarized local history and analyzed foreign affairs. The Regency of Algiers had been governed for nearly three centuries by a garrison of about twelve thousand Turkish soldiers continuously replenished from the Levant. They were generally ignorant, ferocious adventurers, often fugitives from justice; in fact, Barlow reported, "It is a common saying in the Levant that no honest man goes to Algiers." The Dey originally had been elected by the Turkish officer corps to preside over a divan of fellow officers, but for a long time the divan had not met, and the state had degenerated into an Oriental despotism. The present Dey had come into power in 1791 by getting his hands on the gold paid by Spain for a peace treaty and using the money to bribe his way into the office the moment the old Dey died. Then he had eliminated his rivals promptly by the standard procedure of banishment and assassination. When Barlow arrived, Hassan Bashaw was the undisputed master of Algiers and the fancied overlord of both Tripoli and Tunis.

The chief revenues of the state, Barlow continued, came from piracy, the ransom of seamen and cargoes, and frequent peace presents offered by governments unlucky enough to be attacked. To keep his treasury filled, the Dey, therefore, needed frequent wars, and Barlow advised Pickering that he could not expect the American treaty to be honored for more than seven years, assuming they could get it put into effect at all. At that moment the Dey was going to war with the Danes on a flimsy pretext, and afterwards Barlow thought it would be Venice or Sweden. "They will then try Holland again, & perhaps Spain, and our turn will be the next." When the Algerian gangsters had attacked Holland three years before, they had hardly bothered with an excuse. They simply charged that the Dutch had delivered some faulty spars in the naval stores sent annually as tribute. The Dutch offered to make good double, but war was declared immediately. The pirates then brought in several Dutch ships and enslaved seventy seamen, and Holland had to pay four hundred thousand dollars to end the business.

For the rest of March Barlow was left pretty much alone to observe, take notes, and reflect on his new experience. There was nothing to do but wait for the shipment of gold that Humphreys now presumably was trying to get from Hamburg. The process of raising the money had been going on for months; surely it could not last much longer. The Dey, irascible brute, occupied himself with other matters and paid no attention to the Americans. Barlow was hopeful that he could wind up his mission in a few weeks and return to Paris. He was immensely relieved that he had not brought Ruth, and fervently wrote her so on the day when twenty-nine of her letters arrived in one bunch. On that happy occasion his morale soared, and Ruth never seemed so endearing: "You are my light and my blood, my life, my soul, and my spirit; you are more: you are my delight, my nourishment, my hope of real happiness."

He had barely finished reading his bundle of letters from Ruth when the sky fell in. On April second the Dey came out of his trance, flew into one of his fits of ungovernable temper, and sent a message to Barlow and Donaldson. In eight days he would throw the Americans out of Algiers and declare war on the United States. He had waited six months for his money; his patience was exhausted.

In thirty days his corsairs would begin bringing in American ships. At this news the American captives, who had been expecting release any day, were plunged into despair. Barlow wrote Humphreys sadly that he was witnessing among the prisoners "a scene of as complete and poignant distress as can be imagined," and added despondently: "We [are] without the power of administering the least comfort or hope."

But Joel Barlow was a resourceful and lucky man. He was also bold, imaginative, and stubborn. His sense of outrage welled up, and his sympathy for the enslaved American seamen goaded him to think of some way to save the situation. On the same day that Hassan Bashaw uttered his threat, an Algerine cruiser brought into the harbor a Danish merchantman. Then a few hours later came another, and another, and Barlow saw a ray of sun break through his own gloom. Denmark's misfortune, he thought, might have a calming effect on the volatile temperament of the Dey. If this happened, could anything be done to induce him to wait for his money? On the third of April Barlow had an idea. When he talked it over with Donaldson, his assistant agreed that the scheme might work; but it was going to cost forty-five thousand dollars. He did not think they should spend so much without authorization from their superiors.

Expense be damned, thought Barlow, as he made his way to the home of Joseph Bacri, the rich Jewish banker who had more influence with the Dey than anyone else in the city. Barlow already had made friends with Bacri and already had spent an unauthorized eighteen thousand dollars as a retainer to the banker. Bacri was to oil the troubled waters whenever the Dey remembered his grievances against the United States. The scheme that Barlow outlined to the Jewish banker was simple. In return for an additional three months' time, Bacri was to offer the Dey's daughter a gift of a brand-new, American-built, twenty-gun frigate. The idea was a stroke of genius, for the trim, fast-sailing product of American shipyards already had won a great reputation throughout the world.

On the fourth of April Bacri visited the Dey several times on the pretext of other business, but he could not manage to broach Barlow's offer. He tried again the next day and succeeded. The Dey rose instantly to the novelty of the lure, but Hassan Bashaw was cunning. He told Bacri to tell Barlow that the ship must be a thirty-six-gun frigate or he would not even discuss the proposition. Yet the fish had swallowed the bait: the Dey summoned Barlow and Donaldson to see him at once.

Concealing their elation, the two Americans went directly to the palace to repeat their offer (now a thirty-six-gun ship) and to extol the merits of American shipbuilding. They stepped buoyantly across the palace courtyard, entered a central hall, and climbed a winding maze of five flights of stairs to a narrow, dark entry. Then after removing their shoes, they were ushered into a small room about twelve by eighteen feet dimly lighted by high, narrow slits covered with an iron grating. There they saw, as Barlow's successor describes him, "a huge, shaggy beast, sitting on his rump, upon a low bench, covered with a cushion of embroidered velvet, with his hind legs gathered up like a tailor, or a bear. On our approach to him, he reached out his fore paw as if to receive something to eat." When the guide called out, "Kiss the Dey's hand," the Americans stoically did as they were told. The shaggy animal was in a good humor and grinned amiably as he listened to Barlow describe the frigate that the United States would give his daughter.

Back in his room that night Barlow faced the task of explaining to Humphreys and the Secretary of State what he had done. The idea was unique, for no one before ever had offered to give the pirates a warship. It was like offering a gangster a new and improved machine gun as an inducement to stop hijacking one's merchandise. But it was a pragmatic solution to a tough problem. Barlow wrote Humphreys that he was free to countermand the offer, but if he did so, war would be inevitable. Barlow's superiors took him at his word, approved the added expense, and by June began preliminary steps in Philadelphia to build the frigate. When the Secretary of War (there was no Secretary of Navy yet) dallied in carrying out the commitment, President Washington wrote him sharply to get on with the business. Pickering was immensely pleased with Barlow's conduct of his mission, and even in December when he wrote that the ship was probably going to cost ninety thousand dollars, he made no objection. The conclusion of this episode in American relations with Barbary was the delivery of the frigate *Crescent* in Algiers early in 1798.

Barlow heaved a great sigh of relief as he contemplated his successful purchase of three months' delay. The Dey now was in a friendly mood and would accept the consular present. One more improbable episode in the Algerian melodrama was concluded. Even if the State Department vetoed the frigate, as Barlow thought they might, the money for the treaty ought to arrive before a ship could make a round trip to Philadelphia. But where was that money? Humphreys' efforts to provide the funds by this time seemed so ineffectual that Barlow concluded he must lend a hand. He knew from his commercial experience in Hamburg and Paris that transferring money from one European city to another was not so devilishly difficult as Humphreys was making it.

What the situation required, Barlow reflected, was a new approach. He knew that Captain O'Brien in February had brought no bullion from London but that Baring and Company, the United States' bankers, had sent him back to Lisbon with letters of credit on Madrid and Cadiz. He also thought that the Spanish government would not allow the export of gold, and he was pretty sure that if Humphreys was trying to raise the money in Portugal, he would fail. On the other hand, the banking house of Bacri in Algiers had a branch in Leghorn, which in turn had connections in other parts of Europe. A letter of credit to Bacri in Leghorn from Baring and Company in London could be negotiated without delay, and to transfer credit from Bacri in Leghorn to Bacri in Algiers would be very easy. Therefore, Barlow reasoned, the thing for him to do was to send Donaldson off to Leghorn while he wrote Humphreys to have Baring and Company's letter of credit on Madrid and Cadiz transferred to Leghorn.

Donaldson sailed for Italy on April first, and Barlow blew off steam over Humphreys' futilities in a letter to Ruth: "He seems to have too much beef in his head to be a good manager of such affairs. The most conspicuous talent that I can discover in him hitherto is that of keeping a secret, & keeping it from those whose knowledge of [it] is absolutely necessary." Since February Barlow had received no communication from Humphreys, who then merely

168

had said that he could not yet get the money. "All would have been finished before now," continued Barlow, "& sixty thousand dollars saved to the United States, if we had a good banker's clerk at a certain place for a minister."

After Donaldson's departure for Leghorn, Barlow, the only free American in Algiers, was left to deal with a "government that one doesn't know how to describe." Because he had to remain at least two months longer, he provided for his comfort and amusement by renting a country house with garden. There was also strategy in this move, for he fooled the Dey into thinking he was going to settle down as permanent consul and bring his wife to join him. Hassan Bashaw would have blown up another storm if he had known that Barlow was in Algiers merely as a special agent for the treaty. His simple mind grasped only the idea of resident consuls on whom he could keep his beady eyes fixed. As matters developed, the Dey took a great liking to Barlow and now could not do enough for him. To cement the new friendship, he gave him a fine horse, and as May began, Barlow contemplated a horseback tour of the near-by countryside with some of the other members of the Algerine foreign colony.

Simultaneously, however, he was working with a fine Machiavellian hand on another project to buttress his position. He had learned that the banker Bacri, though the most influential person in Algiers, nursed a jealous hatred of the Dey's Christian secretary Cathcart. Nothing would please Bacri more than to get rid of Cathcart. Barlow wondered. Could he devise a plan by which this removal might be effected? The affair would have to be managed with utmost subtlety, for if Cathcart, a decent fellow, were to lose the Dey's confidence through intrigue, he might also lose his head. Barlow thought over the matter carefully, hatched a plan, and called on Bacri. The banker, he explained, might try planting in the devious mind of Hassan Bashaw the notion that maybe he should send someone he trusted to America to expedite the collection and transportation to Algiers of the American naval stores promised in the treaty as annual tribute. The banker, however, should be careful to make the Dey think this plan was his own idea.

Barlow believed, correctly, that the only person the Dey trusted who was also qualified for the mission was Cathcart.

The stratagem worked like magic: on May eighth Cathcart set out for Philadelphia on orders of the Dey. Bacri, of course, was delighted to see the American go, and Cathcart, after ten years of Algerian captivity, was overjoyed to be going home. The Dey was greatly pleased at the shrewd scheme *he* had concocted to speed shipment of his naval stores from the United States, and Barlow, too, was secretly elated. For him the result was protection with double indemnity. Not only had he placed Bacri in his debt, but also he had relieved pressure on himself. No longer would the Dey be after him morning and evening for the peace money and promised tribute, but from now on, the Dey would look directly to Philadelphia for some of his answers. In the weeks ahead Barlow's sly maneuver turned out to be perhaps the decisive factor in saving the lives of the American prisoners.

3: *Diplomatic Sleight of Hand*

The days of May dropped silently away like the sands in an hourglass. By the end of the month two-thirds of Barlow's grace period had expired, but still no money arrived either from Humphreys in Lisbon or Donaldson in Leghorn. The city baked under the desert sun, and Barlow was glad he had moved out to the country. Suddenly the torpid city jolted awake. Rumor circulated, then fact substantiated. Barlow wrote Monroe on the thirty-first: "I have now to add the frightful news that the plague has broken out at Algiers."

In the packed, unsanitary cities rimming the Mediterranean the fearsome scourge struck periodically, carrying off a few hundred or thousands as its virulence rose and fell from year to year. Barlow's letter reported that already one of the American captives had contracted the disease and probably would die. "I am trying to get leave for them to quit their work and come into the country near me . . . to save as many as I can."

His intervention, however, was unsuccessful, for the Dey declared flatly that the prisoners "were not yet paid for; they were therefore the property of the Regency." On June twelfth Barlow wrote in sorrow: "Two of our finest young fellows, Nicholas Hartford of Portsmouth and Abraham Simmonds of Cape Ann, have already fallen." Barlow could do nothing to aid the captives, and four days later Joseph Keith died while two more came down with the plague. Privately Barlow raged at the obstinacy of the Algerian government, its utter indifference to the disease, and its stubborn refusal to take the slightest precautions. Daily Barlow exposed himself to the contagion in visiting the seamen and relieving their distress as best he could.

One day while the plague still raged, Barlow sat down at his desk thinking of Ruth in Paris. The chance of his dying from the plague, he thought, was good. What a miserable way to end fifteen years of happy marriage! Just when the future had turned rosy, he had blithely involved himself in a God-forsaken mission to the hellhole of creation. With such reflections in mind he composed his last will and testament in a long letter to his wife. "I run no risk of alarming your extreme sensibility by writing this letter," he began, "since it is not my intention that it shall come into your hands unless and until, by some other channel, you shall have been informed of the event which it anticipates as possible."

How could he make Ruth see that he had to expose himself? How could he tell her that his obligation to humanity required him to take the risk? She would have to understand. "Though they [the prisoners] are dying very fast," he tried to explain, "yet it is possible my exertions may be the means of saving a number who otherwise would perish. If this should be the case, and I should fall instead of them, my tender, generous friend must not upbraid my memory by ever *thinking* that I did too much." If Ruth were present, his rationale went on, she would see the necessity of his actions. "Were you in my place, you would do more than I . . . your kind, intrepid spirit has more courage than mine." And another consideration: "Many of these persons have wives at home, as well as I, from whom they have been much longer separated . . . having been held in a merciless and desponding slavery."

171

Joel was tired and he paused. He had much to say and he was weary, weary. He felt guilty snatching even this hour from his duties, and he had yet to reach the business of his letter—the will. "Where shall I begin? Where shall I end? How shall I put an eternal period to a correspondence which has given me so much comfort? With what expression of regret shall I take leave of my happiness? With what words of tenderness, of gratitude, of counsel, of consolation, shall I pay you for what I am robbing you of?" Finally he plunged into the statement of his financial affairs and bequeathed to Ruth his entire estate.

He felt obliged to explain why he named no other relatives in his will. "When you gave me your blessed self, you know I was destitute of every other possession. I was rich only in the . . . sweet consolation of your society. In our various struggles and disappointments . . . I have often been rendered happy by misfortunes; for the heaviest we have met with were turned into blessings by the opportunities they gave me to discover new virtues in you." Then he added that since 1791, their most difficult year, he never had been so contented. Since that time he had loved her better; his heart had been more full of her excellence and less agitated with objects of ambition which used to devour him. "I recall these things to your mind," he continued, "to convince you of my full belief, that . . . the competency which we seem at last to have secured is owing more to your energy than mine . . . the energy of your virtues, which gave me consolation, and even happiness, under circumstances wherein, if I had been alone, or with a partner no better than myself, I should have sunk."

Finally he came to the end of the long document: "If you should see me no more . . . you will not forget I loved you . . . [but] let your tenderness for me soon cease to agitate that lovely bosom. . . . It is for the living, not the dead, to be rendered happy by the sweetness of your temper, the purity of your heart . . . your undivided love." Then he closed with one more paragraph: "Farewell, my wife; and though I am not used to subscribe my letters . . . yet it seems proper that the last characters which this hand shall trace . . . should compose the name of your most faithful, most affectionate, and most grateful husband—Joel Barlow."

Having completed the letter, Barlow felt relief and once more plunged into the fatigues of his office. By now the plague had raged for more than a month and taken a toll of five American prisoners. It was July eighth. The Dey's three-months extension of time was up; still no money had come to implement the treaty and to ransom the captives. The crises of Barlow's mission seemed endless; yet when everything appeared lost, his sheer luck and shrewd mind once more retrieved a desperate situation.

What happened in late June and early July can only be called diplomatic sleight of hand. An amazing sequence of events began when into the murky sea of unrelieved gloom one day floated a new face. The newcomer, who joined the foreign colony as a replacement for the former French consul, arrived bearing an unusually brilliant consular gift. So dazzling was the gift that France suddenly became the most favored nation in Barbary. Now nothing was too good for the French consul, who took prompt advantage of his welcome to borrow two hundred thousand dollars from the Dey's treasury. At that moment money was scarce in Algiers, though the government's till was full. Even the firm of Bacri was temporarily embarrassed. The Jewish bankers had their money tied up in the hands of the French government; hence the arrival of a new French consul who could tap the Dey's treasury was to them an important event. Bacri now could get part of his money from the French consul, and France would owe the Dey instead of him. This transfer of funds took place.

Barlow, being privy to the transaction, caught a glimpse of a plan to save the American prisoners. With complete disregard for the laws of probability, he gambled his reputation and perhaps even his personal safety. He went to Bacri and put the matter bluntly. He wanted to borrow that two hundred thousand dollars to ransom the American captives immediately to get them out of Algiers before they all died of the plague. Bacri squirmed and raised objections. Barlow offered to give him bills on Donaldson in Leghorn and a personal guarantee that the bills would not come back under protest. He recalled Bacri's previous wish to lend him money at a time when both men knew there was none in Algiers to lend. Bacri stalled once more; then perhaps he remembered how Barlow had

173

rid him of the hated secretary Cathcart. Perhaps he succumbed to Barlow's talent for winning friends. Perhaps he was touched by a spark of sympathy for the prisoners. Whatever it was, Barlow got the money. Four days after he wrote his last will and testament, he bought the freedom of the American prisoners with the Dey's own gold and whisked them out of Algiers at the first fair wind.

The Americans embarked on a ship named *Fortune*, skippered by one of their number, Captain Samuel Calder, and chartered from Bacri. They carried Barlow's blessing and dispatches for Donaldson, Humphreys, and Pickering. To the Secretary of State Barlow wrote: "This will be presented to you by the remnant of our captive citizens who have survived the pains and humiliation of slavery in this place." Barlow had grown fond of the prisoners and wished the government not to begrudge the expense of liberation. "When we reflect on the extravagant sums of money that this redemption will cost the United States," he continued, "it affords at least some consolation to know that it is not expended on worthless & disorderly persons. . . . Our people have conducted themselves . . . with . . . patience and decorum." He hoped that the men would receive help in rehabilitation when they reached home, for some of them had suffered cruelly in their captivity. "One is in a state of total blindness; another is reduced nearly to the same condition; two or three carry the marks of unmerciful treatment, in ruptures produced by hard labor; and others have had their constitutions injured by the plague."

Three days after the *Fortune* sailed, the Dey discovered that Barlow had pulled a rabbit out of his hat. Fortunately, he did not know that the ransom had come from his own treasury, but he did realize that he no longer held any hostages to enforce payment of the peace money. Barlow had persuaded Bacri to accept responsibility with him for payment of the entire sum, and the banker's assurance, plus the two hundred thousand dollars, had been just enough to obtain the prisoners' release. As Barlow wrote Pickering: "This was only the rattle given to the child while you take away the penknife." But the child soon began to holler. In the Dey's simple mind there was no good reason now why the United States should pay up, since the hostages had slipped from his grasp. He was furious at Barlow and began tormenting him daily for the rest of the promised gold.

August and September were months of hard work, frustration, and harassment. Joel wrote Ruth after getting the captives away: "I am [now] the only American slave in Algiers, and I work like a dozen." Happily, Barlow had only the Dey to contend with, for he won his gamble with Bacri. A few days after the prisoners sailed, news finally came from Donaldson in Leghorn that he had a letter of credit for four hundred thousand dollars from Humphreys. Shipping the specie to Algiers, Bacri knew, was a formality that would be accomplished in due course. The simple-minded Dey, however, understood only the hard metalic clink of gold pieces, and to make Barlow's position almost unendurable, war now closed the port of Leghorn. Napoleon, waging his first great campaign, was driving the Austrians out of northern Italy, and the British navy, like a pack of hounds yapping at his heels, was blockading the coast. If Humphreys only had sent his letter to Leghorn by express instead of normal conveyance, Barlow chided in a dispatch to Lisbon, the credit would have arrived twenty-five days sooner and the money could have been shipped before the blockade began.

Early in September Hassan Bashaw called Barlow in and said again he would wait no longer. He had been bemused a whole year with a string of lies. "Is it possible," he said, "that your money has been dancing all over Europe for a year, & has happened to light at last in Leghorn just at the moment that the English were to blockade the port?" Then he shouted and raved that the Americans had no money in Europe and never intended to pay him at all. "You speak of patience," he thundered; "I have more patience than God. I have resisted all your enemies who have tried to overturn your peace. My heart has struggled against my judgment. I wished to think you honest, but I begin to think you the most faithless nation among the infidels." After this outburst the Dey subsided a trifle and left Barlow alone for a little while.

Then Barlow received a letter from Humphreys on September fourteenth saying Captain O'Brien was on his way in the brig *Sophia* with two hundred and twenty-five thousand dollars raised in Lisbon. This certainly was welcome news, but the dispatch was dated August fourth. O'Brien had been en route forty-one days already on a voyage that should not have taken more than a week or two in the summer. What could have happened? Then Barlow began to figure. He had heard several weeks before that two un-identified ships had been captured by Tripoli; one must have been the *Sophia.* If true, O'Brien would arrive eventually, for he trav-eled under a safe conduct from Algiers and the Tripolitans would not dare to hold him. At all events, he braved the Dey's close little den once more. As a messenger announced the caller, the Dey ex-ploded: "Is it possible that that man has the impudence to appear again in my presence?"

"He has good news to announce to you," the messenger replied.

"Good lies . . . I suppose you mean," the Dey answered. "But let him come."

Once again Barlow turned his charm on the Algerian despot. He explained that O'Brien was on his way with the money and he surely would arrive soon. Also, the thirty-six-gun frigate was being built and would not the Dey rather wait for good workmanship than accept something hastily put together? The Dey looked stern, but Barlow detected an unconcealed trace of pleasure.

"Do you think I believe all this?" asked the Dey.

"Why . . . Effendi, I know you believe it. That severity in your face is but the mask of an excellent heart, and you esteem the Amer-icans in spite of all their enemies."

"We will be friends a little longer," said Hassan Bashaw extend-ing his huge paw to Barlow.

The rest of September passed in another tense period of anxious waiting. Ten days after the interview with the Dey O'Brien still had not arrived, and Barlow wrote Ruth painfully: "It is nine months since I left on this mission. Why did you let me go? . . . If Hichborn had come, he'd have let the treaty go to the devil and returned to his own affairs. I am too obstinate to be discouraged so early . . . I have resolved to contest the ground, inch by inch." He added, however, that his only success was likely to be the free-ing of the prisoners, and he feared that any day he might be thrown in irons. He also worried over the resentment of other nations at his success so far in keeping the Dey from going to war with the

United States. As a result of his diplomacy, the Danes, Swedes, and Venetians already had suffered, and he was sure they all were scheming behind his back. He would have been even more alarmed had he known, as he found out later, that the Spanish consul had orders to get rid of him, if it could be done for fifty thousand dollars.

Barlow's distressing wait finally came to an end on October first. The *Sophia* dropped anchor in the harbor of Algiers, and O'Brien hauled ashore his chest of gold. Barlow no doubt was the happiest man in the city. Success was his at the eleventh hour despite weather, war, incompetence, disease, and intrigue. A seasoned diplomat by now, Barlow lost no time in taking a profit on the sharp rise of American stock in Algiers. He picked up O'Brien and went to see the Dey.

When the two Americans entered the audience chamber and announced the arrival of the money, "the Dey of Algiers changed from a tiger to a lamb." Hassan Bashaw seized Barlow's right hand with his right and put his left on Barlow's heart. Then he said: "My friend . . . I have long admired your constancy & courage. I now find you are true to me, as well as to your country. I have treated you with great severity, but you must allow that I have had uncommon patience. . . . I always felt something at the bottom of my heart which told me, 'That man cannot lie.' . . . We will be friends forever." Then the Dey went on to ask Barlow if there was any favor he could do for him. There was.

"My lord," Barlow answered, "for myself I need nothing." But then he hastened to add that he had yet to obtain treaties with Tripoli and Tunis. "The Tunisians and the Tripolitans make a cruel war against us." The Bey of Tunis, he explained, had agreed to negotiate a treaty but was now going back on his word. The Bey of Tripoli had just captured two American ships, one of which (the *Sophia*) he was afraid to keep because it traveled on an Algerian passport. "Now I ask one letter from your hand to the Bey of Tunis to force him immediately to keep his word and conclude the peace. . . . It is for you . . . to hold these people to . . . their word, and save the honor of Barbary."

Barlow paused an instant to see if his request was getting a sym-

177

pathetic hearing. It was and he continued: "As to Tripoli, I am going to offer forty thousand piastres, in all, for the peace & the prisoners. I ask you for a letter for the Bey, forcing him to give me these terms precisely, to ask your pardon for the insult done to your passport."

"My friend," replied the Dey, all smiles and good will, "You have not asked enough." And with that, Hassan Bashaw offered to lend Barlow money to buy his treaties with Tripoli and Tunis and to send strong letters to the pirates in those cities ordering them to conclude peace immediately with the United States. He was as good as his word, and when Barlow wrote Ruth an account of this remarkable interview, he was ecstatic: "My tears flowed in response." He added: "All is arranged; O'Brien goes tomorrow." In a month, he hoped, the treaties would be concluded and he could depart quickly for Paris. Ten days later he wrote: "Our business goes wonderfully. I shall probably leave in six weeks. I am master of the battlefield." But again disappointment ambushed his irrepressible optimism.

4: *Thousand and One Nights*

Barlow's high spirits continued through the end of 1796. He sent O'Brien to Tripoli with the proposed text of a treaty and engaged a French merchant, Joseph Famin, to represent him in Tunis. He now became known in the foreign colony in Algiers as "the father of all consuls," so dazzling had been his diplomatic legerdemain. The Swedish, Danish, Venetian, and English consuls, all his good friends despite the trouble he was causing them, could only marvel at their colleague's wizardry. Barlow might have taken pleasure in his favored status if Ruth had been there to share it. He wrote her modestly that his success had been due to his "tranquility and constancy" throughout the affair. The Dey finally learned the truth of all Joel had been saying about American intentions, and this "flattered his heart . . . in my favor without knowing why." At the moment, Joel added, the Dey would "give me his beard, hair by hair, if I should ask it; but this humor cannot last long, for caprice is the first of his virtues."

The treaty with Tripoli materialized only a little behind schedule. The Dey of Algiers' strong note to the Bey of Tripoli produced the desired effect, and O'Brien hammered out the treaty in November for forty thousand dollars plus presents and a promised shipment of naval stores. By the end of the month Barlow was in daily expectation of treaties from both Tripoli and Tunis and wrote Ruth that he hoped to leave for Paris in two or three weeks. O'Brien did not appear in Algiers until January, 1797, but when he came back, he carried only the document from Tripoli, which Barlow forwarded to Humphreys for transmittal to Philadelphia.

This treaty, negotiated easily and ratified promptly by the Senate, contained a curious clause which since has raised many eyebrows. Article Eleven begins: "As the government of the United States is not in any sense founded on the Christian religion. . . ." In the context of the complete sentence, however, neither President Washington nor Timothy Pickering nor the Senate found it objectionable. Its meaning was clear: because the United States had not adopted Christianity as a state religion and therefore held no official enmity for Islam, no pretext arising from religious differences should ever produce disharmony between the two states.

If the negotiations with Tripoli went smoothly, the dickerings with Tunis met unexpected obstinacy. Captain O'Brien stopped at Tunis on his return from Tripoli to Algiers expecting to pick up the second treaty, but he found that the Bey of Tunis now wanted more than twice the fifty thousand dollars he carried to buy the peace. Hassan Bashaw's threatening letter to Tunis only made his rival pirate angry and determined to raise the ante. When O'Brien sent this information back to Algiers, Barlow once more went to the Dey to put his friendship to the test.

In his interview Barlow twanged energetically on the Dey's ego and raised a great noise of indignation over the effrontery of the Bey of Tunis. Afterwards Barlow wrote: "The Bey of Tunis is certainly lost . . . he has not three months to live." By the end of the year, however, further threats from Algiers had produced no chastening effect, and Hassan Bashaw had to declare war on Tunis.

Now Barlow reported: "The Dey has sent fifty thousand armed ambassadors on horseback, well armed, to negotiate my affairs in Tunis. These good negotiators ought to bring the head of the Bey to me and his treasure to the Dey. At that price our peace is assured."

Barlow's mission was proceeding so well that he declared a holiday and went wild boar hunting. Invited to a hunt by the minister of marine, Barlow and the English and Swedish consuls joined a party of one hundred well-mounted natives armed with lances in the manner of the ancient Numidians. The expedition rode to a forest fifteen miles from Algiers where the hunters pitched tents for a three-day stay. But the hunt had not progressed far when Barlow found that he had been riding in carriages for too many years. The father of all consuls wrote his wife after the first day's hunt: "Two hours after midday I was so excessively fatigued that I dismounted . . . leaving all the honor to my two sons [the English and Swedish consuls]."

The hunt was an experience, however, that he would not soon forget. "It is unbelievable, the speed and boldness of these Moors in this game," he wrote; "they pursue a beast, run over him, and plant their lances in his body." The beast, he added, was "capable of killing at any moment the horse and its rider, a thing which happens sometimes." On a single day of the chase three or four mounted hunters were wounded and fourteen wild boars killed. One of the hunters gave Barlow an extra thrill by running down a hyena and planting a lance in it only a few feet from where he was sitting.

When the expedition returned to town, the Dey wanted to know why Barlow was fatigued. The minister of marine replied generously that the American rode a vicious, unmanageable horse. "That was a lie," Joel admitted to Ruth; "the horse was excellent, but the horseman is worth nothing." The Dey replied: "I thought I'd given him a good mount; tell him that tomorrow I will send him one of the best from my stable." The next day the horse arrived, a superb beast, conceded Barlow, but "he can give me two hundred; it will never make me a horseman, and I shall never again go to hunt boars."

After the boar-hunting interlude, Barlow again turned to the stalled treaty negotiation. The Dey's war against the refractory Bey of Tunis faded away like a mirage in the desert, leaving the affair where it started. Barlow's troubles were compounded by the indiscretions of American merchants who would not keep their vessels out of the Mediterranean until peace was obtained. Barlow was furious when he heard that the schooner *Eliza* had been captured by a pirate row galley and taken into Tunis. This sort of episode doubled the cost of the treaty by adding the expense of ransom to the price of peace. There was nothing he could do, however, but redeem the *Eliza*, thereby adding another thirty thousand dollars to the bill and running up the Bey's asking price to one hundred and seven thousand dollars. Even after its release the American schooner continued to plague him.

Barlow had to deal with more than just the Barbary pirates. The *Eliza* was captained by a scoundrel, Samuel Graves, who deliberately ignored his orders on leaving Tunis. Graves was either to go to Leghorn, pick up the American seamen ransomed from Algiers, and take them home, or to come directly to Algiers to get dispatches for Philadelphia. In all events, he was to get his ship out of the Mediterranean immediately. Instead, Graves took on board a Jewish merchant from Tunis with goods for Algiers and sailed to Palermo, where he sold the cargo Barlow had ransomed and loaded another for England. This flouting of instructions might not have been serious, but then the rascally captain came close to creating an international incident.

Graves threw the merchant in chains after the ship cleared the port at Tunis and in Palermo subjected him to brutal treatment. He tied a rope around him, plunged him into the sea several times, set him on shore with only the clothes he wore, and robbed him of his goods. The merchant subsequently made his way to Naples, Rome, and Leghorn, where he got passage to North Africa. Then he traveled overland to Algiers and finally arrived there five months after leaving Tunis. Barlow was appalled when he heard the tale, but fortunately he got the news before the Dey.

Barlow had visions of immediate hostilities between Algiers and the United States, a scrapping of the treaty, and the collapse of all

181

his work. There was no time to lose; the story would be all over Algiers in a matter of hours. He went to the Dey and told him the *Eliza* had been battered by a storm and driven in a wrecked condition to Sicily. He said there had been a dispute between the captain and the merchant over property lost in the storm. The merchant, he added, was incensed at the captain, but no doubt both men were at fault. The United States would investigate, discipline the captain and pay damages, if he was to blame. Barlow begged the Dey not to punish the merchant if he exaggerated the story when he arrived. After all, he had been through trying circumstances.

Barlow's quick action prevented an ugly situation from developing, though it cost the United States another six thousand dollars. The Dey took Barlow's word without question and "even threatened the Jew with a thousand bastinadoes, if he should be found to exaggerate." Barlow summarized in his account of the sorry business: "Though the principal weight of the storm is in this manner averted, yet the affair has not failed to produce a great sensation—here and in Tunis. It is a most shameful & humiliating stroke on the American character in Barbary."

For seven weary months after he concluded the negotiations with Tripoli, Barlow waited for his emissaries and the Bey of Tunis to agree on a treaty. Every month he grew more restive; every month he hoped to be off. His stubborn refusal to leave before his mission was completely finished kept him in Algiers well into the summer of 1797. His patience at last was rewarded, but only meagerly. Although the treaty avoided the payment of any annual tribute, it cost the United States the Bey's entire original demand. During Barlow's final months in Algiers there was a procession of occasional intrigues and minor disturbances, such as the *Eliza* business, to deal with. He had to block the scheming of the French consul, a fiery ex-follower of Robespierre, who seemed eager to foment war between the United States and France. He had to pacify the Dey once more—this time over the delay of promised naval stores from America. He had to adjust claims when a cargo of Bacri's wheat on board a ship flying the American flag was captured by the British. But in general Barlow had a superabundance of time on his hands.

During this period he meditated on his past and resolved for his future. "This absence has contributed to my reformation," he wrote Ruth in April; "I will return to you a new man." The passion of ambition, so consuming in his previous careers as poet, land sales-man, and politician, by now was burning out. "In place of grand political philosophy, I'll follow small social and domestic philos-ophy. My first and constant care will be to make my wife per-fectly happy." His new course, he projected, was to work for the good of humanity, though he admitted candidly there might be "a great deal of vanity" driving his humanitarian impulse. But even so, he promised: "Once back in your arms, I shall certainly not leave them again." Ruth, writing almost simultaneously from Paris, was declaring in like vein: "If I am ever so happy as to hold you again in my arms, I will never let you go. . . . I will follow you through everything; I will brave all dangers rather than thus be abandoned by the one who alone can make me happy."

As his reflections continued, Barlow analyzed the relationship be-tween himself and Ruth. He saw more clearly than ever the strength of their union, the complementary qualities that bound them together. "For virtues of the heart and the absence of vices between both of us—*equality*," he scored. For genius, which he divided into three components, imagination, judgment, and taste, the honors were divided. "The taste of both of us is infinitely sim-ilar, a thing which has contributed very much to the happiness of our union. The judgment is more on your side; the imagination on mine." But he admitted that his imagination was not brilliant, even though he owed it the little literary reputation he had acquired. Then in a final flash of insight into his own character, he wrote: "My taste, without being perfect, has directed me happily enough in style, especially in prose. I have always lacked judgment, more or less, as much in literary subjects as in the material and social world."

Sometimes in his musings the Yankee businessman in Barlow over-whelmed the philosopher-poet. On these occasions he totaled up an imaginary balance sheet of the money he could have made if he never had gone to Algiers. Reports from Ruth and his former business associates pricked his envy and made him assert, perhaps correctly, that the mission cost him twenty thousand dollars. When trade was booming in Paris, Ruth wrote: "How much you have lost by this devil of a mission! If you had been here, you would have made a fortune." Barlow was in full agreement and in his depressed moments let his correspondents know it. He wrote Humphreys: "As an individual consulting only my own convenience & prospects, I certainly have reason to curse the day in which I agreed to come." And he wrote Wolcott, now Secretary of the Treasury, that the mission had been undertaken "at the expense of sacrifices which have cost me exceedingly dear. . . . I never shall be able to repair the wrongs I have done to myself by coming here." Considering that Barlow estimated his estate at one hundred and twenty thousand dollars when he made his will in 1796, one is inclined to be unsympathetic.

Yet some of this mood of self-pity was justified. For a year after Barlow ransomed the American captives, he was the only resident American in Algiers. Communications were so poor, the depredations of the warring powers and Barbary pirates so frustrating, that he often felt abandoned in Africa or at least obliged to carry more responsibilities than one man should have to bear. He heard from Humphreys infrequently, and thirteen months after leaving Paris he had received no communication from the Secretary of State. He was afraid his efforts would be repudiated in Philadelphia, and he did not see how the administration or Congress could be persuaded to pay the large extra expenses his mission was incurring. But he was overly pessimistic on this count. His efforts were appreciated, as he realized when he finally received this commendation from Timothy Pickering not long before he left Algiers: "It has been fortunate for the United States that their interests were at so critical a period in the hands of a citizen who had intelligence to discern and confidence to seize the fittest moment to secure them."

Even while bemoaning his losses, Barlow was turning to some account the commercial opportunities in Algiers. He now had friends or acquaintances among the merchants and consuls in a dozen Mediterranean ports. As soon as American ships could navigate the sea, he was on the spot to know it and bought, no doubt at a bargain, two ships, the *Rachel* and the *Friendship*. He operated the vessels for something over a year, then sold them profitably after he returned to Paris. When he answered Joseph Donaldson's later insinuation that he had made ten thousand dollars on a grain cargo during his Algerine mission, he denied that he had cleared more than five hundred; but this shipment involved only one voyage of one of his ships, and when he left North Africa, he wrote his wife: "I have turned some profit during my weary moments in BARBARY. I have even made what we are accustomed to call a little fortune."

On July 18, 1797, the impatient United States agent for Algiers finally boarded ship for Marseilles. After twelve days of easy sailing over a peaceful Mediterranean, he reached the French port. Traveling on his own ship, the *Rachel*, commanded by Philip Sloan, he reported that he never had such a pleasant voyage before, only one day of seasickness, the first day out. His colleagues in Algiers, the French, Spanish, and English consuls all gave him passports to insure that he would get to France without interruption. The Dey sent him off with a handsomer present than usual on such occasions and broke all established custom by sending a gift to Ruth.

When Barlow disembarked from the *Rachel*, he was not yet free to set out for Paris. Coming from a pest-ridden African port, the ship and its personnel had to endure forty days of quarantine. He wrote Humphreys: "I have at last escaped from the infernal regions, & am transferred to the purgatory of the Lazaret. . . . I declare to you that for all the treasure of the United States, past, present, & to come, I would not undertake another such task." But despite the delay of the quarantine, Barlow's spirits were high; he was at last back in France and would see his wife in a few more weeks. Every other day he wrote her glowing letters, which the quarantine authorities dipped in vinegar before posting.

The day after settling down in the lazaret he wrote Ruth gaily: "I wear large mustaches—long, beautiful, and black (a little gray, however). Do you wish me to cut them here, or do you wish to see them and cut them yourself?" Then he explained how he happened to grow mustaches: "As I am a lamb at heart, it was necessary for me to conceal this character beneath the exterior of some

185

other animal, and my mustaches give me very nearly the air of the tiger." He had found a fierce appearance a great asset in Barbary where there was a proverb: "Who makes himself mutton, the wolf eats." Ruth, however, wanted her husband back as little changed as possible and requested that he not return to Paris looking like a Barbary pirate.

The forty days in purgatory finally ended early in September, and after two or three more days in Marseilles completing the sale of the *Rachel*'s cargo, Joel headed for paradise. "I leave tomorrow," he wrote on September tenth in the last letter Ruth was to receive from him for several years, and this time nothing prevented his departure. The trip back to Paris was uneventful, and nearly twenty-one months after leaving Ruth the separation that had seemed a century came to a happy conclusion.

CHAPTER VIII

Transatlantic Politics

1: Imbroglio

In the year 1797 the unbelievable success of General Bonaparte riveted all of Europe's attention on France. After putting to rout the Austrian defenders of Italy, the French armies turned northward to Austria proper. They crossed the Carnic Alps from the plains of Friuli and pursued Archduke Charles' troops to resounding defeat at Neumarkt and Unzmarkt. The Austrians had to sue for peace, and the important treaty of Campo-Formio followed. This brilliant success pushed the frontier of France to the Rhine and cleared the way for General Bonaparte to become Napoleon I. When the future Emperor arrived in Paris on December fifth, there was neither political nor military rival able to eclipse his swiftly rising star.

The city that Barlow returned to in September had just experienced another convulsion in the Revolution of the Eighteenth Fructidor (September fourth). On this day the Directory successfully smashed its opponents in the legislature and gained undisputed control of France. The *coup d'état*, probably masterminded by the wily Talleyrand, was carried out bloodlessly, but it was nonetheless effective. Fifty-five enemies of the Directory in the legislature were instantly arrested and deported without trial, and two dissident members of the five-man Directory were allowed to escape from France.

In the waters surrounding Europe the success of French arms was offset by British sea power. Though the British navy had been rocked the year before by a great mutiny, in February Admiral Sir John Jervis, assisted by Commodore Nelson, won a decisive victory against the French and their Spanish allies at Cape St. Vincent. Eight months later Admiral Adam Duncan met the Dutch fleet, now also allied with France, and destroyed it off the dunes of Camperdown. By the year's end the British controlled European coastal waters from the Mediterranean to the Baltic. The Directory and General Bonaparte then concocted a plan that they hoped would hurt Britain by crippling her power in the Middle East. They undertook the indecisive Egyptian campaign.

Concurrent with these significant events was the rapid deterioration of traditional friendly relations between France and the United States. James Monroe, a warm friend of France, had been recalled during Barlow's Algerian mission, and his successor was Charles Pinckney, a staunch Federalist. This appointment, coming on the heels of the Jay Treaty, greatly irritated the French Directory. They already had been angered when President Washington declared the officious Citizen Genêt *persona non grata*, and now they concluded that John Adams' administration would be ardently pro-British. When Pinckney arrived in Paris the Directory refused to receive him, placed him under surveillance as a suspicious character, and then ordered him out of the country. French ships next were instructed to seize all American vessels carrying goods to or from British ports.

Battles and diplomatic problems, however, did not dim the luster of Paris. The *coup* of the Eighteenth Fructidor was a political event of wide ramifications, but without the tumbrels and guillotine the public took little notice. Barlow returned to the gay, pleasure-loving capital he had left in 1795. Paris was, as always, a city of beautiful avenues, handsome parks, and imposing buildings. The powerful impulse that once sent Jefferson to the Tuileries nearly every day to look at the Hôtel de Salm also sent Barlow roaming the streets. He covered Paris from the Place Vendôme to the Luxembourg Palace and once more delighted in the rich architecture, sculpture, painting, and music that the city afforded.

When Barlow reached Paris after a fast trip from Marseilles, he was not yet aware of the ominous drift of events. He was only glad to be back with Ruth. He returned from Algiers deeply tanned, in ruddy health, forty-three years old. He reported to his old physician and fellow wit, Dr. Hopkins: "I have grown fleshy, weight one hundred and seventy pounds, have contracted no vicious habits, have acquired a moderate but sufficient income, & a pure & undivided taste for tranquility, study, & doing good." When he discovered that Ruth, too, was blooming in her middle years, he felt that life could not hold much more joy. "The health of my precious wife," he also wrote Hopkins, "has grown by degrees much better than when you used to mend it so often, & her temper & taste are perfectly conformable to my own. Indeed I rank myself in the rarest class of living creatures. I am a happy man."

Barlow returned to Paris telling himself that he would collect materials for his history of the French Revolution and then go home. The season would be too far advanced to leave this autumn, but next spring perhaps the sailing could take place. He had many reasons to return to America. Family and friends kept urging him, even though Ruth's brother Dudley finally had given up, declaring that Joel was "so headstrong, it does no good to say anything to him" on that topic. He now possessed the fortune he originally had left America to seek. He had the means to live comfortably, pursue his literary interests, and patronize the arts and sciences. After completing his successful mission to Barbary, he also might have expected to return home modestly triumphant.

The history, however, was really an excuse to put off the departure. Though he was genuinely interested in the work and actually made copious notes and collected a valuable library, he never carried the project very far. Perhaps he did not have the patience to be a historian; certainly he did not have enough motivation. What seems to have kept him in Europe was the prick of hostility he felt in the political climate at home. He had exclaimed, when Adams was nominated to run against Jefferson: "The nomination of Adams to the presidency has almost taken away my desire to see my country again." This outburst was a great exaggeration, of course, but he was keenly disappointed when Jefferson subsequently was defeated by three electoral votes. He hoped that Jefferson as vice-president could offset some of the mischief he feared the Federalists would cause in international relations.

The times conspired to keep Barlow in France as a self-appointed representative of the Jeffersonian minority. By the end of 1797 he no longer needed the projected history as justification for lingering in Paris. Franco-American relations then hung together by such a fragile tie that he felt obliged to stay in France to help avert the disaster of war. Again his destiny thrust him into the cockpit of fateful events, as his brother-in-law, Senator Baldwin, noted: "It has been your extraordinary good fortune to fall by accident into the very place for which your distinguished qualities designed you, and just at the moment when you were wanted." Joel Barlow, citizen of two worlds, could not stay out of politics no matter how hard he tried.

There was another factor, too, that kept Barlow dallying beside the still waters of the Seine. He acquired a new friend and developed a new interest. While he still reclined in the green pastures of his joyful homecoming, he met a young Pennsylvanian who recently had joined the American colony in Paris. This newcomer lodged at the Barlow's own hotel and instantly charmed both Ruth and Joel. They liked his looks, his manners, and his big ideas, and the more they saw of him, the closer the attachment became. Before they knew it, the attractive youth, who was ten years their junior, began to play the rôle of a favorite younger brother. Joel and Ruth then invited their new friend to live with them, and for the balance of their years in France this young man became an increasingly intimate member of the Barlow household. His name was Robert Fulton.

When he arrived in Paris, Fulton already had come a long way from his birthplace on a farm near Lancaster, Pennsylvania. As a youngster, he had been apprenticed to a jeweler and later had become a painter of miniatures in Philadelphia. Because his talent seemed precocious in eighteenth-century America, he aspired to study in Europe, and several years after the Revolution, he borrowed forty guineas and secured a letter of introduction to Benjamin West, the most famous American artist of his day. West lived and worked in London and occasionally took students. Fulton painted in his studio for several years.

What had passed for talent in the United States, however, proved too meager an endowment in England to support a career as painter. Fulton was a realist and soon turned to engineering, for which he discovered a much greater aptitude. During the next few years he absorbed himself in canal-building, then a lively subject of interest and endeavor in commercial and industrial England. He devised a grandiose scheme for linking cities and towns with a network of canals, through which would move strings of towed boats, like railroad cars. When Fulton's path crossed Barlow's, he had gone to France to obtain a French patent for his scheme. Nothing came of the canal idea, but Fulton stayed on in France and launched a new project, a submarine that almost worked.

While the Barlows were getting acquainted with Fulton, a time fuse was burning towards the mysterious XYZ Affair. In America President Adams, though unfriendly to France, had resisted stubbornly Federalist demands for war. When the Directory insulted the United States by refusing to receive Pinckney as minister, Adams then sent a commission, made up of Pinckney, John Marshall, and Elbridge Gerry, to negotiate a treaty and compose differences between the two countries. For all of Adams' efforts to be conciliatory, Talleyrand snubbed the commissioners, then dealt with them through shadowy agents, Messieurs X, Y, and Z. The foreign minister demanded a large American loan for the French government and a tidy little bribe of two hundred and forty thousand dollars for his own services. The commissioners rejected these terms, not because they were shocked by the proposals but because they did not trust Talleyrand, and during the fall and winter they haggled and talked but came to no conclusions.

Barlow watched the futile negotiations as an interested bystander who no longer had any close connections with the government. Three weeks after the commissioners presented their credentials, he wrote a friend that Talleyrand had seemed agreeable at first.

The foreign minister had hinted that if the Americans did not press matters but were patient he would lay the business before the Directory and return with an answer. When nothing happened, Barlow soon concluded that the mission would fail. During the succeeding weeks he reported to his correspondents that the negotiations were stopped on dead center. His information was accurate, for it no doubt came from the one republican among the commissioners, Elbridge Gerry, whom he saw frequently. Gerry was unfortunately, in Barlow's words, "a little make-weight man appointed with the intention that he would have no influence." With Gerry and two pro-British Federalists on the commission Barlow realized there was little hope for success. He probably wished at this point that he still had some friends in the government, but he did not.

The shifting sands of French politics had obliterated his connections during his sojourn in Hamburg and subsequent mission to Algiers. "To aid you with the government here," he wrote a friend on a business matter, "is totally out of my power. I have not the least acquaintance with any minister, or any director, or any of their secretaries or clerks." Then he went on to explain that ever since 1793 "when I came near perishing with the fathers of the Republic, because they were my friends, I have avoided any connection with men in power." And what was more, he concluded, "I do not know any American here who has any influence with the government."

After months of unsuccessful dickering the Federalist members of the American commission left France. Gerry stayed behind until recalled, but alone he could do nothing to arrest the drift towards war. When Pinckney and Marshall returned home and President Adams reported the futile negotiations to Congress, the United States reacted violently. No one had objected to paying tribute to the Barbary pirates to obtain a peace treaty, but the Federalists used Talleyrand's demand for a bribe as an excuse to bludgeon the Republicans. Federalist editors whooped up a noisy inter-party brawl, and the public clamored for war. The administration responded by increasing the army, organizing a navy, and conducting unofficial war with France on the high seas.

Barlow brooded over the failure of the commissioners to obtain a treaty. From his observation point it looked as if President Adams had been incredibly ill advised or downright belligerent in sending Pinckney and Marshall, known enemies of France. He quoted to Jefferson a statement by Talleyrand saying substantially this. What could a private citizen do to help retrieve the situation, he asked himself? Not much apparently, but in the absence of an American minister in Paris, a well-informed compatriot at least could let his prominent Republican friends at home know the real mood and temper of France. With this thought in mind he composed a long, candid letter to his brother-in-law, Senator Baldwin, and sent a copy to Vice-President Jefferson. He entrusted the letters to his friend William Lee, an American merchant who was en route to the United States, and Lee promised to deliver them in person.

In his communication Barlow reviewed with "bluntness and severity" the gradual bankruptcy of American prestige and good will in France. At the beginning of the French Revolution, he said, the American republic was the country most admired by French leaders. They looked on the United States as a nation that already had solved "the frightful problem of representative democracy." George Washington was a great hero to them, and Thomas Jefferson as minister to France had forged strong bonds between the two countries. But then Jefferson had been replaced by the hostile Gouverneur Morris, whose appointment was "an insult" to France "that admits of no palliation." "I have no doubt," Barlow charged, "that after the Austrian & the English Ambassadors retired from Paris, Morris acted as secret agent & spy for both those cabinets."

Next came the affair of Citizen Genêt, the French minister who was declared *persona non grata* by the United States; but this episode, Barlow thought, did not create much French animosity because Genêt had been sent by Brissot, whose party soon was liquidated. More serious deterioration in Franco-American relations resulted from the Jay Treaty and Morris' anti-French activities after his recall. The fortunate mission of James Monroe, which followed next, served to counterpoise the weight of resentment in France against the United States, but then "for the apparent crime of preventing a war" Monroe was recalled and Pinckney appointed. Even after this event, which seemed incomprehensible to France if the United States meant to remain friendly, the Directory decided to take no immediate action. They knew that President Washington was in "the dotage of his natural life," and they hoped that Jefferson would win the presidency in 1796. When Adams was elected, the French government concluded that "the enmity of the old president towards France was now . . . nationalized in America."

After Adams took office, continued Barlow, what did he do but "play the Bully by forcing a man [Pinckney] back who had just been driven out of Paris." If Adams really had wanted a treaty, he should have returned Monroe, or if Madison had been sent, the business could have been concluded in twenty-four hours. At the same time, Adams was telling Congress, so Barlow was informed, "that, though he should succeed in treating with the French, there was no dependence to be placed in any of their engagements; that their religion & morality were at an end; that they had turned pirates & plunderers, and that it would be necessary to be perpetually armed against them, although you were at peace." People in France, added Barlow, wondered that the answer of Congress "had not been an order to send him [Adams] to the Mad-house."

Barlow closed his letter with the hope that good sense would prevail in the Adams administration's dealings with France. Unless the United States intended war, he thought, there was still a chance to avert a complete rupture. "I beg you to remember the warning I now give you," he told Baldwin and Jefferson. If the executive is not willing to appoint someone like Madison or Monroe to negotiate the treaty, war will be the result. "When in God's name are we to expect from America just ideas relative to France?" The answer, of course, was never while Adams was President; but Barlow was too hard on John Adams. The President was a man of complete probity, whose patient diplomacy with France cost him his political career. Almost singlehandedly Adams resisted the demands of his party for war, putting principle above party and peace above re-election.

The consequences of Barlow's letter were more tremendous than anyone could have foreseen. The message did not fall into wrong hands during transit, as Barlow feared it might, and Baldwin made just the use of it that the author intended. He discreetly showed it to other members of his party, but the "bluntness and severity" of the language were high explosives in the arsenal of political warfare. The Republicans and Federalists now were joined in a struggle that asked and gave no quarter, and news of the communication spread widely by word of mouth. One day a friend, who had been entrusted with a copy of the letter, returned to his rooms in a Philadelphia lodging house to find that his locks had been picked. The letter was gone.

Baldwin and his colleagues held their breath waiting to see what would happen. Their suspense was short. Congressman Matthew Lyon of Vermont, a firebrand Republican, printed the letter in pamphlet form on his press at Fairhaven, and the noise of political strife swelled to a deafening fortissimo. Lyon apparently stole the letter and published it in a deliberate effort to provoke a crisis in party politics. Baldwin and the more responsible Republicans were appalled, though they probably were not astonished at Lyon's act. The Vermont Congressman was a brawling, rambunctious fellow who loved to give the Federalists better than he got. He frequently embarrassed the Republican leadership, and Baldwin called him a "beast" and "atrocious liar" in denying to Barlow Lyon's claim that he had been given a copy of the letter.

From Lyon's point of view the timing of his blast was brilliant. The Adams administration had just rammed through Congress the four notorious Alien and Sedition Acts, among which was the law forbidding any person to "write, print, utter, or publish . . . any false, scandalous, and malicious writing or writings against the government of the United States." Clearly, under terms of this law Lyon was guilty of seditious libel for publishing Barlow's letter. He was daring the government to enforce its law.

The administration moved quickly to accept the challenge. An indictment was brought against Lyon and his trial scheduled for the fall term of the Vermont district court. His prosecution was the first under the Alien and Sedition Acts. The jury, which had no concern with the constitutional issues involved in the case, had no choice but to find him guilty as charged. The federal judge then sentenced him to four months in prison and a fine of one thousand dollars. He went defiantly off to jail, unrepentant and still full of fight.

Subsequent events proved that Lyon had gauged shrewdly the public reaction to the repressive laws. As a result of his unscrupulousness, he became something of a martyr whose trial helped turn opinion against the Adams administration. From Barlow's letter to Lyon's pamphlet to the sedition trial ran a chain reaction that did not stop until the Federalist Party was shattered. While Lyon was serving his sentence, he ran successfully for re-election to Congress. At the same time, the Republicans captured Vermont and in two more years were able to elect a president.

The Federalists, as well as Lyon, used Barlow's blunt letter as ammunition in the political wars. Baldwin was overcome by mortification at what had happened and had to endure the agony of reading the letter in one Federalist newspaper after another. He belabored "Old Pick [Timothy Pickering] and the rest of them" for widely reprinting a letter sent in confidence, but he could do nothing more than rage inwardly and hope the noise soon would subside. No doubt he dreaded the day Barlow would hear about the episode. The Federalist papers, or perhaps Lyon himself, doctored the text a little by inserting adjectives like "bullying" and "stupid" before "speech of your president" and "answer of your Senate." But even without changing a comma they had an inflammatory document and worked themselves into a fine frenzy of righteous indignation over Barlow's plain language. They boiled particularly at his implication that President Adams must be insane.

The *Columbian Centinel*, published in Federalist Boston, was the most violent in its attack, although the Hartford *Courant* was the first to print the letter. The *Centinel* appended to its version half a column of editorial abuse. Barlow's letter, accused the *Centinel*, undoubtedly was written in Talleyrand's office, while the French foreign minister, "arch apostate, sat at the elbow of the duped American and dictated every word. A greater quantum of folly, arrogance, egotism, and falsehood could not be condensed within equal limits." Then to administer the *coup de grâce* to Barlow, the paper thundered that the letter was a betrayal "compared with which that of *Judas Iscariot* is but a foible." Among other papers that took up the cudgel, the New York *Commercial Advertiser* delivered its opinion that "the Gallic revolution destroyed the character of Barlow's mind, and his residence in, or near, the French republic has rendered him a traitor to his country, and a blasphemer of his God."

Some of the attacks were delivered with a lighter and perhaps more devastating touch. Barlow fell victim to the same sort of satiric verse that he had written himself a decade before as one of the Connecticut Wits. Richard Alsop, in *The Political Green-House for the Year 1798*, presented the "Hasty-Pudding" bard to the readers of the Hartford *Courant:*

> His wandering wits, and cunning call'd in,
> Writes o're "*his book*" to Parson Baldwin. . . .
> What eye can trace this Wisdom's son,—
> This "Jack-at-all-trades, good *at none*,"
> This ever-changing, Proteus mind,—
> In all his turns, thro' every wind;
> From telling sinners where they go to,
> To speculations in Scioto, . . .
> From morals pure, and manners plain,
> To herding with Monroe and Paine,
> From feeding on his country's bread,
> To aping X, and Y, and Z [ed],
> From preaching Christ, to Age of Reason,
> From writing psalms, to writing treason.

Distressing as they were, scurrilous attacks in the papers were the usual thing in eighteenth-century America. The Republicans had plenty of newspapers that defied the Alien and Sedition Acts, and Barlow's supporters rallied around. But hard to bear for any sensitive man were the attacks of old friends whose political views now severed the bonds of former affection. One of these was Noah Webster, who wrote a sizzling attack on France and Barlow in the New York *Spectator*. Declaring, among other things, that Franco-American friendship was the "greatest scourge ever inflicted upon our country, not excepting the plague," Webster argued the familiar Federalist position. At the end he addressed his former college classmate: "One word more, Sir, from an old friend who once

197

loved and respected you. The contemptuous manner in which you speak of the President and the Senate of America is a striking proof of the effect of atheism and licentious examples on the civility and good manners of a well-bred man. You went from America with a good character . . . in divesting yourself of religion, you have lost your good manners." Webster's assault was only the first of many such blows that rained on Barlow in the next few years.

He eventually learned to live with his virtual proscription in his native New England. Months later, after he had heard of the furore caused by his letter, he observed to Wolcott: "I understand . . . that you & Meigs are the only friends that remain to me in Connecticut . . . the only two republicans existing in that state among my acquaintance." This situation, which seemed almost impossible to believe, strengthened his resolve to remain abroad until the dispute with France was settled. Yet he could hardly credit, as he had been told, that there was "no state in the Union where every principle of liberty" was "so much discarded" as in Connecticut. He commented sadly: "It is a little strange that a people so enlightened, as we used to call ourselves, should have carried on a long war and made such sacrifices for a thing they did not want."

2: *Joel the Peacemaker*

Even before Barlow knew the fate of his letter to Baldwin, he continued his efforts to serve the cause of Franco-American peace. He wrote a second letter, this time to another old Yale friend, James Watson, who was Senator from New York. He shifted tactics somewhat, for Watson was not pro-French. Four months had passed since he had written Baldwin and sent a copy to Jefferson; now Talleyrand and the Directory seemed to have second thoughts about their relations with the United States. The first warships of the American navy already were at sea, and Congress had authorized merchant vessels to arm themselves in self-defense. Barlow reported to Watson that France wished unequivocally to avoid war between the two republics. The Directory, he said, was ready to name a minister to treat with anyone who should be named by the United States. All claims for loans and all offensive speeches on either side would be ignored. "This is considered here by all parties," he summed up, "as a more pacific overture than was expected, after the irritations that have been offered on both sides. It is retreating to open ground. . . . A refusal on your part . . . would be considered as a declaration of war."

Barlow's efforts to smooth a path for Federalist diplomats was appreciated neither in Philadelphia nor abroad. Watson answered the letter with a truculent message, suggesting in effect that Barlow mind his own business. He rejected out of hand all the proposals that seemed so conciliatory to an American Francophile in Paris. He forwarded the letter to Wolcott saying: "Although there are few men I have loved so much, there are few whose present conduct I detest more." Meantime in Europe, the American minister to Holland, William Vans Murray, was sputtering with anger over the meddling of Joel Barlow and Colonel Hichborn. He regarded them as traitors to their country and held them chiefly responsible for stiffening French resistance to an accommodation with the Federalist administration. But he boasted that they would fail: "They are the mud on the lion's mane; they can stain, though they cannot clog his vigour when he rises in rage."

Between the writing of Barlow's letter to Watson on July 26, 1798, and its receipt in the United States, another American joined forces with Barlow. This was George Logan, Philadelphia Quaker, who arrived in France in August on a private mission solely for the purpose of staving off the threatened war. Back in Philadelphia Logan had watched the drift to war with the same sense of dread and futility that Barlow experienced in Paris. When the XYZ Affair exploded, Logan packed his bags and embarked for Europe on his own initiative. Arriving in France when Talleyrand was looking for a way out of the impasse, he was allowed to persuade the Directory to lift the embargo on American shipping. For a brief period Logan was the hero of Paris. Barlow and Fulton were delighted to meet this earnest Quaker and entertained him cordially during his three-week stay in Paris. But Logan's efforts received no praise from the State Department after he returned. "The gov-

ernment does not thank you for what you have done," Timothy
Pickering told him at the end of an icy interview; and in retaliation
for Logan's trip the Federalists pushed through the next session of
Congress a law to prevent private citizens like Logan or Barlow
from undertaking independent diplomatic missions.

Meanwhile, unaware that his Baldwin letter had stirred up a
hornet's nest, Barlow went right on with his attempts at unofficial
diplomacy. Four days before Matthew Lyon's trial in Vermont, he
wrote a third letter from Paris, this time to George Washington.
The ex-President had been called out of retirement to become commander-in-chief in a new time of crisis, and Barlow addressed to
him a fervent appeal for sober statesmanship. Happily, Washington never had read the Baldwin letter referring to him as in the
"dotage of his natural life." Barlow sent the new epistle to his
brother-in-law requesting that it be sealed and forwarded to Washington unless "you find that neither this nor any other statement
of facts is likely to calm the frenzy of him & his associates." If
such is the case, he continued, "I should think it best to publish it
[the letter] with my name & his that our countrymen may see . . .
that one of their chiefs at least has had a warning in proper time
and from an unsuspicious quarter."

Barlow deluded himself in thinking that his views ever could be
regarded as impartial. Even if the Baldwin letter had not been published, his close connections with France and warm support of
Jefferson's party would have made him anathema to the Federalists. It was true, as Watson's hostile note sharply reminded him,
that he had been away from home too long and no longer knew
the temper of the United States. His efforts at mediation served
chiefly to anger the noisier Federalists who panted for war. Washington and Adams, however, both were calm, dispassionate men
who genuinely wanted peace. The former remembered Barlow's
able service in Algiers and was not prejudiced as he might have
been if he had read the blunt language of the Baldwin letter. The
latter considered Barlow's communication because he was responsible for the nation's destiny and could not afford to ignore pertinent data even though he despised the source.

In the letter to Washington Barlow repeated the points he had made to Watson in July. He appealed to the former President and soldier to use his vast influence to head off the imminent war. "I see two great nations rushing on each other's bayonets without any cause of contention but a misunderstanding. I shudder at the prospect, and wish to throw myself between." Again he insisted that the Directory was really conciliatory, really desirous "for the restoration of harmony upon terms honorable to the United States." Without rehearsing again all the causes of the misunderstanding, he begged Washington to persuade the government to send a new minister to France for another try at negotiation.

Washington received the letter from Baldwin on January 31, 1799, and sent it to the President the next day. "I have conceived it to be my duty to transmit it to you without delay," he wrote Adams; "and without a comment; except that it must have been written with a very good, or a very bad design; which of the two, you can judge better than I." Barlow, he pointed out, was a man of parts and such a letter could not be the result of ignorance, "nor, from the implications which are to be found in it, has it been written without the *privity* of the French Directory." The elder statesman asked Adams to let him know what reply to make. He would be happy, he said, to write Barlow a letter that might in a small way restore "Peace and tranquility to the United States upon just, honorable and dignified terms."

Barlow's letter raised John Adams' blood pressure several points, but it went just the same into his dossier on Franco-American relations. He already had received communications from Murray in Holland and a copy of Barlow's letter to Watson. The latter had been placed before him despite Watson's conviction that Barlow was wrongheaded and officious. Also in the dossier were letters from Richard Codman, Boston merchant, and Nathaniel Cutting, American consul at Le Havre, plus data on Logan's unsponsored visit to Paris. These documents corroborated each other and led inescapably to the conclusion that Adams should try negotiating with France once more. Accordingly, on the eighteenth he nominated Murray to take charge of reopening efforts to get a treaty.

How much weight Adams gave to Barlow's two letters is a moot point. The day after making his decision he answered Washington's letter and denied that Barlow's advice had any influence. A note from Talleyrand communicated through regular diplomatic channels, he insisted, had been the heaviest factor in making up his mind. But the vehemence of his denial suggests that the cool lawyer's mind had imposed a reasoned consideration of all the evidence while the matter was open. Once the conclusion was reached, however, Adams indulged himself in saying what he really thought of Barlow. "It is not often that we meet with a composition which betrays so many and so unequivocal symptoms of blackness of heart," he wrote Washington. "The wretch has destroyed his own character to such a degree, that I think it would be derogatory of yours to give any answer at all to his letter. Tom Paine is not a more worthless fellow."

Some years later, after the heat of party politics cooled, Adams took a more temperate view of this episode. From his retirement he wrote: "I . . . considered General Washington's question, whether Mr. Barlow's [letter] was written with a very good or a very bad design; and as, with all my jealousy, I had not sagacity enough to discover the smallest room for suspicion of any ill design, I frankly concluded that it was written with a very good one." The former President followed his successor's advice and returned no answer to Barlow's communication.

This entire situation is nicely tinctured with irony. There was Barlow in Paris innocently offering his services as peacemaker while raising in America a violent party controversy. There was President Adams in Philadelphia loathing Barlow while using his reports to help reach a peaceful decision that would make enemies in his own party and no friends among Republicans. Finally there was Murray in Holland raging at Barlow for impeding American diplomacy while owing his enemy a debt for a chance to negotiate the treaty. The last was the crowning irony, for Murray would have plucked out his tongue rather than say anything good of Barlow's character. He was at that moment advising John Quincy Adams never to traffic with such public scribblers: "Like the toad the more you caress and pat the animal, the more he puffs and swells," and Barlow was the worst kind of writer.

The Federalists were simply wrong when they impugned the

motives of Barlow and other Americans in France. The American maxim, "Politics ends at the water's edge," had not yet been invented. The expatriates were anything but neutral in promoting French interests at the expense of England, but they had opposed the Jay Treaty earlier because it discriminated against France, and they firmly believed that friendship between the two republics should be, for practical and ideological reasons, the cornerstone of American policy. They also were businessmen who owned ships, bought and sold cargoes, and believed that what was bad for business was bad for the United States. War for any reason, they held, was a poor solution to international problems, costly in human resources and economically disruptive.

Barlow's efforts to prevent a war with France were not motivated by a desire to discredit Federalist policy or to promote the Republican cause. Proof of this lies in the archives of the French foreign ministry in a document appealing to France to take the initiative in reopening negotiations with the United States. This unpublicized appeal is dated February twelfth, six days before President Adams nominated Murray to treat with France. It is signed by Joel Barlow and his new friend, Fulwar Skipwith, Consul-General in Paris and the ranking American official in France. Skipwith, a holdover Jefferson appointee, joined with Barlow to urge the French government to make an overt gesture of friendship towards the United States. They advocated that France not wait for President Adams to take the first step. They were sure that the President eventually would appoint a new minister, but they argued that France by acting first could silence the Federalist opposition to a new treaty.

3: Apologia pro Vita Sua

During 1799 commercial relations and communications between the United States and France were virtually cut off, but on the third of March, one year less a day after writing Abraham Baldwin, Barlow chanced upon a copy of the *Columbian Centinel* containing his private letter. He must have been jolted by it like a ship hitting

203

a rock. Before him lay his confidential remarks spread out over four columns of the hostile newspaper. At that instant he realized for the first time that party politics in the United States had descended to unbelievable depths of bad taste and dishonor. When he read the editorial abuse that splattered the page, he knew that no reputation was safe from the character assassins. The next day, trembling with anger and choked by the indecency of the whole business, he began a public letter in his defense.

By now an old hand at pamphleteering, Barlow rose to an eloquent apologia which combined a stout vindication and a bold attack. Perhaps he can be pardoned for not remembering the bluntness of his earlier language and for declaring categorically that his letter had been garbled almost beyond recognition. "Every part of it is mutilated and distorted," he wrote; "there is not a paragraph without some omissions, additions or changes, which . . . give a bitterness . . . I did not mean . . . render me unintelligible . . . vulgarize the style, vitiate the grammar, and make the phrases ridiculous." His assertions here simply are not true, though he no doubt believed them. The *Centinel* certainly was capable of any alterations, but the letter as published was just about as written.

What Barlow found most unfair in the publication of his letter was the impression he gave of being totally blind to French shortcomings. He at once set the record straight on this matter. France, he declared, had committed innumerable acts of violence and piracy against American shipping. These he certainly did not condone; in fact, he had made the strongest representations against them that an individual citizen could. His private letter had been intended only to inform his friends of the French point of view and not to give a complete exposition of Franco-American relations. "You might as well say that I believe in the doctrines of Mahomet, because I do not go out of my way to refute them," he complained.

Then Barlow launched an attack on the Federalist policies that he regarded as subversive of democratic government. These he believed were derived from Federalist aping of British institutions. Government borrowing during recent years of peace, he charged, was an iniquitous practice that ought to be prohibited by constitutional amendment. This borrowing, he added, had been inspired by the British funding system. "Your physicians have gone to a decrepit, intemperate old man [England], and borrowed his strong cordials, his bandages, and gouty velvet shoes, to administer them with cruel empiricism to a sturdy plowboy." And what is more, he went on, the rupture with France has cost the United States sixty million dollars and required the creation of a navy, "a terrible scourge" on the resources of the country. The funding system and the navy "are certainly calculated for the destruction of liberty in the United States." Finally, he addressed his countrymen: "If you really have no talents among you of a higher nature than what is necessary to copy precedents from old monarchies, I pity you, and call on you to pity me. It is time to despair of the perfectibility of human society."

Barlow finished his letter in a fury and sent it off to be printed. When copies were delivered to him, he mailed some to America, one going to Dr. Hopkins in Hartford. In the covering letter he wrote his old friend: "In answer to the calumnies which must be familiar to your ears, against me, I send a pamphlet, which I wish you would cause to be reprinted." He supposed that Hudson and Goodwin, Hartford publishers of the *Courant*, "who have been kind enough to supply their quota of abuse," would not mind printing it, "especially as they may make money by it. For the name of an Arch Traitor like your old friend, may excite a curiosity very useful to Booksellers." But Hopkins either was unwilling or unable to get Barlow a hearing in Hartford, and the letter was not published in New England until 1806.

Having defended himself once, Barlow returned to the political arena with all the zest of his earlier polemics in England. The threat of war had subsided, allowing time for considered reflection on past events and future possibilities. A few days before Christmas, 1799, he finished a thoughtful essay addressed to his fellow citizens, "On Certain Political Measures Proposed to Their Consideration." It was the work of a mature political philosopher who had been through two revolutions, observed the operations of Old World monarchy and Oriental despotism, and drawn sober conclusions on the nature of man and government. Felicitously written in clean, vigorous prose, the pamphlet argued republican principles with cool logic and warm conviction.

Barlow began with some obvious truths drawn from the history of human polity. Whoever looks back over history, tracing the abandonment of brute strength for law and order, he wrote, "must be convinced of a progress in human affairs, and of a tendency towards perfection." No longer was he sure that human society moved *inevitably* forward, but he could see at least a *tendency* towards perfection. The mistakes of the French Revolution illustrated the shortcomings of human wisdom, for France had not followed the best system for governing a large political entity. The strength of the United States rested on two principles: federalization of states and representative democracy. France was too large to be governed from Paris as a monolithic state; hence the Revolution regressed to autocratic government. The hope for Europe lay in an association of republics, a "United States of Europe," organized on the federal system. He dismissed as unworkable the plan for perpetual peace worked out by Henry IV and "embellished with the nervous eloquence of J. J. Rouseau," a plan that envisioned a community of states governed by their traditional political systems. A council of princes, each responsible to himself and not checked by representative government, could not preserve the peace.

After these introductory remarks, Barlow turned to the problem of maintaining liberty and preserving the United States. He aimed his heavy artillery, as before, against the national debt and standing armies (or navies). Because the American states were bound only by ties of convenience and common interest, he believed that excessive taxes and a heavy debt structure would drive states to secede. And he also thought that a military establishment of any size was incompatible with political liberty. Defense of the nation he would provide for by universal military training and a standby militia.

In the less complex world of the eighteenth century Barlow's ideas were sound. Debt was unnecessary, and the deer rifles of Kentucky hunters or the muskets of Concord minute men could defend the United States from foreign aggression. In addition, he would provide for further shoring up of liberty by universal education. "Ignorance," he wrote, "is everywhere such an infallible instrument of despotism, that there can be no hope of continuing even our present *forms* of government . . . but by diffusing universally among the people . . . instruction . . . sufficient to teach them their duties and their rights."

Moving from domestic policy to foreign affairs, Barlow next considered "The Means of Vindicating Our Commercial Liberty." This was a subject he had given much thought to during his years of foreign residence and business activity. He had just written an essay on the same subject for the French government and hoped it might be included in the latest French constitution just drafted. Barlow wanted France to define the rights of neutrals in time of war and to accept the principle that the flag covers the cargo. But the framers of the new constitution, he wrote, were in too big a hurry to listen and tabled his proposal. His suggestion, however, may have served a useful purpose, for this principle was incorporated in the treaty that the United States signed with France the next year.

Barlow could see clearly that modern wars were becoming increasingly economic in their origins and that modern nations must trade to live. If blockades and privateering could be outlawed, commerce between nations would be completely free. Then nations could not be strangled economically, and wars would no longer be practical. Since France was an agricultural nation, he argued, her interest would best be served by respecting neutral rights and allowing neutrals (the United States in particular) to enter and leave her ports freely. If France respected neutral shipping, England also would have to respect it, or face American hostility. And if the seas were free, Barlow thought, American ships would capture much of the business now carried by the large English merchant marine. England thus would suffer economically; France and the United States would benefit; commerce and industry would thrive in a free, competitive world society.

This reasoning led Barlow to propose a "Maritime Convention" formed by as many powers as might be induced to join. This organization would wield economic power on an international scale. The convention would define and declare the rights of neutral commerce, set up a world court to adjudicate disputes, and enforce its principles by the withdrawal of commercial intercourse from any nation refusing compliance. Barlow was proposing to preserve peace and free commerce by the use of economic sanctions, an idea not much different from Article Forty-one of the United Nations Charter. He realized, however, that his plan was ahead of its time; but even so, he urged, the United States ought to begin it alone and induce other nations to join later. All Europe, he wrote, needs American trade, and suspension of it, an embargo, would be a serious thing that would bring the European powers to terms and show them the advantages of associating with the United States. When the "Maritime Convention" became a practical reality, the need for navies would end and wars would be eliminated.

Barlow completed his pamphlet with a sense of finality. He had spoken his mind on vital issues, drawing on the ripe wisdom of his middle-aged liberalism, and there was nothing more at present he wanted to say. Moreover, he was weary of controversy, though not yet done with the noisy reverberations his letters had started. He already felt, as he wrote later: "I wish to live in the error [of republicanism], if it is one, and die in it. I am too old to examine reasons for discarding a system from which I have never yet deviated." How successful his efforts had been, he could not say of course; but war had been averted, the new treaty soon would be negotiated, and his essays were being widely read by Republicans in America. He may have realized, too, that the bitterness of his attackers proved his arguments to be effective. But he certainly did not claim as much as the editor who printed his political letters in 1806: "His exertions had a much greater effect in healing the rupture between the two countries than those of the six Ambassadors who were sent in two triplicate assortments."

Meantime, events in France and at home were moving swiftly. Even before Barlow wrote his second letter, General Bonaparte had staged the coup that put him in absolute control of the destinies of France. The French Revolution had come full circle, betraying the hopes of 1792, and the bright new day had dawned gray and threatening. From across the Atlantic, however, the clouds were parting.

Barlow had been right when he wrote Dr. Hopkins that "things in America are drawing fast to a crisis." The people were about to reject the Federalists and return to Republican principles. Before another year was out, Jefferson would be elected President and Barlow could breathe freely in the knowledge that liberty was secured in his native land. He could withdraw from the political firing line and devote himself exclusively to Robert Fulton's projects.

CHAPTER IX

Retired Leisure

1: *Patron of Science*

"*Politicks,* how I hate the mischief-making word!" exclaimed Ruth
Barlow to a friend during the first year of the nineteenth century.
And she added: "How does it blacken characters, separate friends
& ruin families! I have no patience upon that subject." Joel might
have seconded these sentiments if he had written a postscript to
his wife's letter. Between the end of his pamphleteering and the
start of Jefferson's presidency, Barlow cooled in limbo for more
than a year. His bruises healed inevitably, but until news arrived
of the Republican victory, he could only wonder if the struggle
had been too costly. During this interregnum he wrote Baldwin:
"It seems that your wind is changing & that your big pilot having
carried away his top-gallant-royals is putting about." But this remark alluded only to John Adams and the averted war with France.
Barlow still had to wait six months more to learn that a Republican
crew now was refitting the Federalist ship of state.

Fortunately, Fulton's submarine kept him well occupied until
communications caught up with events. For more than two years
Barlow and his younger friend had talked over the submarine idea
and tried out models on the Seine. Where the suggestion for this
submarine originally came from is unknown, though the idea of

attacking ships from under water is ancient. One submarine pioneer known both to Barlow and Fulton was David Bushnell, who had been a senior at Yale when Joel was a freshman. In 1775 Bushnell had built an ingenious one-man submarine, the *Turtle*, which almost succeeded in blowing up a British ship in New York harbor. But the *Turtle* failed because it was too small and hard to maneuver. It could do little more than drift with the tide, slightly awash, and could not fully submerge. Fulton used Bushnell's screw-type propulsion but designed a boat that was a true submersible. In the summer of 1800 he obtained permission from the French government to build an underwater craft that could either sail conventionally or dive and navigate without connection to the surface. The result was the *Nautilus*, launched at Rouen in July.

During the next month Fulton and the Barlows went to the coast to try out the submarine. Fulton towed his craft down the Seine to Le Havre behind two barges, arriving there on August third, and the Barlows met him at the port. Joel settled Ruth in the Hotel Bien Venu in Fulton's charge, stayed ten days to watch the *Nautilus* perform, and then returned to Paris. His part in the project henceforth was to help pay the bills, look after Fulton's other business, and to interest the minister of marine in the invention. He also had another important errand which took him to the city: he had to find a new and larger place for the three of them to live.

During his weeks in Paris he kept in close communication with Fulton and Ruth. The former sent him glowing reports of the submarine, and the latter praised the healthful effect of daily sea baths. Joel wrote his brother-in-law that he left Ruth "under the pretense of health . . . jumping into her big *baignoire* every morning, and then driving round the country with her sweethearts every day . . . She is growing fat & handsome & young." In reply to Fulton's account of his successful dives and daily exertions, Barlow sent fatherly advice to Ruth: "Tell Toot [Fulton] that every strain and extraordinary exertion in middle life [Fulton was thirty-five], and cold & damp, and twisting & wrenching, and unnatural & strained position that our bodies are exposed to . . . tend to stiffen the nerves & joints, & muscles, & to bring on old age prematurely." Warming to his sermon, he continued: "The machine of his body is better &

more worthy his attention than any other machine . . . preservation is more useful than creation; unless he could create me one exactly in the image of himself . . . he had better preserve his own." Then Joel directed Ruth: "Read this lecture to him . . . every morning at breakfast."

Fulton was out in the submarine nearly every day enthusiastically learning how to handle his invention. His boat carried four men and enough compressed air in its tank to remain under water for several hours. When the craft was above water, it operated with sails and mast like any small boat, but when Fulton gave the order to dive, the crew struck the sails and unstepped the mast. Then they closed a water-tight hatch, submerged by means of moveable planes and water ballast, and propelled themselves with a hand-operated screw. The device actually worked and could move under water at about two and one-half miles per hour. Fulton was elated with his submarine and made plans to use it to deliver a torpedo. He asked Barlow early in September to report his success to the minister of marine and to get him a commission to sink British warships off the coast. He was confident that the French government would grant his request.

When Barlow received the letter, he went to the minister's house at nine the next morning, sent up a letter "concise and clear, explaining the affair," and said he would stay for an answer. There was no response. The minister was uninterested, could not be bothered, and the porter who delivered the note said Barlow might as well not wait. When he called the next day, the minister stalled once more, and when Barlow demanded an answer, he was referred to an underling. His persistence, however, obtained the commission at last, and Fulton took his submarine to sea. But British intelligence alerted the blockading warships, which sailed away before Fulton could get close enough to dive with his torpedoes.

Barlow and Fulton, strange as it may seem today, were not averse to selling a torpedo-carrying submarine to the French government. There was no conflict between the pacifism they preached and the device they were trying to perfect. In the naïve year 1800 the submarine seemed only a defensive weapon, albeit a device of startling effectiveness. A submarine in the hands of the French navy could

make impossible the British blockade of Continental ports. Thus
the first casualty of the new weapon, Barlow and Fulton thought,
would be England's navy; and because France had a feeble navy,
the net effect would be the abolition of sea war. When Barlow
described the invention to Jefferson, he promised that it would
destroy "the whole system of naval tyranny & civilized piracy" and
provide a cheap method of securing free commerce for all nations.

Meantime, Barlow in Paris was househunting diligently but not
very successfully. He tramped about the city day after day in the
hottest weather he ever remembered in France. He wrote Ruth at
the beach that he could not work at his desk without stripping off
everything, including underwear, and he was sleeping at night without even a sheet. But worse than the weather was the fact that
furnished houses or apartments were extremely scarce. He was
tired of living in hotels but did not own any furniture. After ten
days of futile searching, he concluded that the best solution was
to buy a house, and having made that decision, he found the possibilities abundant.

The house that most excited his imagination was an elegant, un-
occupied mansion at 50 rue de Vaugirard in Saint Sulpice parish.
To inspect it, he walked east from his old lodgings farther up the
same street until he came almost to the Luxembourg Palace. The
property, which was across from the Luxembourg Gardens, was
everything the agent told him it would be. As he approached number fifty, he saw first a long frontage on the street (one hundred
and forty feet, he later found), along which had been constructed
a solid building occupied by kitchen, servants' quarters, and stables.
It was pierced by the most magnificent gate he had seen in Paris.

Entering the gate, he found himself in a courtyard with upper
and lower levels connected by a handsome terrace. To his right
and left were wings running from the street-front building towards
the main house. The house itself extended the entire width of the
lot and formed a hollow square with the wings and street building.
Barlow entered the mansion through an elegant vestibule that
opened into a grand salon seventeen feet high. On each side of the
main entrance he found complete apartments, and behind the grand

213

salon was a grand dining room and a large library. It took Joel a long time just to look over the entire establishment.

The second floor of the house, the street-front building, and the wings contained twenty-two lodging rooms, stables for twelve horses, and *remises* for five carriages. The twenty vaulted cellars under the house were capable of holding five hundred wine casks, and the garden behind it, which was reached by three sets of stairs, the central one being thirty feet wide, covered an acre. The grounds were planted with three hundred bearing fruit trees and a wide variety of other ornamental trees and shrubs. To these Barlow added a good many more of his own choice.

This impressive *hôtel* had been built only ten years before at a cost of some eighty thousand dollars, not including the land. But the Revolution had occurred immediately, wrecking the fortunes of the nobility, and great houses in 1800 were hard to sell. The owner, a former *émigré*, was back in Paris but too poor to maintain his expensive home. Barlow was able to get the place for about a quarter of its original cost. Though it was the establishment for a millionaire, which he certainly was not, he bought the house as an investment. When he heard a year later that Lady Hamilton was looking for a place in Paris, he wrote her a glowing but unsuccessful letter offering her his small palace for thirty-two thousand dollars. He never tried to staff it with a full set of servants or furnish it completely; yet the one-time Connecticut farm boy got a great deal of pleasure out of owning it. As soon as he bought the house, he called in painters, paperers, and wall washers to put the interior in order before Ruth's return from Le Havre. He could hardly wait to show her the place.

His companion during the househunting was the Baron de Min, a fluffy little white dog, who was equally eager to have Ruth come home. The Baron had been left in Paris with the servants when the household went to the coast. "Poor Min," wrote Joel on the day after he returned to the city, "every time I come in he devours me, & when I go out he sets up his yowl . . . He looks on me only as a . . . forerunner or a harbinger, but not as the true Messiah . . . When I got up this morning, he seized hold of me as usual for a moment, & then whirled round as though the Devil had struck him & sprang to the bed with the loudest expressions of joy thinking Wifey was between the sheets." Joel added parenthetically: "I wished she had been as much as he, though I did not make such a noise about it." To prepare for Ruth's coming, Barlow the next day gave the dog a good "bathing & scouring" followed by "the usual sacraments of combing & fleaing." He then reported that Min was "as pure & white and as full of grace as a new-dipped Methodist." After the deed for the house was signed, he took the dog to the new place and turned him over to the servants once more. Min sniffed Ruth's things and felt himself master of the establishment. Joel left for Le Havre immediately to bring Ruth back to Paris.

The Barlows and Fulton settled down that autumn at 50 rue de Vaugirard to a season of intellectual activity. One room that Barlow did furnish properly was the library. His collection of books continued to grow until later in America he had one of the best libraries in the United States. He and Fulton began a heavy reading program, though they also continued to plan new trials of the submarine. Fulton, with Barlow's help, made up for his lack of a formal education during his years in Paris. Joel coached him in French, Italian, and German, literature, and philosophy. Together they studied higher mathematics and absorbed themselves in physics and chemistry. Fulton also studied perspective, and though he never again tried to be an artist, he subsequently painted a portrait of Joel that is probably the best canvas he ever did.

The two friends had a great many interests in common, literary as well as scientific. Barlow rekindled his interest in poetry and projected a work in four books to be called "The Canal: A Poem on the Application of Physical Science to Political Economy." Barlow was to supply the versification and historical background and Fulton was to furnish the scientific knowledge. It began:

> Yes, my dear FULTON, let us seize the lyre,
> And give to Science all the Muse's fire,
> Mount on the boat, and as it glides along,
> We'll cheer the long Canal with useful song.

The poem never got beyond half of one book, but it revived Barlow's muse and set him to planning a rewriting of the *Vision of Columbus*, a project which eventuated in the *Columbiad*. Fulton entered enthusiastically into this revision of the early work and took the initiative in sketching illustrations for an elaborate edition of the poem. Fulton's scientific projects, however, received top priority, the most immediate of which was the submarine.

The tests of the *Nautilus* continued the next year under government sponsorship. Though the minister of marine opposed further development because Fulton had failed to sink a British warship, two prominent mathematicians, Gaspard Monge and Simon Laplace, came to the inventor's assistance. They introduced Fulton to Napoleon in December and persuaded the First Consul to overrule his minister. Napoleon then appointed a new commission consisting of Monge, Laplace, and Barlow's friend Constantin Volney to investigate the submarine. As a result, the boat was refitted in the spring and taken to Brest. There in July Fulton submerged his craft, cruised under water for several hours, and blew up a sloop anchored in the harbor for the test. After accomplishing that feat, Fulton dismantled his boat, which was leaking badly after two summers of trials, and sold the parts. When Napoleon wanted to inspect the submarine, there was nothing left to see; nor would Fulton let anyone examine his plans. He expected the French government to buy his invention on the basis of eyewitness reports of its performance. Napoleon had more important matters, domestic and foreign, to think about, and the submarine project was dropped.

There is a sequel to the submarine story, though it does not concern France. When Napoleon was elected Consul for life, Barlow and Fulton (also a good republican) watched with dismay the return of hereditary monarchy to France. "Bonaparte has thrown back the progress of civilization & public happiness about one age," sourly commented Barlow in August, 1802. This was the year of the Peace of Amiens, really a truce, between France and England, and for the time being no country needed a submarine. In less than two years, however, the General became Emperor and marched off on the road leading ultimately to Waterloo. Constitutional monarchy in England at once began to look better than French despotism. When the British government in 1804 asked Fulton to build a submarine for England, he went to London with Barlow's blessing. He then worked in England as hard as he had in France four years before, this time, as he put it, to "remove from the mind of Man the possibility of France making a descent on England." The British admiralty dropped the submarine project and directed Fulton to make torpedoes propelled by rafts to blow up Napoleon's invasion fleet across the Channel. Fulton tried, but his efforts, though generously compensated, were not very successful. Then the Battle of Trafalgar took place in 1805, ending England's immediate need for torpedoes and submarines, and Fulton returned to the United States to build the *Clermont*.

Napoleon's loss of interest in the submarine already had turned Fulton's and Barlow's attention to the steamboat. The submarine had seemed more important because it offered a hope for stopping Europe's endless wars, but the steamboat also had interested them for years. They both had been in England when James Rumsey arrived from America to promote his invention, an early unsuccessful effort to move boats by steam-operated jet propulsion; and they knew of John Fitch's moderately successful steamboat built on the Delaware River ten years before. When France would not buy the submarine, they began serious work on the steamboat and once again experimented with models on the Seine.

2: *Tale of Three Cities: Paris, Plombières, London*

Scientific projects occupied only part of Barlow's restless energy. His tinkering with models of submarines, canals, and steamboats sent him into his library for research in the history of science, and soon he widened his reading to include a great quantity of general history and poetry. His projected account of the French Revolution remained in a pigeon hole gathering dust, for he was done, temporarily at least, with politics. He apparently even had finished with writing on the topic as history. Mythology and religion now became the subjects that engaged an increasing amount of his attention. He began filling notebooks from the *Encyclopédie* and other reference works under such headings as "*théisme*" and "*athéisme*." In his research he traced the history of modern religious practices back to primitive mythological origins. He was amazed, for example, to learn that the liberty pole and May pole of his day derived from the Phallic symbol of the ancient religious fertility rites.

Barlow's interest in religion and myth as separate topics began long before he ever left the United States, but he probably never linked the two subjects until he encountered the brilliant conversations of Tom Paine. *The Age of Reason*, which Barlow had published during Paine's imprisonment, must have made a powerful impact on him. The book's withering fire of logic trained on the historical truth of Scripture confirmed his rejection of the Bible as literal history. To a friend he wrote privately in praise of *The Age of Reason:* "I rejoice at the progress of Good Sense over the damnable imposture of Christian mummery." Barlow was not an atheist, as his enemies charged, but a deist, and along with Paine, Jefferson, Franklin, and all the other deists, he believed wholeheartedly in Christian ethics but could not accept as fact such matters as the Virgin birth or miracles. To an eighteenth-century rationalist, a fundamentalist reading of Scripture perpetuated ancient superstitions and imposed a roadblock in the way of human perfectibility.

Barlow's private letter praising Paine's book dogged his footsteps for years. It too suffered the public fate of the Baldwin letter. Political enemies managed to get and print it to prove that the Arch Traitor also was a blaspheming atheist. A Connecticut clergyman who turned deist committed the unpardonable sin, and in New England, at least, Barlow never lived down his apostasy. Protest as he might that he never had departed from the basic beliefs of his Puritan childhood, he never convinced old friends like Noah Webster that he still was pure in heart. Eventually he stopped trying, and when he gave his sister a Bible for Christmas one year, he wrote in it:

RETIRED LEISURE

To Huldah Bennet, Nathan's wife,
Her Brother sends the Book of life;
He begs her kindly to receive it,
Though Tories say he don't believe it.

His interest in religion and mythology led also to the translation of a controversial book, *Ruins; or, Meditations on the Revolution of Empires* by Constantin Volney. Barlow knew Volney socially as a friend of Jefferson and professionally as a member of the submarine commission. Jefferson had begun a translation of the book during the author's visit to the United States in 1797, but he never got beyond chapter twenty. After becoming President, Jefferson must have decided that he could not finish the work, or if he did, he would be indiscreet to publish it. The *Ruins* was as radical a book as *The Age of Reason* and damned in the same breath by the clergy. Jefferson apparently suggested to Volney that Barlow might like to complete the task and wrote after Barlow's services had been secured: "I am glad you were able to engage so fine a writer . . . A better hand you could not have found." The President already had sent Volney the manuscript of his unfinished translation.

The *Ruins* originally had appeared in the first year of the French republic when reason seemed to be sweeping away the cobwebs of old superstition. The work took the form of a meditation over the ruins of ancient civilizations in the Middle East. What had caused the glories of old cultures to pass away, Volney asked himself? The answer, which he argued with elaborate documentation and pitiless logic, was religion. History revealed that the great princes of the past always had perfected systems of tyranny to keep man in bondage. The result of bondage was invariably dejection and misery. To make the slavery of this world bearable, man therefore imagined "another country, an asylum where, far from tyrants, he should recover the rights of his nature," and thus life became a toilsome journey to be endured only in anticipation of a happy afterlife. This, explained Volney, resulted in stagnation and decay and the eventual extinction of old despotisms. He then went on to apply this thesis to an extensive discussion of comparative religion.

Volney's work was a persuasive, provocative book that Barlow took pleasure in translating. He labored over his manuscript, as Volney wrote Jefferson, "with the talent that you know and the zeal of friendship that he has for you." He completed the task by the following year, and the author had the translation published in Paris. The book subsequently was printed and reprinted in the United States and attacked as a radical document throughout the Nineteenth Century. To begin the translation, Barlow cut short a vacation trip and missed an enjoyable mountain climb in central France.

In late April the Barlows had traveled south to the foothills of the Massif Central for several weeks at Moulins. When Joel returned to Paris, Ruth stayed a little longer to visit Puy-de-Dôme, a commanding peak in Auvergne. She climbed the mountain in a gay company of ladies and gentlemen and looked from the summit on the most sublime view she ever experienced. When a June thunderstorm came up, she thought she never had seen so grand a spectacle. "The mountains below peeked their heads out of the flying clouds," she wrote, "whilst all the world seemed stretched in immensity around . . . I should suppose it might have been there that *Satan* took Jesus to show him the kingdoms of the earth, had not the good book told us it was in another country."

The fall and winter of 1801-1802 was another quiet time at 50 rue de Vaugirard. Barlow and Fulton again returned to their books and plans. French troops evacuated Egypt and were ferried home on English ships, and the autumn began with news of a truce between the two warring powers. Barlow spoke once more of sailing for home as soon as he could wind up his affairs, by which he meant finding a buyer for his house and completing some commercial engagements he still had an interest in. He wrote Jefferson that he now intended to devote the remainder of his life to the solid improvements of the United States—moral, political, and economic.

The President's cordial reply whetted his renewed desire to go back to America. Jefferson reported that everywhere the Republicans were gaining strength at the expense of the Federalists, and he urged Barlow to set out immediately. He even suggested a house on the outskirts of the new federal city that could be purchased at a bargain, "a lovely seat . . . on a high hill commanding a most extensive view of the Potomac." Jefferson had a particular reason for wanting Barlow to settle in Washington: "Mr. Madison and myself have cut out a piece of work for you, which is to write the history of the United States, from the close of the war downwards. We are rich ourselves in materials, and can open all the public archives to you; but your residence here is essential because a great deal of the knowledge of things is not on paper, but only within ourselves." What was more, added the President, John Marshall was in the midst of writing a life of Washington "intended to come out just in time to influence the next presidential election." Barlow was to supply a counterbalance.

Ruth's health, unfortunately, threw an obstacle in the path of an early departure. In the spring she detected strange, hard places on her body, which were diagnosed as tumors. Her doctor prescribed a strenuous course of mineral baths to dissolve the growths, and Barlow made immediate plans to send her off to Plombières in the Vosges Mountains. Fulton, who was momentarily between inventions, offered to escort "Ruthinda" to the spa, while Joel stayed behind to close his affairs as soon as possible. The doctor thought a few weeks of the medicinal waters would cure Ruth, and Joel hoped there still would be time to sail before autumn. Accordingly, the Barlows' phaeton drawn by two white ponies left Paris for points east on April twenty-sixth. The baths, of course, served no purpose except to keep the Barlows separated, and though the tumors proved benign, Ruth stayed at Plombières until mid-September, hoping vainly for the cure the physician kept promising.

Meantime, Joel wrote long, chatty letters nearly every day. Their friends kept his social calendar so full that he soon began making excuses to stay home. He dined out eighteen times during the first three weeks and had standing invitations with the Robert Livingstons and his neighbor, Madame de Villette, who lived at number fifty-four. Madame de Villette, widow of the second Marquis de Villette, advised him on servant and household problems and gathered in her salon friends who shared her consuming interest in Voltaire. Joel also saw a great deal of the Mark Leavenworths, the James Swans, and his friend Fulwar Skipwith. Helen Maria Williams, the English poetess and former friend of Mary Wollstone-craft, held open house nearly every night and urged him incessantly to attend her *soirées*, but her parties—sometimes as many as fifty people—became a burden by mid-summer.

After going there two nights in a row, Joel wrote: "Helen really runs us down with her great parties . . . It is quite stifling. English lords & ladies, Italian princes & duchesses brought together to inhale each other's exhalations & judge of the state of each other's lungs by a free exchange of expirated gasses, compliments & politics." Joel added that he was going to "find a little system of excuses that may serve me the rest of the season." When Madame Merinska invited him to celebrate the anniversary of the Polish constitution, "which has long ceased to exist," he also begged off and explained to Ruth: "I suppose next Vendémiaire we shall be called upon to celebrate the anniversary of the French Republic, which has never existed at all."

Barlow also wrote his wife full details of the domestic establishment. On May seventeenth he picked the first strawberries from the garden and enough currants for a pie. A rain the night before had ended a forty-day drought, and he noted that the peas were now in bloom. A few days later an unseasonable frost damaged a few plants but did not hurt the fruit trees loaded with apricots, pears, plums, cherries, and apples. By the end of May there were "millions of pinks" in bloom and a few roses. When he invited Skipwith and his bride to a Sunday breakfast, he set a table in the garden with great bowls of strawberries and cherries as big as one could lift. A month later the strawberries still were bearing, and he also was picking raspberries and gooseberries.

The house was lonesome without Ruth, but it never was empty. Barlow had the porter, cook, and housekeeper to supervise, and he occasionally invited friends to join him. When Congressman John Dawson arrived from America bringing diplomatic dispatches and a letter from Jefferson, Barlow invited him to be a house guest and asked the Polish patriot Koskiusko in to dine. Meantime, Ruth's little dog also was company. "Min and I," Joel wrote, "go out and work in the garden about an hour every morning as soon as we are out of bed, while they make the room and bed and breakfast."

In fact, both the dog and Joel were in blooming health. "Min is more sociable and lively than he used to be," Joel reported, "because in Wifey's absence he doesn't get as much to eat. He is quite happy & can jump into the armchair easier." Joel also was simplifying and cutting down his own diet, at least when he was not dining out. "I have grown wonderfully temperate. I don't eat above half as much dinner as I used to & drink but little wine." He also wrote that he planned to have the cook make him some breakfast *polente*, as the French call it, "who know as little about a hasty-pudding as they do about a republic."

Barlow worked hard to keep up his wife's morale during the futile baths. He was delighted therefore when he met Madame Pestalozzi one evening and was charged to send love to Ruth and to ask if she had yet been *"sur le trou des Capucins"?* Formerly, he reported quoting the lady, the spa was noted for "putting women into a state to make children, but then there was a convent of fat Capuchins who used to visit the baths every day to whom you must give alms." Madame Pestalozzi, he said, supposed that since "these beggar gentlemen are no more there . . . the place is no more remarkable for making children than other mountainous places." Later Joel urged his wife to "give the waters fair play, *trou des Capucins* & all. I reckon those ladies who come for the purpose of making babies may find the same instruction & spiritual edification from Toot [Fulton] as they used to do from the barefooted brotherhood."

In serious vein, Barlow's letters often relayed political news, which daily became more disillusioning. He commented scornfully on the referendum to make Napoleon consul for life, a measure that was to be submitted to the people to vote yes or no. "They are very sure nobody will write *no!*" Later, on Napoleon's birthday, as bells rang and cannon fired all over the city, he wrote in disgust: "High mass and *Te Deum* all over France; more powder burnt than would serve to conquer half [of] Europe. And this is to conquer the French people!"

On another occasion when the government introduced a bill to establish slavery in French colonies, he exploded: "No legislative body till the tenth year of the French Republic has outraged human

223

nature so far as to make a law to establish it [slavery]." Barlow felt strongly the iniquities of slavery and ardently wished it abolished in his own country. When the Louisiana Purchase later was made, he wrote Wolcott expressing hope that slavery would be barred from the new territory. "A race of hereditary masters cannot be a race of republicans ... [slavery] in every point of view, moral, political & economical, is perhaps the greatest blemish & may become the greatest scourge to our country."

Soon after the middle of June Barlow decided to make a quick, unpublicized business trip to London. He had not been there since 1792 when the climate was distinctly unhealthful for republicans, but now England and France were at peace, and he thought he could go without incident. He hoped by a personal appearance, apparently in an admiralty court hearing on a captured cargo, to get "double the amount" of the award but this business actually took another year and another visit to London to accomplish. Before leaving, however, he took care that Rufus King, American minister to England, should inform the government that his business was "of a private & commercial nature." Then he traveled quietly across the Channel, rode into London incognito, and put up at the Grand Hotel in Covent Garden, where he believed no other American would be staying.

Barlow thought he could get in and out of London without looking up any of his old friends or getting his name into the papers. But on the first day he narrowly missed recognition. As he returned from a business call, a waiter at his hotel asked if he knew an American gentleman, Mr. Cutting, who lived there and had a brother in Paris. Barlow certainly did know him but most emphatically did not want to meet him: "To see Mr. J. B. Cutting . . . would be to give your name to the bell-man to cry it through the town." He packed his bags quickly, paid his bill, and moved to a hotel in Grosvenor Square. But his efforts at anonymity were a failure. Somehow his name got into the papers. Joseph Johnson immediately looked him up, and in the coach on the return trip to Dover a republican passenger recognized him, having heard from

MRS. JOEL BARLOW
(Ruth Baldwin)

Drawing made by Charles de Villette, son of Barlow's
neighbor in Paris, Countess de Villette, probably between 1801 and 1804; owned by Mr. S. L. M. Barlow.

JOEL BARLOW

Portrait by Robert Fulton, owned by Mr. S. L. M. Barlow of New York City. An engraving of this painting was used as frontispiece to the deluxe edition of the *Columbiad*.

Frick Art Reference Library

ROBERT FULTON

Portrait by Charles Willson Peale, 1807. Now in the Independence Hall collection.

National Park Service Photo

Horne Tooke the day before that Barlow was in town incognito.

The visit to London, though it lasted only two weeks, turned out to be more than a simple business trip. He dined with his old publisher Johnson and relived the strenuous days of a decade before when the *Advice to the Privileged Orders* was trumpeting the brave new world. "He took me by the hand, shaking his sides," related Barlow, "& the first word was 'Well, you could not get me hanged. You tried all you could.'" Johnson had been imprisoned for nine months for selling a seditious pamphlet (not Barlow's) during the witch-hunting Nineties. Barlow also visited Rufus King, whose son was in school in Paris under Joel's eye, and saw a good bit of George Erving, American consul in London, whom he later came to know well. One day he even stopped to watch the King go to Parliament to "*prorogue* the *rogues*," after which he reported gratuitously of George III: "He looks as much like a Beef as ever."

The most moving experience of the short visit, however, occurred on the day Barlow walked along Oxford Road and "sheered off into Litchfield Street, guided by an unaccountable attraction." He walked until he came to number eighteen where he and Ruth formerly had lived. He climbed the steps to see who now occupied the premises and above the brass plate reading "Snowdon, Cabinet Maker" was a paper advertising their old apartment: "First floor to let, genteelly furnished." Joel wrote Ruth: "Never did I resist so strong an inclination to go into a house. I wanted to hire that lodging if it was only to sleep one night in the back room."

The day before leaving London, Barlow had a memorable experience of a far different kind. He went to Henry Bromfield's house to look at three trunks he and his wife had stored there before leaving England. When he opened the first two, containing his clothes, he discovered a considerable amount of moth damage. Then he lifted the lid of Ruth's "round hair trunk, where I suppose, had been folded & packed & stowed & treasured up so many of her precious things of this world." The contents, he reported, "offered a mournful lesson to those who put their trust in earthly trunks." Time and corruption had destroyed everything. It was a fit subject for the moralizing of a Sancho Panza:

Seest thou that lady's trunk? What a mine of moral reflection is to be found in that . . . cave . . . where lie the shreds and remnants of what once was garment . . . Lo, the lank skeleton of that once envied tippet! Not a hair . . . no sign by which it can say, "I once warmed a marten on the frozen banks of Hudson, and then passed to the most consummate seat of earthly splendor—curled round the neck and panted on the bosom of the loveliest of her sex." Alas, poor Tippet! a long, thin, brittle strip of untanned leather . . . And thy fond sister Muff—Ah, me! her fate is thine . . . [But] the lining of the muff is left entire, for it was made of silk. Worms eat not silk . . . flax or cotton . . . Learn hence, my brethren, to line your souls with conscience soft as satin, white as cambric, and strong as corduroy, and then, when it comes your turn to be closed up in that sable trunk that shall yield your bodies to the worms, they can never eat your souls.

Barlow was full of observations on his visit to London and went right on amusing Ruth during her rustication at Plombières. Women's fashions next caught his eye—particularly the vast contrast between styles in the English and French capitals. "The ladies dress astonishingly different from what ours do," he informed Ruth after returning to Paris. "Why, they cover their bubbies & bosoms & necks and gorges quite up to the chin . . . and they cover their shoulders & armpits & elbows, and I am positively assured by those who pretend to be well informed that they wear petty coats." On the subject of corsets, he continued: "They wear nothing but stays as long as your arm . . . the milliner shops & haberdashers' warehouses are full of them. I would lay any money that there are ten thousand pounds' worth of stays in Bond Street alone now for sale. . . . It is a frightful thing to think of."

In fact, London was a rather dull spot, he reported, and he did not get out to such public places as the opera and Vauxhall. Such excursions were more fun in Paris where "one goes to see infinite quantities of bare bubbies & shape of mootens." But in London "you see nothing but white chip-hats and muslins . . . *Quelle difference!* Madame Recamier made a great figure in London . . . chiefly owing to the display of the striking features of womanhood . . . It was the reason why London was so remarkably crowded this season . . . Country gentlemen came from all parts of the kingdom to see & stare . . . Parliament continued its session uncommonly late, not being able to get through the business. And if Mme. Recamier had not left London, it is supposed the agricultural & manufacturing interests would have suffered very much from this new species of French invasion."

Ruth was delighted with Joel's wit and reported that she thought the baths really were doing her some good. But when he urged her in August to stay another month, she demurred and wanted to know why he was so anxious to keep her out of Paris. Towards the end of the month he sent thirty louis for the return trip, and Fulton brought his "Ruthinda" back in the phaeton behind the white ponies. Ruth still had her original complaint, but the summer in the mountains had been invigorating. A friend who saw her there reported to Joel that she seemed prettier, happier, younger, and fatter than before. Her throat and bosom were filled out, her complexion and hair were beautiful. She also had a character "soft, celestial, and spirited."

3: *Fulton's Steamboat*

Back at 50 rue de Vaugirard the consuming interest of the next year was Fulton's steamboat. During the summer at Plombières Fulton had experimented with a model that Barlow had ordered for him. At that time the question was not yet settled how best to propel steam-driven boats. Rumsey's idea of jet propulsion—taking water in at the bow and forcing it out the stern—still had advocates, but Fulton's practical engineering sense soon demonstrated the superiority of paddle wheels. While Fulton was still at Plombières, he drew Ruth Barlow a prophetic picture showing a steamboat loaded with passengers, moved by sidewheels, and captioned: "The Steamboat from New York to Albany in 12 hours." After returning to Paris, he set about making this dream come true.

In the French capital, meanwhile, there was a newcomer whose arrival held critical significance for the ultimate success of the steamboat. He was Robert Livingston, who had reached Paris the preceding November to take up duties as the American Minister to France. A man of means and powerful political connections in New York, Livingston already had backed other efforts at home to build a practical steamboat. His previous partners, however, had failed, though he had been able to get from the legislature exclusive rights to navigate New York waters with steam. He met Fulton in Paris and was impressed.

In July Barlow had written Fulton: "I had a great talk with Livingston. He says he is perfectly satisfied with your experiments . . . You have converted him as to the preference of the wheels above all other modes." By October Livingston was thoroughly enough convinced of Fulton's genius to sign a partnership agreement with him for the further development of the steamboat. Fulton then built a new model, four feet long and operated with clock springs, and continued experiments at Perrier's Pond and on the Seine during the winter. When spring came, he and Livingston ordered construction of a boat seventy feet long powered by twelve-foot paddle wheels and rented an eight-horsepower steam engine to move it.

Barlow was relieved to get out from under the financial drain of the steamboat. He already had spent several thousand dollars on Fulton's projects and was eager to transfer his money to the United States. Barlow, once bitten by the submarine's financial failure, was twice shy in the steamboat venture. He was willing to support Fulton's experiments with generous outlays from current income, but he was glad when a rich man came along to back the invention. He had enough to live on comfortably and did not want to risk his capital in a large-scale promotion. Fulton was properly grateful for Barlow's financial aid and assigned him a part interest in his boat, though the arrangement was later cancelled by mutual consent after Ruth Barlow inherited some money. Joel desired to spend the rest of his life revising his poem, writing a history of the United States, reading his books, and getting worthy projects started.

In August, 1803, curious spectators along the Seine saw a strange craft tied up at the Quay de Chaillot. It was "equipped with two large wheels, mounted on an axel like a chariot," behind which was a "kind of stove with a pipe." When the crew boarded the boat, they fired up the stove and cast off the moorings in a cloud of smoke. An eyewitness of the trial run reported: "At six o'clock in the evening, aided by only three persons, he [Fulton] put his boat in motion . . . and for an hour and a half he produced the curious spectacle of a boat . . . provided with paddles . . . moved by a fire-engine." Pedestrians along the banks of the river could keep up with the steamboat, but the craft operated under its own power and maneuvered in the Seine with complete success.

Fulton's contribution to applied science lay not in the idea of moving ships by steam or even of moving them by paddle wheels. Neither suggestion was original with him, but his genius was in engineering—the successful application of theory to a practical result. He recognized this himself when he later wrote that the real invention was in knowing what were the proper relationships of size, proportion, horsepower, velocities of engine, paddles, and boat. These matters he was able to calculate as the result of his experiments, and what followed was a boat that could carry passengers and cargoes quickly and economically. After the slow, clumsy first boat steamed up the Seine under its own power, Fulton knew that he needed only a better powerplant to build a boat to navigate the Hudson. He then ordered a larger and more powerful steam engine from Bolton and Watts in Birmingham, England, and after some delay in obtaining an export license took it to New York to put in the *Clermont*.

While the steamboat was under construction, Barlow made another business trip to London. Apparently he represented Fulton and others in the same commercial matter (the cargo of the ship *Neptune*) that took him to England the year before. The award he previously had hoped to get did not materialize, and he had to file suit to enforce his claims. The litigation kept him in England from April to August. The trip was not especially profitable, because he only charged his friends for his expenses; yet he eventually completed the business and obtained ten thousand pounds for one owner and about one-fifth as much for Fulton. On this visit the pleasures of returning to England after a long absence were no longer able to absorb him. Barlow chafed at the law's delay, but while his suit was pending, he also seems to have had a few irons in his own fire. He wrote Ruth from London that he was attempting to get her a "little solid income." As he explained it, he was trying to hold "with fingers frail/ The eel of fortune by the tail."

Before Barlow left London, James Monroe arrived from Paris with first-hand news of the Louisiana Purchase just concluded. As Jefferson's special emissary, he had gone to France to assist Livingston in buying enough territory from Napoleon to secure American use of the Mississippi River. The negotiations, which began and ended while Barlow was in England, created a sensation everywhere. The United States not only obtained access to the Mississippi, but it also acquired the entire tract extending from the river to the Rocky Mountains. Barlow and Monroe celebrated this triumph, which nearly doubled the size of the United States, and renewed an acquaintance that had been carried on only by correspondence for eight years.

Bad news from 50 rue de Vaugirard accompanied the exhilarating public announcement of the Louisiana Purchase. While Barlow completed his business in England, Fulton wrote that Ruth was quite ill, and when Joel reached home, his wife's condition alarmed him. What her trouble was the doctors apparently did not know (they called it dropsy), and for nearly two years she languished. During the next spring, when the Barlows definitely had planned to return to the United States, her health grew worse. Relatives back home were notified that Ruth was "very sick & not likely to recover." Her constitution, however, was not that fragile, and she had many years ahead of her. Nevertheless, the departure scheduled for 1804 had to be delayed. Barlow, meantime, continued transferring his money to America in anticipation of the earliest possible sailing, and Fulton left Paris to fulfill his commitment to build a submarine for England.

When French doctors failed to cure Ruth, Joel decided to take her to England for further treatment. After a disheartening summer in which she was confined to the house, her health mended a little in September, and together they set out for London by way of Holland and Rotterdam. At last they were on their way home, though they still faced a winter in London and another ten months of exile. They bade goodby to Paris with a sense of relief, for that city, despite its memories and blandishments, had become increasingly uncongenial. Soon after reaching London, Joel wrote his brother-in-law: "You must not imagine that we have the most distant idea of staying in this country or of ever setting our foot again in the land of the Corsican. I have disposed of the property I had there, & have quitted with great joy a nation that had long become insupportable to me, from the follies of the many & the rogueries of the few."

Barlow's disillusionment with France soon was compounded. He learned that his move to London was viewed in Paris as an unfriendly political mission. Because he had sponsored Fulton for so many years, some Frenchmen and American expatriates assumed that he had crossed the Channel to assist his protégé with the submarine. He pretended not to care what people thought, but he felt obliged to write a long explanation to his friend William Lee, now American consul at Bordeaux, and to send a copy of the letter to President Jefferson. His trip to London, he protested, was motivated solely by the desire to obtain excellent medical treatment for his wife, and he was happy to say "that the event has thus far justified" his action.

Then he angrily attacked his slanderers—"the idle babble of men to whom nature has dealt out understanding with a miser's measure." Protesting rather too much, he presented a long bill of particulars: His attackers were men "whose narrow comprehension never gave them a glimpse of the progressive improvements of mankind or of the political events which lead to such improvements;

who attach themselves to men & not to principles & are royalists or republicans as circumstances chance." He went further: "Calumny is the natural effervescence of such minds. They take pleasure in condemning what they have not the capacity to comprehend. Let these men enjoy their contemptible amusement."

Barlow disclaimed any connection with Fulton's commission to build a submarine for England, but he rallied to a vigorous defense of his friend's acts and motives. Fulton, he asserted, believed that the submarine would "check tyranny & diminish the frequency of wars & promote the interest of America by giving her a free commerce." He was determined furthermore to advance his ideas "in whatever country he can find a footing for his machines, regardless of the momentary opinions of his friends or enemies." Barlow declared finally that Fulton was attached to the "true republican interests of his country" and possessed of an "excellent moral character [that] would make few men who should know him . . . fear to be his friend."

Despite minor vexations the Barlows settled down to a quiet winter in England. They took an apartment in London, and Ruth began consultations with the best British doctors. Fulton joined them after a seven months' separation, and they renewed other former associations. Old friends like Horne Tooke and Joseph Johnson had mellowed and aged since the radical ferment of 1792. Others, like Mary Wollstonecraft and James Mackintosh, were no longer present. The former had died giving birth to the future Mary Shelley, and the latter, now Sir James, was a judge in India, having been, as Barlow put it, silenced and bought off by the government. The intimates of this winter often were Fulton's one-time teacher, old Benjamin West, whose work Barlow admired extravagantly, and Earl Stanhope, a noble lord who still was an unreconstructed radical. Stanhope retained his gloomy views about the future of British monarchy but contented himself with science and mechanics. He was an old friend of Fulton's through their common enthusiasm for canal-building in the mid-Nineties.

By March Ruth was well enough to sail for home, and though the embarkation did not take place till summer, this time the Barlows actually left Europe. Their ship cleared England about the middle of June and began a voyage as stormy and rough as a winter crossing. Ruth died a half dozen deaths during the fifty-two-day trip, and Joel suffered his usual torments from seasickness. At last they arrived in New York early in August, and thus ended an exile that for Joel had lasted seventeen years.

CHAPTER X

Mr. Jefferson's America

1: Homecoming

The Barlows spent the first month of their repatriation in semi-seclusion in a New York hotel. Joel had been abroad for seventeen years, Ruth for fifteen. They had to sort out their emotions and get used to being back in the United States. They were thoroughly disenchanted with Europe and determined never to venture abroad again. Even before returning, Joel had written his brother: "Do not give them [your sons] a taste for roving over the world. There are very few young men who are sent to Europe for the sake of seeing the world who are not ruined." At the same time, their delight in coming home was tempered by a few misgivings. They were a little apprehensive upon regaining their native soil, as all exiles have been from Ulysses down. They wondered if their New England relatives would receive them, and they wondered further if America might not have changed so much that they never again could feel at home.

Soon after they disembarked, they sent off letters to friends and relatives and began charting their course for the coming months. They tentatively planned an immediate trip to the national capital to see Ruth's brother Abraham and Mr. Jefferson, but they discovered that official Washington had dispersed for the summer. The

President sent a cordial invitation for them to visit Monticello, but when they simultaneously learned that Baldwin was in Connecticut, they decided to go north first. In declining Jefferson's invitation, Barlow wrote: "I intend to pass the winter at the seat of government, chiefly for the sake of being near you, for I have much to say to you & a great deal to learn from you." Early in September they left New York.

Old acquaintances in Redding and New Haven found Joel and Ruth much changed. They had left America in their early thirties and were returning at fifty-one and forty-nine respectively. Ruth wrote her brother from New York: "Prepare yourself to see your once-blooming sister an infirm old woman that you would not know were she not announced." This was an exaggeration written before she had fully regained composure from fifty-two days at sea, but friends agreed that she was greatly altered and seemed to cling to life precariously. Joel, on the other hand, returned ruddy and hale. He was a big man for his day, well filled out, and about five feet, ten inches in height. He still retained his long, raw-boned farmer's fingers. Though his manners were not courtly, they were grave and dignified, and the impetuous optimism of his youth had given way to a more reflective manner. In company he was often silent when the conversation was frivolous but talkative and animated on topics which excited his imagination.

One of the first persons the Barlows saw in New Haven was Noah Webster, who had branded Joel an atheist and Jacobin nearly seven years before. He wrote somewhat smugly to another Yale classmate that their old friend Barlow wore "a downcast look" that "masked great depression of mind." He seemed "a little convalescent, chiefly by means of Bonaparte's *harsh* remedies for new philosophy," but "his *constitution* is much impaired . . . a radical cure is impossible." Webster no doubt saw what he looked for, and Barlow, wishing to be friends again, conducted himself as deferentially as he could. Towards Ruth, Webster was more charitable. Though he noted her "dropsical manner," he was chiefly interested in her from a professional viewpoint. He wrote: "She is far more precise & formal in her speech than before she left America—but extremely well informed—retains her Americanisms—& is very agreeable."

In the twenty-ninth year of American independence Thomas Jefferson began his second term as President of the United States with a clear mandate from the voters. Having won all but fourteen electoral votes, he faced the road ahead with a secure hand on the reins of his Republican Administration. The United States was prospering and growing—faster than it ever would again—at the rate of thirty-six per cent per decade. Four new states had been added to the Union since the Barlows first went to Europe, and the population now numbered about six million. The country was still, as Jefferson hoped it always would be, a nation of farmers.

American relations with the major powers in Europe were at the moment not too unsatisfactory. As England and France struggled for supremacy, draining into their armies and navies thousands upon thousands of young men, American merchants expanded their fleets and captured a large part of the carrying trade. But in this year, the Battle of Trafalgar, which destroyed the remnant of France's navy, and the Battle of Austerlitz, Napoleon's brilliant victory over Austria and Russia, promised intensification of the struggle. The American merchant marine again would fall between the hammer and the anvil, and Jefferson, before his second term was out, would have to impose his unpopular embargo. Meantime, the infant United States Navy, inspired by Stephen Decatur's bravery, had just forced Tripoli to make peace with America.

For the United States the course of empire clearly lay westward. When Barlow's ship landed in New York, the Lewis and Clark expedition was toiling over the Continental Divide toward the headwaters of the Columbia River. The Louisiana Purchase had stirred the public imagination with dreams of power and glory and spurred on the tide of migration to the West. More than a million people already lived beyond the line of settlement permitted when the country was a British colony. Any able-bodied man with a few saved dollars could make the down payment at a government land office for his quarter section of black Illinois or Indiana farmland at two dollars an acre. Pittsburgh and Lexington already were roaring frontier towns; Cincinnati and Nashville were villages that would become cities before the pioneers had time to grow old.

Life in America in 1805 remained relatively simple and crude. Most people lived in the country and tilled the soil in the same way their grandfathers had before them. The Barlows who still farmed at Redding, Connecticut, occupied the same saltbox houses, wore the same clothes, grew the same crops, used the same wooden plows, sickles, and flails. City dwellers, the few there were, enjoyed some amenities, but Boston, New York, and Philadelphia were still the chief cities. Although New York reminded Barlow of Europe, only the lower tip of Manhattan was settled, and only Philadelphia had well-paved, well-lighted streets, good drainage, and a water system. The explosion of technology had yet to remake the face of America.

The political life of the United States in 1805 was ardent and partisan. Under Jefferson's expert leadership the Republicans had smothered the Federalists at the polls but not silenced them. The struggle went on in the public prints, as newspapers and magazines proliferated, and the battle continued within the government. John Adams had filled every vacant appointive position before he left office, and the Federalists, led by Chief Justice John Marshall, successfully resisted most Republican efforts to alter the status quo. Jefferson and his Secretary of State Madison often raged inwardly at the roadblocks they encountered, but they bowed to the necessity of making haste slowly.

Barlow poked his toe gingerly into the domestic waters when he arrived home from his long foreign residence. He wondered at first if he ought to chance a visit to his native New England, the last stronghold of Federalism. He remembered only too well the showers of abuse aimed his direction six years before, but the XYZ Affair certainly was ancient history by now. War with France had been averted, a new commercial treaty was in effect, and republican principles had been vindicated in Jefferson's election and reelection. When he decided on a return to Connecticut and Massachusetts, he braced himself for what might come, and it was well he did.

In mid-October the *Repertory* greeted his arrival in Boston for

a brief visit with a blast as intemperate as anything published in
1799. The editor of the paper resurrected an old slander known as
"The Guillotine Song." A parody of "God Save the King," these
verses first had appeared in a scurrilous work by the venal journalist William Cobbett (Peter Porcupine), who claimed that Barlow
had written the song for a Fourth of July celebration during his
residence in Hamburg. The blood-thirsty doggerel went like this:

> God save the Guillotine,
> Till England's King and Queen,
>   Her power shall prove;
> Till each appointed knob
> Affords a clipping job
> Let no vile halter rob
>   The Guillotine.
>
> Fame, let thy trumpet sound,
> Tell all the world around—
>   How Capet fell.
> And when great George's poll
> Shall in the basket roll
> Let mercy then control
>   The Guillotine.
>
> When all the sceptered Crew
> Have paid their homage to
>   The Guillotine,
> Let Freedom's flag advance,
> Till all the world, like France,
> O're tyrants' graves shall dance,
>   And peace begin.

After printing the song, the *Repertory's* editor aimed another
meat-cleaver blow at Barlow. He recoiled in horror, he said, from
a man with such a "passion for murder, that the sacrifice of Louis
and his Queen, on the scaffold, was made the theme of his exulta-
tion, and bacchanalian orgies." Barlow was such a scoundrel that
he could "dance on the graves of those hapless victims of popular
frenzy." Just in case anyone missed "The Guillotine Song," three
days later the editor reprinted, out of context, garbled parts of the
letter to John Fellows of 1795 praising Paine's *Age of Reason*, ac-

cused Barlow again of atheism, and warned him to get out of town.

The expatriate, happy to be back home, took the attacks in stride. In New Haven at the end of October, he answered the libels with unruffled composure in an impersonal public statement; then he wrote his former partner, Elisha Babcock of the *American Mercury*, asking him, if he would, to give the editor of the *Repertory* a "knock on the empty skull for his elegant samples of Boston hospitality." He also denied to friends his authorship of "The Guillotine Song," though he did not bother to disclaim it in public. Such attacks, he declared, "are scarcely to be considered as personal to me. Their authors must have the name of a living man to stick them on . . . the name of Philo would do as well as that of Barlow for the purpose of the romance."

Barlow's reception in New England was not entirely hostile. Republicans were plentiful and articulate, and when he visited New Haven, a committee of Republicans in the legislature drafted an address of welcome and offered him a public reception, which he modestly declined. The address praised him for services to the republic and expressed the hope that he would make Connecticut his home. When he declined the large public celebration, he accepted a dinner in his honor given by Abraham Bishop, Collector of the Port. More than one hundred and fifty persons attended. On that day Barlow thanked his old friends and noted with pleasure that "the malicious calumnies . . . published in the American papers against me . . . have made no impression on your minds." Then he added: "I flatter myself that you believe with me that they have been . . . promulgated with no other view than to destroy my usefulness in the cause of liberty."

There was no warm welcome awaiting Barlow at his alma mater, however. Yale was firmly run by Barlow's ex-friend Timothy Dwight, a strong and able teacher but a political troglodyte. Before Josiah Meigs left the Yale faculty to become president of the University of Georgia, he had incurred the wrath of the president by keeping Barlow's portrait over his fireplace. "I was actually advised to hide it, which I did not," he wrote his friend in a letter that referred to the president as "that Lapland Wind Merchant Dwight." Before leaving Europe, Barlow had wanted to enrich

Yale's library with a set of French classics in every branch of science, art, and literature and to send the latest French chemical apparatus; but of these desires he had written Meigs: "I suppose . . . every French book that should come openly among you would be burnt . . . and everything coming from me would be sedition or treason." Barlow regretted, he wrote his nephew later, that such a bigot and tory as Dwight should be at the head of an important school.

At the end of November the Barlows left New England for Washington by private carriage. They had to wait in Philadelphia for the weather to clear and the soggy autumn roads to become passable. After spending five days getting from Philadelphia to Baltimore, Barlow wrote that they had been "jogging on slowly without the least accident & only praying that Maryland would mend its ways." The state could not mend its bridges, he added, until it had built some. When they had to get out and walk around the sloughs and claypits, they probably regretted not taking the packet which sailed from Market Street in Philadelphia every morning and connected with a daily stage for Washington twenty-four hours later. The contrast must have been painful between smooth, hard-surfaced highways in France and the rutted wagon tracks in America. Arriving in the capital on November twenty-ninth, the Barlows found lodging for the winter at Mrs. Doyne's boarding house. They paid forty dollars a week for board, parlor, bedroom, quarters for two servants, and stable.

Barlow reached Washington eager to begin promoting his first project for the improvement of American society. He knew Jefferson believed as he did that education was the footing on which democracy must rest, and for years he had thought about American education. One good result of the French Revolution and Napoleon's rise was a reformation of the schools in France. Barlow had visited European schools and observed details of their administration and organization. As early as 1798 he had written to General Ira Allen about plans for public education in Vermont: "It is certain that if we wish to preserve the principles and practice of liberty . . . we must proceed by instruction. This is not only the most pacific, and the most legitimate way of changing or ameliorating the condition of men, but it is the most energetic & the most effectual."

Two years later Barlow saw a copy of George Washington's will which bequeathed a sum for the establishment of a national university in the new federal city. This apparently gave him an idea for a specific educational project, and he wrote Jefferson right away. He wondered if the government could not take advantage of the country's veneration for Washington and carry out the desires of the will in truly effective fashion. "In all our colleges and universities with which I am acquainted there are so many useless things taught and so many useful ones omitted that it is difficult to say whether on the whole they are beneficial or detrimental to society." He proposed to Jefferson an "institution of much more extensive and various utility than anything of the kind that has hitherto existed." The President was enthusiastic and Barlow continued working out his ideas.

The first thing he did at his desk in Mrs. Doyne's boarding house was to put his plans for a national university into a prospectus. He finished this in January and sent it to Jefferson; then he called at the White House to talk over the proposals. The President approved the plan with only minor revisions and asked Barlow to draft a bill to carry out the project. Meantime, another person who was intensely interested in the university joined Barlow in his efforts. This was George Logan, the Philadelphia Quaker, who now was a Senator. Logan introduced the education bill in the Senate on March fourth with a carefully prepared speech in its behalf. Then he served on a special Senate committee to which the plan was referred.

To interest Congress and the public in the university, Barlow published his proposal in a pamphlet: *Prospectus of a National Institution, to be Established in the United States.* His purpose, he stated at the outset, was to advance knowledge by two means: the association of scientific men and the instruction of youth. His idea was to create a university in Washington which would combine the best features of an institution like the Royal Society of London with a college like Yale. The most distinguished scientists and scholars would be brought together to carry on basic research and

241

give instruction in all branches of the arts and sciences. Barlow envisioned the National Institute as the focal point for a related series of regional colleges—all receiving inspiration and stimulation from the central organization, which also would train professors for the subordinate units.

Barlow's proposal contained additional novelties. He wanted to establish a printing press for the use of the institute to publish scientific and scholarly findings, an idea anticipating the modern university press. He also suggested that the press supply text books for the elementary schools throughout the country. This device, he explained, would distribute school books widely and cheaply and "by an able selection . . . give a uniformity to the moral sentiment, a republican energy to the character, a liberal cast to the mind and manners, of the rising and following generations." The *Prospectus* further advocated removing the patent office from the State Department to the National Institute and setting up a laboratory to "expose to public view such impostors as sometimes apply for them [patents], with the intention of imposing on the credulous." Here Barlow's notion looks ahead to the establishment of the Bureau of Standards.

In many respects the *Prospectus* outlined an organization that was far ahead of its time. Barlow saw the United States on the threshold of great new advances in the arts and sciences. He wanted to teach and sponsor research in mineralogy, botany, chemistry, medicine, mechanics, hydraulics, and mathematics. He also wished to strengthen literature, morals, government, and law, for he argued that scholars in the humanities were capable, if provided the encouragement, of going far beyond the elementary research accomplished so far. His plan, in summary, projected an institution very much like a great modern university where basic research, graduate training, and undergraduate teaching go on simultaneously. Unfortunately, the United States had to wait until Johns Hopkins was founded in 1876 to obtain its first real graduate school.

Despite the Logan Committee's enthusiastic support, the Senate failed to pass the bill for a National Institute. George Washington's deathbed wish to establish a university in the national capital did not secure bipartisan support. The Federalist opposition feared that the Institute would become an instrument of political control, and the Republican majority in Congress, which could easily have passed the measure, was unable to generate sufficient interest. Both Barlow and Jefferson saw the Institute as a means of preserving republican principles, but they planned to give it complete independence. The *Prospectus* called for the President to appoint the chancellor and members of the board of trustees, but thereafter the governing body would be self-perpetuating. Barlow's bill was sent back to committee at the third reading, and there it died.

When Jefferson submitted his next annual message to Congress, he tried to revive the education proposal by tying it to more practical matters. He declared that the Federal treasury was piling up available surpluses that ought to be used for education, canals, and roads. Since the Constitution did not specifically provide for federal expenditures for public improvements, he urged passage of a constitutional amendment to authorize the government to undertake such projects. But even the President could not get the National University established and had to content himself after retirement with setting up the University of Virginia. Barlow's plan did not die completely, however, for some of his friends kept it alive and after his death founded privately both the Columbian Institution for the Promotion of Arts and Sciences and Columbian College. Barlow's old friend Josiah Meigs was the first president of the Institute and an incorporator and member of the first faculty of the college. In 1832 Congress granted the college twenty-five thousand dollars and gave the Institute some land. Ultimately the college became George Washington University.

While the plan of the National Institute was before the Senate, the Barlows received a letter that came "like a shipwreck." In this communication they saw the end of "our most brilliant projects of domestic happiness." Fulton had written from England that he planned to get married. When Joel and Ruth had sailed from London the summer before, Fulton intended to follow them as soon as the torpedo project was finished. Apparently they never expected that Fulton, who had not found a wife by the time he was forty, ever would break up their contented threesome. Joel answered his friend's letter with a heavy heart: "We can say nothing to your proposal except that you ought by all means to pursue your own ideas of your own happiness, well weighed & well considered." Then he proceeded to fill several pages with every argument he could think of against Fulton's marriage.

The girl's education, habits, feelings, character, and cast of mind were English, he argued, and because she had a fortune, as Fulton had stated, she could not be happy in the simple society of the United States. "Your mind is American; your services are wanted here." Furthermore, Fulton's proposed bride apparently was a widow with several children, and Barlow declared that he would rather have yellow fever than bring up children with ideas of affluence and ease. One ought to have children when young and poor, he declared, and bring them up to labor. In addition to these drawbacks, the plans that he and Fulton had made for living together in America, finishing the poem on the canal, and pursuing scientific projects would have to be abandoned.

So far the objections raised seem within the legitimate province of an older man's advice to a younger friend. But next Barlow employed a questionable use of the love that bound Fulton and Ruth. "She thinks she has given her full & free consent to your proposal," Joel wrote of his wife. "She would not for the world stand in the way of the least ray of happiness that was lighting on you . . . But, my friend, you don't know her so well as I do." Then he went on to say that the news of Fulton's impending marriage had "cut deep into her soul, constitution, health. It has settled there a grief unmixed with any active emotion—a calm, hopeless, heart-sinking, life-mining grief, which deceives herself as much as her letter will deceive you." And still going on with his recital, he claimed that Ruth's health, which had been mending for the past six months, was now undone. "Seeing her constantly in tears, unable to eat and sleep, and relapsing into bodily sufferings without her usual flow of spirits to support them, you may conceive of my distress."

Fulton's state of mind when he received this letter cannot be determined. Maybe he was persuaded by it; maybe the lady in England would not have him; but whatever the result, he wrote again in September that he soon would be home. He had finished his arbitration with the government and received a total of fifteen thousand pounds, part of which he already had spent in developing the submarine and torpedo. He expected to sail from Falmouth in October and reach America in November, "perhaps about the fourteenth, my birthday; so you must have a roast goose ready." He did not arrive in time for his birthday, and he never again lived permanently under the Barlows' roof, but he landed in December and spent most of the winter with his friends.

2: *The Columbiad*

The Barlows had left Washington by the time Fulton reached America. After a summer at Rockaway Beach and Ballston Spa in New York they moved from Mrs. Doyne's boarding house to rooms at 312 Market Street in Philadelphia, one block from Carpenters' Hall and two from Independence Square. There they lived for over a year while Joel tried once more to be a national poet. There the *Vision of Columbus*, transformed into the *Columbiad*, came from the press of Fry and Kammerer. The event was parturition with great labor—a literary anti-climax but a graphic arts triumph.

Vanity and lost opportunity! Barlow squandered his months in fanning the thin, feeble coals of poetic fire when he might have been writing the history of the United States. In doing so, he missed a chance that comes to few men. Jefferson and Madison were urging him to write the history and were offering the resources of government archives and their own files. They also were ready with their memories and interpretations of men and events. In July, 1806, the President sent Barlow four boxes of papers and pamphlets for use in the history, but always there was another more pressing project, and at this moment it was the *Columbiad*.

Barlow felt compelled to rewrite his poem. In the twenty years since the *Vision of Columbus* first appeared the world and Joel Barlow had changed astonishingly. The loose federation of states that had won independence from England was becoming a nation of consequence. European history had run full cycle from monarchy to revolution to monarchy again, and the *Vision's* dedication to Louis XVI sounded very strange in the first decade of the Nineteenth Century. Barlow, a republican and deist, had traveled a long road figuratively and literally since his Connecticut youth. He knew more of the world certainly and thought he knew more about literature than at the age of thirty-three.

The process of revising the *Vision* began tentatively after Barlow brought out a Paris edition during the Terror (1793). Subsequently, he was too busy making money in Hamburg and negotiating treaties in Algiers to work on the poem, but eventually he returned to the project. Three complete, extant manuscripts of the *Columbiad*, plus some notes and fragments for a revision, show the painstaking attention he lavished on the work. By 1802 he had cut apart the leaves of a 1793 edition of the *Vision* and interlarded the old pages with scores of new ones. He cancelled many of the early lines and emended countless others. He added hundreds of new couplets and one entire book. The face-lifting was so complete that the reader of the *Columbiad* had to look twice to recognize the earlier *Vision*. Yet the two poems are the same under the skin, and if anything, the youthful blemishes are more attractive than the middle-aged remodeling.

Fulton, a better engineer than literary critic, was accessory before the fact of the *Columbiad's* appearance. Full of enthusiasm and affection for Joel, he encouraged his friend to bring out a sumptuous edition befitting his affluence and *soi-disant* status as poet of America's rising power and glory. Fulton planned a large, illustrated volume and drew the sketches for it himself. After Barlow spent a thousand dollars to commission paintings by a prominent artist, Robert Smirke, Fulton added five thousand of his own to have the paintings engraved. The eleven illustrations, plus a frontispiece of Barlow engraved from Fulton's own painting, went into the book. Fulton had the plates made and the prints struck off just before winding up his own business in England.

Magnificent illustrations from paintings by a member of the Royal Academy required a handsome book, and Barlow moved to Philadelphia to see that he got it. Conrad and Company agreed to publish the poem and engaged Fry and Kammerer to print it.

The work went slowly and exactingly, but the result, typographi-cally, was worth all the effort. The publisher brought out in No-vember, 1807, the most beautiful book yet manufactured in America. It was printed in a handsome, eighteen-point, specially made type on fine paper in quarto size and bound in leather with gold stamp-ing. Even the caustic Francis Jeffrey in the *Edinburgh Review* said he never had seen a more attractive book published in England. He conceded: "The infant republic has already attained to the very summit of perfection in the mechanical part of bookmaking."

Americans took a national pride in the beauty of the book, but for Barlow the elegance was a little embarrassing. He had to recon-cile his republican ideals of simplicity and modesty with the fact that the book cost ten thousand dollars to publish and sold for twenty dollars a copy. With artful disingenuousness he rational-ized his predicament in dedicating the book to Robert Fulton: "This poem is your property. I present it to you in manuscript, that you may bring it before the public in the manner you think proper . . . You designated the subjects to be painted for engravings; and, un-able to convince me that the work could merit such expensive and splendid decorations, you ordered them to be executed in my ab-sence and at your own expense." To this he added that the work had cost him nothing except the "leisurely and exhilarating labor in which I always delight."

There is only a kernel of truth in those statements. Alone, Bar-low might have issued a less pretentious work, for he had a native New England frugality that curbed expensive impulses. Yet he certainly would have published a handsome revision of his poem, Fulton or no Fulton. He let his friend persuade him easily and sub-sequently took delight in seeing the *Columbiad* achieve distinction in the history of American graphic arts. Charles Willson Peale put the book in his Philadelphia museum and reported two or three months later that visitors called for it so often that he was afraid his copy would be damaged.

If Peale feared that the poem could not be replaced, he need not have worried. There were plenty more books in stock in Conrad and Company's warehouse, and five years later five hundred and fifty-four copies remained unsold out of the original edition of nine hundred and twelve. Even today this beautiful volume can be found in second-hand bookstores for less than its original sales price. The poem was not a failure, however, because a modest, two-volume edition issued in 1808 sold well enough to support another printing the following year. The poem also was reprinted in London, Paris, and again in the United States in 1825.

In preparing his revised poem for publication, Barlow felt obliged to add a preface to the *Vision's* old historical introduction. In his editorial foreword he announced the poem's two objects—one poetical and the other moral. His poetical object was the same as it always had been: the depiction of America, past, present, and future, the unrolling of a rich panorama of historical and topographical detail. His moral aim, however, was now frankly political. Earlier he had believed in America's inevitable destiny and had inhaled only a few heady draughts of current European philosophy. He had not yet witnessed the tough and sometimes losing struggle on two continents to establish republican principles. He stated his purpose clearly: "I wish to encourage and strengthen, in the rising generation, a sense of the importance of republican institutions; as being the great foundation of public and private happiness, the necessary aliment of future and permanent ameliorations in the condition of human nature."

Barlow's new poem was in every way more pretentious than the *Vision*. He had refrained from calling the previous effort an epic, thinking of it rather as a philosophical poem; now he gave his work an epic title, the *Columbiad*, and began in epic fashion:

> I sing the Mariner who first unfurl'd
> An eastern banner o'er the western world.

He seems to have thought of the poem as a kind of modern and improved *Iliad* or *Aeneid*. He believed, as his preface states, that most epics of the past have had an evil moral influence. He thought that both Homer and Virgil taught the "pernicious doctrine of the divine rights of kings" and "false notions of honor." In sending a complimentary copy to Jefferson, he wrote modestly: "As a poem of the Epic character it can never rank high. As a patriotic legacy to my country, I hope it may prove acceptable."

The first five books of the *Columbiad* do not depart significantly from the original *Vision*. In them Barlow describes America and narrates the history of the Western Hemisphere from the Inca Empire to his own day. He substitutes for his Miltonic angel, who reveals the future to Columbus, a mythological "Hesper," the spirit of the Western World. But the epic still is a vision poem in which Columbus is whisked from his prison at Valladolid to a lofty mountain to survey the panorama of history.

When Barlow reaches Books VI and VII, he expands his account of the American Revolution into three books. His aim is to make the heroes of the war more heroic, the action more epic, and the subject matter more detailed. These books, the most successful lines in the poem, have a genuine epic quality about them. The British are now sinister tyrants, and Washington strides across the continent like Milton's Michael leading the cohorts of Heaven against Satan. Barlow now shows his reader American captives rotting in a British prison ship and England's allies, the howling Mohawks, murdering fair Lucinda as she waits in a thicket for her soldier-lover. He also employs the traditional supernatural machinery of the epic. As Washington's army crosses the Delaware, Hesper contends successfully with an evil spirit, Frost, to aid the patriot army.

Book VIII contains Barlow's most concentrated homiletics. It retains the original hymn to peace but is lengthened to include an address to the patriots who survived the war. Exhorting them to preserve the liberty they have established, Barlow writes:

> Think not, my friends, the patriot's task is done,
> Or freedom safe, because the battle's won.

On every shore at all times "stalks the fell demon of despotic power" who "treads down whole nations every stride he takes." The poet also admonishes his countrymen to remove the blemish of slavery lying like a curse on their free society. "Equality of Right is nature's plan," and woe to the nation that flouts this truth. The result can only be

A vengeance that shall shake the world's deep frame,
That heaven abhors, and hell might shrink to name.

Book IX, containing Barlow's scientific and philosophical ideas, required a complete overhauling. He had to update the scientific theories of the *Vision* and remove ideas that he no longer believed in. For his earlier Biblical story of the creation he substitutes a remarkably modern concept of the earth's evolution:

Millions of generations toil'd and died
To crust with coral and to salt her tide,
And millions more, ere yet her soil began,
Ere yet she form'd or could have nursed her man.

The moral world that Hesper shows Columbus is no longer informed by revealed religion. Barlow's reading of contemporary thought, his study of science and mythology resulted in a more utilitarian and rational philosophy. Jeremy Bentham's principle of self-interest ("enlighten'd interest" in the poem) directs human relationships towards a peaceful, orderly world. Society will pass through the time of error and blinding passion to reach a millennium of reason.

The final book of the *Columbiad* once more scans the future to reveal a union of all men and an assembly of united nations. But there is a difference, for the *Vision's* unity came from a vague, inevitable progress. Now unity results from a carefully thought out historical process. In the final scene the great day of truth and harmony dawns, and the peoples of the world trample in the dust "the mask of priesthood and the mace of kings." Then shall

One centred system, one all ruling soul
Live thro the parts and regulate the whole.

While the *Columbiad* was in press, Barlow made two trips back to Washington. The first was in January with Fulton to attend a testimonial dinner for Captain Meriwether Lewis, who had just returned from his trek to the Pacific Ocean. All the prominent Republicans gathered to honor the explorer and to praise the wisdom of their party in acquiring the vast Louisiana Territory. Captain

Clark did not arrive in time for the dinner and thus missed Barlow's poetic tribute to the expedition, which was read amidst the numerous toasts. But Captain Clark did not miss much, as readers of the Republican newspaper, the *National Intelligencer*, noted when the verses appeared in print. Among other things, Barlow invoked the spirit of Columbus, apropos of the expedition's leader:

> With the same soaring genius thy Lewis ascends,
>   And seizing the car of the sun,
> O're the sky-propping hills and high waters he bends
>   And gives the proud earth a new zone.

He also urged metrically that the name of the Columbia River be changed to Lewis:

> Then hear the loud voice of the nation proclaim,
>   And all ages resound the decree:
> Let our occident stream bear the young hero's name
>   Who taught him his path to the sea.

Senator John Quincy Adams read Barlow's verses and nearly choked. When he pulled himself together, he wrote a parody and sent it to the *Monthly Anthology:* "Gentlemen, The following 'elegant and glowing stanzas' [quoting the *Intelligencer*] are not from the pen of Mr. Barlow, nor were they recited by Mr. Beckley at the 'elegant dinner' given . . . to Captain Lewis":

> GOOD people, listen to my tale,
>   'Tis nothing but what true is;
> I'll tell you of the mighty deeds
>   Achieved by Captain Lewis—
> . . . .
> What marvels on the way he found
>   *He'll* tell you, if inclined, sir—
> But I shall only now disclose
>   The things he *did not* find, sir.
>
> He never with a Mammoth met
>   However you may wonder;
> Not even with a Mammoth's bone,
>   Above the ground or under—
> . . . .

251

And from the day his course began,
  Till even it was ended,
He never found an Indian tribe
  From Welchmen straight descended:
. . . .
We never will be so fubb'd off,
  I'm sure as I'm a sinner!
Come—let us all subscribe, and ask
  The HERO to a dinner—
And Barlow stanzas shall indite—
  A bard, the tide who tames, sir—
And if we cannot alter *things*,
  By G—, we'll change their *names*, sir!

In March Barlow rushed to Washington when he heard that
Abraham Baldwin was critically ill. Ruth was ill once more and
unable to go, and even though Barlow traveled posthaste, he arrived twenty hours after Baldwin's death. The senator died, with
characteristic quiet and lack of fuss, the day after Congress
adjourned. When Barlow saw him, "every sentiment of conscious
dignity and self-approbation seemed to be painted on his pale and
placid face: he seemed to say, 'Here I am; my work is finished.' "
Most of the Senate and many other Congressmen and government
officials stayed for the state funeral and accompanied the coffin to
the cemetery five miles outside Washington. Barlow wrote home
sadly the next day to reconcile Ruth to her brother's death: "He
had suffered no pain during his last illness, and his serenity, be-
nignity, even good-humor remained till the last . . . He talked as
long as he could talk at all, of the affairs of the public." Barlow
remained in Washington long enough to settle his brother-in-law's
affairs and to write his obituary for the *Intelligencer;* then he returned to Philadelphia feeling that part of his life had ended with
the loss of his old friend. In May he wrote a Yale classmate: "We
belong to the generation that is going off the stage."

The next six months in Philadelphia were meager in accomplishment. Barlow went back to find the printers working like snails on
the *Columbiad*, and Ruth's health was no better. He frittered away
the days in the minutiae of book manufacture: selecting the paper;

supervising the typesetting, printing, and binding; reading proof and making an index. Though he was interested in the mechanics of publishing, the procedure already had lasted six months and the novelty was wearing off.

Philadelphia, fortunately, was an attractive place to await the appearance of the poem. He was a frequent visitor to the museum and studio of Charles Willson Peale, who painted portraits of Fulton and Barlow to hang in his Temple of Wisdom along with other good progressive Jeffersonians. In addition, he called often at the near-by headquarters of the American Philosophical Society, which later elected him to membership in 1809. The city lost one of its attractions, however, when Fulton left for New York a few days after Barlow's return. He went to supervise the construction of the *Clermont*.

The Barlows kept track of Fulton and the steamboat's progress by correspondence. Fulton's work moved forward swiftly and he finished the *Clermont* by mid-summer. On August seventeenth he began his historic voyage to Albany. As soon as he got back to New York, he wrote the Barlows an account of the trip:

> My steamboat voyage . . . turned out rather more favorably than I had calculated . . . I ran it up in thirty-two hours and down in thirty. I had a light breeze against me the whole way, both going and coming, and the voyage has been performed wholly by the power of steam. I overtook many sloops and schooners beating to windward and parted with them as if they had been at anchor . . . The morning I left New York there were not, perhaps, thirty persons in the city who believed that the boat ever would move one mile an hour or be of the least utility, and while we were putting off from the wharf, which was crowded with spectators, I heard a number of sarcastic remarks.

Fulton's success with the *Clermont* ended his intimacy with the Barlows. Building steamboats kept him in New York, whereas Joel and Ruth wanted to settle permanently in Washington. But he wished to spend as much time as possible with his closest friends and agreed to share expenses with them in buying a country house near the capital. This arrangement might have worked if Fulton had not at last found a wife. Less than five months after the *Clermont's* maiden voyage he married Harriet Livingston, a cousin of his partner Robert Livingston.

Fulton naïvely hoped that his marriage would make no change in his relationship with the Barlows. Five months after the wedding he wrote "Ruthinda": "Shall we unite our fortunes to make Kalorama [the new house] the centre of taste, beauty, love, and dearest friendship, or by dividing interests never arrive at that comfort, elegance, or happiness for which our souls are formed?" He added that he wanted Harriet to study the example of "Ruthinda, dear Ruthinda, heart of love" in order to "acquire all that is [in] her most endearing." But Ruth never accepted Harriet and put up with her only because she could no longer have Fulton alone. The result of Fulton's marriage was estrangement between the Barlows and Fulton. No doubt Harriet too was jealous of Ruth and could not tolerate a continuation of the old affection.

The estrangement was not permanent, however. When Fulton realized that two families could not possibly live together, he wrote a long, candid letter to Joel to untangle the emotional snarls. "Believe me, my dear Barlow, your ease and happiness and that of the dear and amiable Ruthinda is as dear to me as my own." He patiently pointed out all the reasons why he had to live in New York and why two families could not share the same roof. He also totaled as best he could from memory Barlow's capital and expenditures to show that the new house would not be too expensive for the Barlows alone. In its whole tone and content the letter was a model of fraternal conciliation and apparently satisfied Joel. But Ruth continued to pout.

Fulton had too much good sense to let her go on sulking for long. One day business took him to Washington, and he went to see the Barlows without announcing his arrival. Afterwards Ruth wrote her sister that Fulton had "popped in upon us yesterday morning without the smallest notice. I was never more surprised. You see, I had no opportunity to say no, and now I am glad he came this way." Ruth's jealousy of Harriet, however, did not change, even though Harriet named her son Barlow and kept Ruth with them a long time after Joel's death and Ruth's return from Europe in

1813. When Fulton died, Ruth wrote her sister: "In him I have lost a sincere friend; in spite of her, he was such."

When the *Columbiad* came from the press, there was nothing to hold the Barlows in Philadelphia any longer. All that year they had been considering the house that Jefferson had praised as "a most lovely seat" five years before. It now was empty again and they bought it. In the autumn, after packing their personal effects, they returned to Washington to live, so they thought, for the rest of their days. As they began their residence in the capital, they awaited the critical reception of the *Columbiad*.

CHAPTER XI

Squire of Kalorama

1: *Elder Statesman*

"Barlow's house is a miniature palace. It is situated on a high hill surrounded with about fifty acres of large forest trees . . . He has Washington, Georgetown, the President's house, the Capitol, Alexandria, & the majestic Potomac in full view . . . He keeps four horses, three carriages . . . and eight servants." Thus wrote a visitor to Kalorama during Barlow's happy years near the seat of Republican government. When the new owner of the house invited guests to visit him, he instructed them: "In passing over the plain by the President's house, you have ours in sight on the hill. You turn off at the seven buildings, a half a mile beyond." Kalorama no longer exists, but it stood at the top of what is now Twenty-second Street, about three hundred yards east of Rock Creek. S Street between Massachusetts and Florida Avenues now passes through Barlow's former front yard.

The new house and grounds were a delight in every way, Barlow wrote his nephew on November sixth, two or three weeks after taking possession. The place lacked only a few improvements that he planned to make before it would be a little paradise. His first act was to change the name from "Belair," which was much too common, to "Calorama," from the Greek signifying "beautiful

256

view." This place presents one of the finest prospects in America, he declared at the time he bought the property. He later changed his "C" for a "K," and the house remained Kalorama for eighty-one years. During the Civil War it served as a hospital; then it was torn down in 1889 to make way for subdivision and progress.

Barlow soon added on to the house, enlarged the stables, cut a new road, and laid out paths to wind through his picturesque, wooded acres. About half of his land was forested, the rest laid out in lawn, garden, and orchard. He puttered contentedly about the place, landscaping and gardening, redecorating and building a little here and a little there, as long as he lived at Kalorama. Fulton urged him to build a piazza across the back of the house for coolness during Washington's muggy summers and to construct a summer house, for which he sent suggestions and a sketch. Benjamin Latrobe, official surveyor of public buildings, came in to design a gardener's lodge and to install marble fireplaces in the main house. Barlow also added a mausoleum at one corner of the estate and immediately had Senator Baldwin's remains brought there.

Kalorama was a well-known landmark long before Barlow bought and improved it. Anthony Holmead, one of the original proprietors of the land chosen for the federal city, built the first house in mid-century and sold it about 1795 to Gustavus Scott, one of the commissioners appointed to build the new capital. After Scott died in bankruptcy in 1801, Jefferson recommended the house to Barlow, but when Barlow did not come home for another three years, the estate passed into the hands of William Augustine Washington, nephew of the first President. All the owners added to the original house, which was a three-story, masonry building with mansard roof and simple façade ornamented by unobtrusive pilasters and shuttered windows. The front door was covered by a modest portico, probably added by one of the later owners. Barlow paid fourteen thousand dollars for the house and thirty acres of land and later added another twenty acres for fifteen hundred dollars.

Furnishing the house was a slow process. Many boxes and trunks shipped from Paris had remained in storage in Philadelphia ever since the Barlows arrived in America. In March, 1808, Charles Willson Peale had their goods shipped to them in the capital, including a mangle and washing machine brought home from Europe. Other possessions still to be collected had been sent home years before addressed to Oliver Wolcott. Because they had owned little furniture in Europe, they were obliged to spend five thousand dollars equipping Kalorama in a manner befitting the author of the *Columbiad*. The library again was Barlow's particular interest, as it had been at 50 rue de Vaugirard. In fact, the library already was about complete, for Barlow had acquired so many books in Europe that he found five hundred dollars' worth of duplicates to sell to James Madison. By the time the Barlows finally were settled in their new home, they already had entered fully into the life of the national capital.

Washington in 1808 was still a backwoods Athens. The District of Columbia had about twenty-four thousand inhabitants, but the city of Washington held only a third of them, and the village of Georgetown was half as large as the capital. During his first term Jefferson described Washington as "a pleasant country residence, with a number of neat little villages scattered around within the distance of a mile and a half, and furnishing a plain and substantially good society." The region surrounding the new government buildings was undeniably attractive. Lush green woods sloped gently down to the quiet Potomac, which averaged half a mile in width where it passed the city. The White House, usually called the President's house, and the capitol building already had been put up at opposite ends of Pennsylvania Avenue, though much of L'Enfant's plan existed only on paper. The south wing of the Capitol, the foundation for which had been laid in 1794, was finished in the year Barlow bought Kalorama. The north wing had been completed during Jefferson's inaugural year.

The President tried to give a homespun character to his Republican administration. He dropped the pomp and ceremony of the Federalist years and abandoned Washington's and Adams' practice of delivering messages to Congress in person on the grounds that such speeches were too much like addresses from the throne in a monarchy. He ignored diplomatic protocol at White House social functions and insulted the British minister by receiving him in old clothes and carpet slippers that were down at the heels. He compounded the insult later at a state dinner for the British minister by escorting Dolley Madison to the table instead of the guest of honor's wife. He also irritated the vain little Spanish envoy, who nursed his injured ego over similar slights and boycotted the President's house.

Nevertheless, rustic simplicity and urban pleasures existed side by side in the national capital. When Ruth Barlow wrote her sister that her radishes were nearly ready to pull in mid-March, she also added that Mrs. Madison's cucumbers were in bloom and her lettuce ready to eat. Joel Barlow, like the country squires who led the Republican Party, farmed his acreage, cutting hay for his own horses and raising vegetables for his own table. Meantime, when Congress was in session, the town was full of belles and beaux. The girls might trail their homemade gowns in the mud en route to a party, but there were half a dozen big weddings during any winter, and assemblies in Washington and Georgetown took place at least once a fortnight. In the summer the Fourth of July was always an occasion for great dinners and balls, and the arrival of a new minister to swell the diplomatic corps often brought prominent citizens an invitation to dine with the President or Secretary of State.

One of the noteworthy features of the federal city was its women. At the top of the hierarchy was Dolley Madison, the capital's acknowledged social leader. She occupied this place both as wife of the Secretary of State (because Jefferson was a widower) and later as First Lady. A card to one of her parties was a summons seldom ignored. But she was only one of many charming hostesses in a city known for its bewitching women. The unattached ladies were in great demand by bachelor Congressmen, who married them and spirited them off to the provinces. One disgruntled resident complained: "Washington thus resembles a nursery, where fine plants are annually transplanted to a foreign and less congenial soil." Diplomats used to the sophistication of Paris or London, however, were not always charmed by Republican women. A member of the British legation wrote home: "The women here are in general a spying, inquisitive, vulgar and most ignorant race . . . many of them daughters of tavernkeepers, boarding housekeepers and clerks' wives and yet as ceremonious as ambassadresses."

All things considered, life was relatively simple and certainly different in Washington in 1808. The barber arrived on horseback every morning to shave his customers and work in with the bay rum a daily budget of gossip. Hostesses sent around servants with invitations to summer teas on the day of the party. Gentlemen asked out to dine drank a toddy before the meal and often at the table sat apart from the ladies. Men wore their hats in carriages, and both sexes carried umbrellas.

The newspapers, too, advertised a life far removed from the Twentieth Century. As they ran ads for lost cows and runaway slaves, a prosperous citizen might broadcast his desire to buy a young Negro girl "well acquainted with house work." The papers announced the winners of well-patronized state lotteries, and they publicized the government's call for bids to supply the Capitol with one hundred cords of good hickory for the next winter. Meantime, stores urged their customers to come in for prime mackerel, spermaceti candles, muscatel raisins, fine yellow cheese, Lisbon salt, and Jamaica rum.

Lying an easy carriage drive from the President's house, Kalorama became a gathering place for official Washington. The Barlows struck up a close friendship with the Madisons, and Joel renewed his earlier acquaintance with President Jefferson. Secretary of War Henry Dearborn and his wife were familiar visitors to Kalorama; so were Gideon Granger, Postmaster-General from Connecticut and Yale, and the Benjamin Latrobes. The Barlows regularly entertained most of the prominent members of the Republican Party and kept their place full of house and dinner guests. Joel, who devoted much of his abundant spare time to thinking about public affairs, considered himself a kind of elder statesman and was accepted as such by the President and Cabinet.

No one can be sure whether or not Barlow had any real influence on matters of state. Certainly he was listened to respectfully, and his advice on foreign relations probably helped determine policy. The British chargé d'affaires during Madison's first term believed that Barlow exerted a considerable influence on the President's opinions, and Jefferson had earlier invoked the Embargo against England and France, a measure Barlow strongly advocated, during the year that Barlow bought Kalorama. Yet both Madison and Jefferson made up their own minds, and most of Barlow's ideas harmonized with the general position of the Republicans. One can record only that Barlow had been preaching to Jefferson for fifteen years the efficacy of economic warfare. He always was ready to, and often did, defend his view that England and France needed American shipping more than American merchants needed foreign markets. He was right, even though the Embargo Act was politically unpopular and had to be repealed. It was an effective, though double-edged, weapon and might have forestalled the War of 1812 if the public had been willing to try it longer.

The letters which passed between Jefferson and Barlow during two decades abound in evidence of Joel's promptings from the wings. Once he wrote enclosing a plan for dealing with England in which he suggested that the British might be persuaded diplomatically to stop molesting American ships. It was important, he felt, not to wound their *amour propre*. At another time he reported a talk with the Tunisian minister, an old friend, who he thought might be useful in arranging an accommodation between the United States and Barbary. On a third occasion, because of his experience in North Africa, the President asked him to propose someone competent to go to Tunis as consul. After moving to Washington, Barlow sometimes forwarded to Jefferson letters detailing matters of commerce and diplomacy from the viewpoint of commercial friends abroad.

Most of their interchanges, however, oral and written, concerned domestic matters of science and education. Once at Barlow's suggestion Jefferson asked Fulton (who was too busy with the steamboat) to go to New Orleans to survey the ground for a canal linking Lake Pontchartrain and the Gulf of Mexico. At various times the President discussed with Barlow the plan for a national institute and ways and means of obtaining Congressional approval for it. But when Barlow forwarded a plan for establishing a veterinary college, Jefferson disparaged the project, arguing that medical science was primitive enough in human beings, who could describe their diseases, but non-existent in dumb animals. Later Jefferson was more interested in the French Institute's report on Gall's theory of the brain, which Barlow sent him, for he certainly agreed with the accompanying remarks: "The cultivation of the sciences is becoming so essential . . . that I think it should be ranked among the duties of the federal government to give a certain public importance to scientific research."

Barlow cashed drafts on his intimacy with the President and the Cabinet only at rare intervals. On one such occasion Henry Baldwin's father-in-law, Andrew Ellicott, who was a well-known surveyer, mathematician, and astronomer, needed a job. A convenient postmastership at Lancaster, Pennsylvania, was vacant, and Barlow struck a blow for federal patronage of science and art. He wrote Postmaster-General Granger that "in all our country there is evidently too little attention paid to men of science as well as men of literature." The more he thought about it, the angrier he became, and he aimed a withering blast at the "inordinate and universal pursuit of wealth as a means of distinction" in America and the neglect of scholars and scientists like Ellicott. What he meant was something like this: "If I find that writing the *Columbiad* . . . will not place me on a footing with John Taylor, who is rich, why, then . . . I'll be rich too. I'll despise my literary labors . . . & I'll boast of my bank shares . . . I'll teach my nephews by precept . . . that merit consists in oppressing mankind & not in serving them. Excuse me, my dear sir, this dull sermon & make Andrew Ellicott postmaster of Lancaster."

The fall and winter of 1808-1809 brought Jefferson's retirement from public life and Madison's succession as the fourth President. During the last year of Jefferson's second term, uninhibited protests of merchants, farmers, and tradesmen suffering from the effects of the Embargo Act raised a noisy clamor. The President's popularity at the time of the Louisiana Purchase ebbed away as the death struggle between England and France involved the United States in problems no American chief executive could solve. By election day in 1808 the Federalists were enjoying a reprieve from the political boneyard, but despite an emotional campaign issue in the Embargo they could not defeat Madison, who carried all the states outside of New England. Before Madison was inaugurated, however, the Embargo was repealed, and the new President took office in an atmosphere of relaxed tension.

The Barlows joined the throng of enthusiastic Republicans who attended the inauguration ceremony at the Capitol and the accompanying social functions. The attempt to save seats at the swearing in for the ladies of public characters failed completely, "for the sovereign people would not resign their privileges." One could hardly elbow one's way to a point of vantage through an estimated ten thousand spectators. Afterwards at the Madisons' home on F Street the crowds were nearly as thick, and carriages jammed the streets so completely that guests were half an hour in getting to the house. Inside, the Madisons stood in the drawing room receiving, Dolley beautiful in a plain cambric dress, round in the neck, with long train, bonnet of purple velvet and white satin trimmed with white plumes. Jefferson stood beside them. When Ruth Barlow's friend Mrs. Samuel Smith reached the ex-President, she said: "You have now resigned a heavy burden."

"Yes, indeed . . . and am much happier at this moment than my friend," replied Jefferson.

Later the festivities shifted to the inaugural ball at Long's Hotel where the jam of well-wishers was, if anything, greater than before. Dolley Madison again was the center of attraction but nearly suffocated before someone broke the upper sashes of the windows to let in air. Guests a few feet from the President and his wife had to stand on benches to see what was going on. Two hours after the band had announced the arrival of the retiring President and the President-elect, Jefferson withdrew leaving Madison and the stunning Dolley alone with the crowd. But while he was there, he beamed at his successor and Mrs. Smith noted: "I do believe father never loved son more than he loves Mr. Madison."

If Jefferson felt a fatherly interest in the man he picked as his successor, he maintained an avuncular interest in Barlow. The squires of Kalorama and Monticello corresponded with each other at fairly regular intervals after the latter left Washington. Soon after his retirement Jefferson resumed his urgings that Barlow get on with the history of the United States. He wrote in October that he was reading John Marshall's fifth volume of the life of Washington and would make annotations in it for Barlow to use. He would correct what was wrong and commit to writing such facts and memoranda "as the reading of that work will bring to my memory." A little later when Barlow reported that building and gardening at Kalorama were taking up a lot of his time, Jefferson admonished: "You owe to republicanism . . . a faithful record of the *march* of this government . . . your principles, and your means of access to public and private sources of information, with the leisure which is at your command, point you out as the person who is to do this act of justice."

The two men also corresponded on agricultural matters. Soon after Jefferson reached Monticello, he discovered that one of his trunks containing a dynamometer just received from France had been stolen. He had planned to use that instrument, which measures muscular effort, to design a new and improved plow. He thought Barlow had a dynamometer, wanted to borrow it, and would send his nephew to get it. Barlow replied, however, that he did not have one and did not know where another could be obtained in the United States, but he was full of suggestions for building a homemade instrument. He also responded to Jefferson's offer of a plow: "I am not much of a farmer . . . but . . . shall be very thankful for one of your plows whenever it shall be convenient to spare me one."

Correspondence was not enough to satisfy either Jefferson or Barlow, and when the President was at Monticello he repeatedly invited the Barlows to visit him. After they had landed in New York in August, 1805, he urged them to come directly to Virginia. "The mountains among which I live will offer you as cool a retreat as can anywhere be found." The stage from Washington via Fredericksburg, he said, passed within one hundred rods of his door "where we shall receive you with joy and be glad to retain you as long as your convenience will permit." If the Barlows came in their own horse and gig, they should take a shorter and better route via Centerville, Culpepper Court House, and Madison's home at Montpelier. When the Barlows decided to go to Connecticut instead of Virginia, they postponed their visit to Monticello.

Later the President extended another invitation, which Barlow eagerly accepted, though he had to go alone because Ruth was not up to the journey. The weather was hot, the time being mid-September, 1808, and Jefferson advised his guest to travel over the hilly roads only during the early morning and evening. In that way he could make the trip easily in three days without inconvenience to himself or his horses. Jefferson sent even more detailed instructions about the route than before. He starred all the places along the road where the beds and food were good. There was a "superlative good" inn at Fauquier Court House but a "wretched" one at a place called Jefferson nine miles farther on.

The president had built Monticello on a single, cone-shaped mountain overlooking Charlottesville. Before Barlow reached the village, he turned off the road from Walton's Tavern at Jefferson's gate and began to ascend a primitive pair of tracks winding upward through virgin forest. There was no hint of the President's husbandry for the first few hundred yards. Then suddenly he came on a cornfield, and presently he burst on to the summit of the mountain. For miles in all directions below him stretched a countryside covered with woods, plantations, and houses. On the western horizon lay the Blue Ridge Mountains. The classic brick house with its pillars, dome, and outbuildings stood in the center of a fine lawn that contrasted sharply with the wild approach.

Barlow found Jefferson surrounded by his children and grandchildren, a family of twelve in all. At five o'clock they were called to dinner, over which Jefferson presided like a patriarch. The table was plentifully but plainly spread, except for Italian and French wines from the host's well-stocked cellar. After dinner Jefferson conducted a social hour that lasted till nine o'clock, following which the host and his guest separated. The next morning Barlow met Jefferson again at the large family table. Breakfast was a substantial meal: coffee or tea, several kinds of hot breads, cold ham, and butter. About ten o'clock everyone dispersed once more. Jefferson went to his ample library to work or supervised the operation of his farm, while Barlow was left to his own devices until a few minutes before dinner. After a few idyllic days at Monticello, Barlow returned to Washington.

2: *Honors and Obloquy*

Life was very pleasant at Kalorama during the first two years of Madison's initial term. Barlow's acres and buildings responded well to his energetic landscaping and improving, and he enjoyed fully his position in the capital as the most important political figure who held no office. When the *Columbiad* appeared, his Republican friends began honoring him publicly. The American Philosophical Society elected him to membership; so did the short-lived United States Military Philosophical Society, which had headquarters at West Point and the ex-President as patron. Josiah Meigs, President of the University of Georgia, conferred on him in absentia an honorary doctor of laws degree, and the citizens of Washington asked him to make the Fourth of July oration in 1809.

Barlow responded to this last honor with an address admirably suited to a patriotic gathering of citizens in a young republic. His ideas were no novelty to any of his friends, but the speech reflected accurately his preoccupations and outlook in his fifty-fifth year. He reiterated his belief that America's potential was magnificent, and he looked forward to the day when United States might contain two hundred million inhabitants. He was thoroughly disenchanted with European politics and wished his listeners to guard well their uniquely successful political institutions. But his speech contained relatively few glittering generalities.

The broad concern of American citizens, he urged, should be public improvement and public instruction. "They are both necessary to the preservation of our principles of government; they are both necessary to the support of the system into which those principles are wrought." By improvements he meant roads, canals, bridges, such things as would bind the states and people together and prevent the fragmentation of the Union because of its huge size. Education, the subject closest to his heart, received his most eloquent words. "A universal system of education . . . is incontestably one of the first duties of government, one of the highest interests of the nation, one of the most sacred rights of the individual . . . without which your republic cannot be supported." Every citizen is a voter, he went on, and if he has not the instruction necessary to withstand the intrigues of the wicked and to preserve what is right, he immediately becomes a tool for knaves, an object and an instrument of corruption.

Fourth of July celebrations in the early years of the republic were gala occasions, and this one was no exception. After the oration Barlow and his friends gathered for a handsome dinner laid at the Center Market. Barlow presided at the head table, assisted by General Mason. Both the attorney-general and the postmaster-general were there. The Marine Band played, and the *National Intelligencer* reported that seventeen regular and many volunteer toasts were proposed, one of which was to Joel Barlow—"American patriot and philanthropist." This was a memorable and satisfying occasion, and when Barlow sent Jefferson a copy of the oration, his friend replied gracefully: "I was doubting what you could say equal to your own reputation on so hackneyed a subject [as the Fourth of July], but you have really risen out of it with lustre."

The only bitterness in Barlow's cup at this period came from the critics who attacked the *Columbiad*. By 1809 the pretentious quarto had been distributed everywhere, and the reviewers had spoken their pieces. Since the dwindling Federalist Party still had a noisy claque, the poem gave anti-Jeffersonian editors a chance to belabor a prominent Republican. The fact that the poem contained many pompous absurdities made the game even more exciting for the Federalist reviewers. Even if the *Columbiad* had been another *Iliad*, it is doubtful if the critics could have read it objectively. Political enemies damned the poem, and political supporters exhausted their superlatives.

The *Port Folio*, magazine edited in Philadelphia by Federalist Joseph Dennie, expressed as well as any publication the case against the *Columbiad*. Its anonymous reviewer dismissed the poem generally as devoid of interest. The work lacked sustained narrative, overdid the allegory, and piled up a discordant mass of characters.

It was full of repetitions and recurring themes. "His sages are presented to your view (as you may see portraits in the window of a print-shop) surrounded by air-pumps and telescopes, piles of books and heaps of chemical apparatus." This critic explained to Barlow how he should have written the poem and only at the end of his essay made the grudging admission that the *Columbiad* was not the worst poem he ever had read. He ranked it with Robert Southey's *Madoc*, another long poem that has achieved among modern readers a massive indifference.

Dennie's publication, however, pretended to be a literary magazine, not a political organ, and when readers complained of the caustic review, the *Port Folio* reprinted a glowing notice from the *London Monthly Magazine*. Dennie insisted: "We know Mr. Barlow only as a poet, and in that capacity he is amenable at the Bar of Criticism." The favorable review went to ridiculous extremes of praise, calling the *Columbiad* "magnificent . . . beyond anything which modern literature has to boast, except the Paradise Lost of Milton." This critic thought some of the images as sublime as he ever had read and found "remarkable variety of scenery and sentiment." He singled out for special commendation the denunciation of slavery and rated the description of Raleigh conducting the first colonists to America as "one of the most finished pictures we have ever seen." The plaudits of this reviewer are so uniformly enthusiastic that one wonders if Federalist Dennie was not subtly sabotaging the *Columbiad* with a surfeit of uncritical approval.

The most serious review of the poem came from the influential pen of Francis Jeffrey in the *Edinburgh Review*. Jeffrey wrote a sixteen-page essay which shows a thoughtful reading of the poem and neither damns without reason nor praises to excess. Commenting unfavorably, he noted: "Mr. Barlow, we are afraid, will not be the Homer of his country . . . in his cumbrous and inflated style, he is constantly mistaking hyperbole for grandeur, and supplying the place of simplicity with huge patches of mere tameness and vulgarity." Jeffrey followed his strictures with nine pages of quotations and a generous summation: "We have no hesitation in saying, that we consider him [Barlow] as a giant, in comparison with any of the puling and paltry rhymsters, who disgrace our English literature by their occasional success. As an Epic poet, we do think his case is desperate; but, as a philosophical and moral poet, we think he has talents of no ordinary value."

The truth of Jeffrey's conclusion was proved by reaction to the poem's ideas. Barlow must have realized that the old charge of atheism would be leveled at the deistic ideas worked into the *Columbiad*. If he did not anticipate such a response, he got a taste of what was to come from Noah Webster, to whom he sent a copy of the poem. His old friend had come to an accommodation with his apostasy so that the two men were able to discuss fruitfully Webster's spelling books and dictionary; but Webster could not bring himself to review the *Columbiad* favorably. "Of the poem, as a poem, I can conscientiously say all, perhaps, which you can expect or desire; but I cannot, in a review, omit to pass a severe censure on the atheistical principles it contains." He went on to repeat privately what he once had written publicly: "No man on earth, not allied to me by nature or marriage, had so large a share in my affections as Joel Barlow, until you renounced the religion, which you once preached, & which I believe." Therefore, he concluded, he would say nothing in print about the *Columbiad*, either for or against.

No such scruple prevented another old friend from leaping into print with an attack on Barlow's so-called atheism. Henri Grégoire, former Bishop of Blois and a leader of the French Revolution, promptly published a pamphlet in Paris: *Critical Observations on the Poem of Mr. Joel Barlow*. Grégoire attributed the excesses of the Revolution to its godlessness and believed that if Europe ever staged a comeback towards moral order, it would do so under the aegis of Christianity. He saw in the *Columbiad* an attack on the Church and felt compelled to demolish Barlow because he was "placed at the summit of the American Parnassus." Grégoire had been disturbed particularly at the poem's final illustration, which shows the destruction of prejudices as the world enters its final state of universal peace and harmony. One of the symbols of prejudice in that picture, along with the crowns of temporal monarchs and the devices of Eastern religions, is the cross, and Grégoire took for his text the sight of the cross lying discarded on the ground.

Though he was a sincere man, his assault on Barlow was really intemperate and uncalled for. Jefferson commented after reading the pamphlet, that Grégoire "must have been eagle-eyed in quest of offense to have discovered ground for it."

Barlow was stung by the criticism of this old friend and had to answer the attack with a pamphlet of his own. It was his only reply to the critics and was a soft answer aimed at turning away wrath. "You have done right in giving him a sugary answer," wrote Jefferson, "but he did not deserve it." Barlow protested that he was not opposed to Christianity and that if he had foreseen the effect of that illustration, he would have suppressed it. The picture of the cross was only a symbol of corrupt, institutionalized Christianity, not of fundamental doctrines. He had no wish to overturn religion and denied that he ever had renounced Christianity. He explained patiently that he had grown up in New England where the Puritan sect allowed no bishops, no mitres, no crucifixes, no censers. If his ancestors had participated in the Crusades, he said, they would have carried no cross but marched without a standard. "The best of Christians of one sect may consider the Christian emblems of another sect, as *prejudices* of a dangerous tendency, and honestly wish to see them destroyed." Then he went on to say that if all Catholics were like his old friend Grégoire, the world would contain nothing but Catholics. He admitted that the *Columbiad* was not a work of genius, "but I *know* it is a moral work."

Barlow's letter to Grégoire was a shrewd defense of a difficult position. The author was still a deist, but he wished to disarm the religious objection to his poem so that the political principles could obtain a hearing. After all, under the Constitution of the United States religion was a private matter. His pamphlet may have convinced readers that he was not a dangerous atheist, but his answer was necessarily ambiguous, as the *Panoplist and Missionary Magazine* pointed out in siding with Grégoire. Yet Barlow mollified his critic somewhat, and the good priest wrote a conciliatory letter the next year. He took pains to absolve Barlow from the charge made against him in America that he once had appeared at the bar of the French National Convention to declare himself an atheist. This, said Grégoire, "is an infamous calumny." He went on generously:

"I likewise remember that you often grieved with me at the sacrilege and cruelties that dishonored certain epochs of the French Revolution, and desolated the hearts of all good men . . . To be calumniated is said to be a tax that the good man pays to the wicked." And he ended his letter by saying: "Our opinions disagree on the principles of religion, but they will always be in unison as to the obligation of loving our fellow creatures and laboring for their happiness."

The wound that Grégoire's attack opened did not heal immediately. When Barlow sent a copy of the cleric's letter with his reply to his Yale classmate Stephen Jacob, he wrote somewhat plaintively that he hoped his old friend would read and understand. He wanted people to think well of him so that he could go on with his plans to do good for his country. "I am now perhaps the only man in America who has sat down with a fixt design to devote his whole resources of mind & industry to the benefit of his country." He added that he had rejected public offices many times to carry out his projects, but despite his intentions, he was misunderstood both in his objects and in his character.

The controversy damped down in time, and the year 1810 began in promising fashion. In the spring Ruth Barlow's health grew better than it had been for years, and life at Kalorama ran on serenely. Barlow went about his planting happily, and early in the season produced salads from his hot bed. By summer Ruth reported to her sister: "Hubby has been so busy, so *busy*, making roads, making hay, and potatoes and cabbages, and at the last he has been making earth," by which she meant he had dug the foundation for his gardener's lodge. In July the Barlows were able to plan their first pleasure excursion since buying Kalorama, and at the beginning of August they departed for a trip into Pennsylvania. Their itinerary led them northwest from Washington into the Allegheny Mountains to Bedford Springs.

The first leg of their journey took them up the Potomac River to its confluence with the Shenandoah at Harper's Ferry. This was the spot that Jefferson called one of the most stupendous scenes in nature: "You stand on a very high point of land. On your right comes up the Shenandoah, having ranged along the foot of the mountain an hundred miles seeking a vent. On your left approaches the Potomac, in quest of a passage also. In the moment of their junction, they rush together against the mountain, rend it asunder, and pass off to the sea." Ruth wrote her sister that the country was sublime. "Mr. Jefferson in his notes on Virginia has so well described it; there is nothing left for me to say."

When the travelers turned north from Harper's Ferry, they had to balance the scenery against the vexations of primitive hostelries. For the first day they had tolerable roads, but when they lodged for the night, Ruth got no rest, "for the bedbugs . . . swarmed not only on the bedstead but on the floors of the chamber." The next day they bounced over rough mountain roads that tore Ruth to pieces. "We made only eighteen miles and stopped to feed the bugs in another place and so continued to the end of our journey, which lasted five days." At Bedford Springs they found a small, clean room, and though Ruth admitted she had "hardly room to swing a cat," she added happily: "Yet I am now quite contented and comfortable . . . Hubby is getting fat and handsome and amiable . . . as an angel."

Before this pleasant vacation ended, however, a minor disaster overtook the Barlows. They were returning home tired and eager to end the trip. On the last day out, night fell when they were within a few miles of Washington. Because neither of them wanted to spend another day on the road, they whipped up the horses and drove on after dark. Within a mile of Kalorama their carriage ran off the road, dashed over a six-foot embankment, and turned over. The vehicle landed upside down and smashed to splinters. Luckily, the horses broke loose from the wreck and ran away, but Joel and Ruth were left struggling in the pitch blackness in the wrecked carriage and "assuring each other . . . that we were still alive." In writing to Clara Baldwin, Joel described Ruth's injuries: "My poor wife found the blood gushing from her face, which is beat to a pummice, both lips cut quite through . . . She had many other bruises about the limbs [but] no bones broke." He hoped the wounds would heal in about a month. Two weeks later Ruth was able to write her sister not to worry about her: "Husband is not yet to be gratified with a young wife. He can't even break his old wife's neck, nor yet her heart."

This optimistic note was followed by a minor chord almost immediately. A week later Ruth came down with a fever, and a month afterwards Joel daily expected to lose her. When General Dearborn wrote to inform them of his wife's death, Joel replied that he dared not break the news to Ruth. "For there is little prospect of her being able to continue many days. The crisis that I have been dreading several years is now at hand & must soon be decided." Then he explained the details of the accident and went on brokenly: "My loss will be greater than yours, for you have children on whom you can rest your affections . . . I have but this one tie to life. That once broken, there is nothing left for me. All that I have seemed to live for is gone."

But the crisis passed, and Ruth recovered, though October and November, 1810, were months of great anxiety. During the following April Joel was able to write General Dearborn again saying that Ruth had made an astonishing comeback: "The shock she received in her fall . . . brought on a total revolution in her system, & though it threw her into a fever which left no hope for two months . . . yet for the last three months she has now been gaining a state of firmness & solidity of constitution greater than she has known for twenty years."

The Barlows were not destined to live quietly after Ruth's recovery. Before the winter ended, they accepted a proposal that would change their fortunes unalterably. The happy life at Kalorama was about to end, despite all previous intentions of remaining in Washington for the rest of their days.

CHAPTER XII

Minister to France

1: *Nomination and Preparation*

By 1811 the final act in one of the great dramas of modern history was beginning. The curtain had gone up on the storming of the Bastille, and it presently would ring down on the Battle of Waterloo. Americans, who had done little more at first than carry spears as supernumeraries, eventually acted important roles. The United States was to emerge at the end of this vast spectacle as a world power, no longer a collection of weak states flung up and down the Atlantic Coast of North America. But first it would have to fight the War of 1812—a conflict that did credit to neither participant but produced important ramifications.

The foreign policy of Washington, Adams, and Jefferson had been aimed at reconciling desire with reality. As a struggling, small nation, the United States had to live with the major powers whose strength and resources were manifestly superior. Washington's administration had negotiated the Jay Treaty, humiliating in some ways but actually the best accommodation that could be obtained. John Adams had resisted the warmongers in his own party and borne the bitter scorn of the opposition to negotiate with France and avoid war. Jefferson had tried economic pressure with the Embargo Act but failed to make England and France drop their systems of blockades under which American ships were pawns in Europe's wars. Nothing short of war seemed to work.

It was inevitable that the United States should become embroiled in Europe's convulsions. Between 1792 and 1807 the annual value of foreign goods (mostly French and English) carried by American ships increased from about half a million dollars to sixty million. Despite blockades and depredations American skippers went everywhere; the number of American ships increased tremendously. Because a cargo of coffee, for example, could be sold in Amsterdam in 1804 for a profit of one hundred thousand dollars, one should not wonder that Yankee merchants took every risk and tried every dodge to keep their ships sailing. American vessels sometimes carried duplicate papers to prove their cargoes either British or French, as the necessity arose. They took advantage of capricious winds that made blockading difficult and slipped into ports they knew were besieged. They loaded produce in the West Indies and tried to claim its origin as the United States by touching at New York or Boston before sailing for Europe. In this international game of hare and hounds hundreds of ships were captured; thousands more eluded the blockades.

As British seapower and French landpower increased simultaneously, the vise tightened on American shipping. The British, after annihilating the French fleet at Trafalgar in 1805, blockaded the coast of Europe from the Elbe to Brest. Napoleon retaliated the next year by issuing his famous Berlin Decree, which declared the British Isles under blockade. Though he had no navy to enforce the order, nevertheless he decreed that any ship stopping at a British port first would not be admitted later to the Continent. England then issued Orders in Council extending the blockade to the entire coast of France and requiring all neutral vessels to clear from British ports and secure licenses before they could be passed through the Continental blockade. Napoleon countered with his Milan Decree, which threatened to seize and confiscate any ship bound to, or coming from, a British port or even stopped for search by a British warship on the high seas.

By the time James Madison was inaugurated as President, the international situation had become incredibly complex. Napoleon

275

went on issuing decrees which harassed American shipping, and the British went on enforcing their Orders in Council. The American government found no way to solve its problems. When the Embargo Act, which closed American ports to all foreign shipping, became such a political liability that it had to be repealed, Madison's administration passed a non-intercourse act. This measure, though less drastic, was designed to exclude French and British goods from the United States and to prevent American ships from trading with England and France. It also produced no happy results and was followed by still another effort, the Macon Bill, which dangled a special inducement before England and France. In this bill the United States offered to resume trade with either country if it would repeal its decrees or orders against American shipping. But by the middle of 1810 America was close to war with both countries. Eventually the American ministers to France and England came home and left only chargés d'affaires representing the United States in London and Paris.

Both France and Britain had given the United States ample grounds for war, but fighting two major powers at once was beyond American capability. Napoleon fortunately provided a way out of the dilemma. Late in 1810 he pretended to have revoked both the Berlin and Milan decrees against American shipping, and President Madison accordingly proclaimed that the non-intercourse act henceforth would be invoked against England. To a Republican President, America's traditional friend France seemed the lesser enemy, and Madison tentatively decided to send another minister to Paris in hopes that Napoleon could be held to his word. The President had little confidence that any emissary could do it, but there seemed no satisfactory alternative to this plan. The United States really was not prepared to fight anyone.

The President had no trouble picking a well-qualified man to send to France. His obvious choice was Joel Barlow, his public-spirited neighbor who knew France intimately. Madison's chief task was to persuade his friend to accept the mission, for Barlow knew as well as anyone in the Administration that the chances of success were pretty slim. He had meant it in 1804 when he resolved to leave France for good, and since establishing himself at Kalorama, he had realized that he was growing old. The time had come to trim his sail to the storms of time. The President, however, apparently made a strong call to patriotism and probably a subtle appeal to ego, for he succeeded in winning Barlow's consent to return to France.

Madison was a shrewd judge of men and a hard person to resist. When he offered the appointment to his friend, he knew that Barlow was not so reluctant to accept public office as he pretended to be. Fulton had written Madison before the inauguration that Barlow would make an excellent Secretary of State and said further that Barlow would accept the position if it were offered. When Madison realized that Barlow was hankering after a cabinet post, he wrote him directly to explain that he already was committed to name someone else Secretary of State. The President broke this news to Barlow with masterful tact: "I owe it to my high respect for your talents, and my confidence in your principles, and the purity of your patriotic zeal, to say that no abatement in the continuance of either of those sentiments is implied by the course which I have deemed . . . most advisable for the public service."

Barlow had immediate misgivings about accepting the subsequent appointment as Minister to France. He wrote General Dearborn that "the sacrifice of ease & comfort on my part is too great & the prospect of doing good to the public too little" for him to take any pleasure in the coming mission. To Jefferson, who congratulated him on the appointment, he replied: "I have seen too much of the world to promise myself any pleasure from a further acquaintance with it." Jefferson agreed with his pessimism: "Your doubts whether any good can be effected with the Emperor of France are too well grounded . . . Of the principles and advantages of commerce he appears ignorant, and his domineering temper deafens him moreover to the dictates of interest, of honor and of morality. A nation like ours . . . can never enjoy the favor of such a character."

At the end of February the President sent Barlow's nomination to the Senate, and the next day the upper house debated his fitness. The opposition made a strong attack, charging Barlow with a long list of derelictions, moral and political. They said he stood debtor to the United States treasury for a large amount that dated back to his mission to Algiers. They claimed that he had gone to France poor and returned rich without any proper explanation of how he made his money. It was hinted, furthermore, that he had speculated in American claims against France by inside knowledge of the Louisiana Purchase. Other opponents objected to him because he had lived in France too long and was a French citizen. Some opposed him on grounds that he was an atheist. They even complained that Barlow was a poet, a dealer in visions, and thus not a suitable person to deal with things of this world. Finally, it was said, Barlow was not fit because he had had no mercantile experience.

When the opposition completed its innings, Barlow's supporters answered the attack. Henry Clay produced a letter from the Treasury Department saying that Barlow's accounts were closed and that he owed the government nothing. As an amateur diplomat Barlow never had known until his nomination that his accounts were any concern of the Treasury. Putting matters straight, however, required only the merest formality. Clay went on to observe that if being an honorary citizen of France were an objection, then neither George Washington nor Alexander Hamilton would have been suitable men to send as Minister to France. The most surprising defense of Barlow's fitness came from that rabid New England Federalist Timothy Pickering, former Secretary of State and then Senator from Massachusetts.

Pickering had listened to the objections and made notes as the debate went on, and after Clay sat down, he took the floor. He may have hoped to infuriate Madison's Republican enemies by supporting the nomination, but in any event he proceeded to put a few matters in proper perspective. He had to admit first that he had no reason to be pleased with Mr. Barlow: "On the contrary, his conduct, at the time when the French Directory most grossly insulted the Government of the United States, appeared to be very reprehensible." Nevertheless, continued Pickering, he had known Mr. Barlow as chaplain in the Revolutionary army, and at that time he had sustained a good character. He had maintained it until 1788 when he went to France—that "Whore of Babylon which had polluted the world." There he had renounced his belief in Christianity, though he had not become an atheist. Barlow was a deist, but his being a deist could not be a serious objection to the majority of people of the United States "who raised to higher offices—the highest in the nation—men whose faith was doubtless the same."

Answering further charges, Pickering went on to say that he did not know how Mr. Barlow got rich in France, but if he were objectionable because he was rich, he could not also be objectionable because he was a visionary poet. The Senator observed dryly that apparently Mr. Barlow understood the world as well as poetry. Furthermore, Pickering declared, the fact that Barlow had lived in France for a long time did not mean he was attached to France at the expense of his own country. On the contrary, he had lived there long enough to become perfectly acquainted with the French government and disgusted with it. He concluded by saying that Barlow had an intimate knowledge of France, was widely read, and well qualified as a diplomat. Therefore, he was disposed to vote in favor of the appointment.

Pickering's defense assured Barlow's easy confirmation despite the bitter attacks of General Samuel Smith, Madison's implacable Republican critic from Maryland, and a scattering of Federalists. When the nomination was voted on, it passed by twenty-one to nine. George Erving, soon to be Minister to Denmark, was there and wrote: "Our General S. raved like a madman about it; he called B. a man of small talents!! . . . Pickering looked him full in the face & told him that there was no man amongst them so fit for the office." Erving noted also that the appointments of Monroe, Livingston, and Armstrong, Barlow's predecessors as Minister to France, had been approved by smaller majorities.

Before Barlow left for France, the State Department blew apart in a very public explosion. The demolition crew was the Smith brothers of Baltimore: Samuel, the general and Senator, and Robert, a mediocrity. The former planted the charge when he forced the President to accept the latter as Secretary of State in the interest of party harmony. Madison had to fire Secretary Smith in mid-March after two years of accumulating differences. Smith opposed the administration's conciliatory stance towards France and its stiff attitude towards England and tried ineptly to sabotage the President's foreign policy. The Secretary's ouster need not have been noisy, for Madison offered Smith the position of Minister to Russia to save face. But Smith did not go quietly to St. Petersburg. Instead, he talked to his brother and other dissident Republicans, who aroused his anger and then were unable to keep him from digging his political grave. In June, 1811, Smith embarrassed the administration by publishing a pamphlet revealing policy differences within the Cabinet. He printed confidential documents in a highly improper manner and thus complicated the President's already difficult job of dealing with England and France.

The defection of Secretary Smith could not go unchallenged. Some articulate spokesman close to the President would have to answer the attack. Barlow was willing and able. Within a month after Smith's blast appeared, he issued a pamphlet in rebuttal: *Review of Robert Smith's Address.* Barlow wrote Fulton on July seventeenth: "The review of Smith's address will appear in a day or two in a pamphlet in Philadelphia. Binns writes that he is publishing an edition of five thousand copies. It must not be known who wrote it." With Barlow at Kalorama when he wrote the pamphlet, was his old friend William Lee, consul at Bordeaux, who jotted down ideas and supplied him with up-to-date information about France.

Barlow responded to this summons like an old bird dog recalled for a final hunt. The zest of his early political pamphleteering returned, and he dropped the elevated tone of his recent essay urging a national university and his Fourth of July oration. His review of Smith began: "An opinion had long prevailed with many persons, both in and out of Congress, that Mr. Secretary Smith, from want of capacity and want of integrity, was quite unfit for his place." He went on to cite the "miserable intrigue" that originally got Smith into the Cabinet and damned the ex-Secretary's pamphlet as a "gross immorality" and "a stab into the vitals of Executive Government." When he warmed to the attack, he wrote: "The Ex-Secretary complains that he was often opposed, reined in and goaded on by the President. An animal with longer ears than Mr. Smith . . . would utter the same complaint." And again: "Robert Smith never opposed anything in the cabinet. He had not vigor of mind enough to support an argument, even on the right side of a question."

In addition to the ridicule and blunt censure, Barlow addressed himself seriously to Smith's attack on Madison's conduct of foreign policy. Barlow argued that the non-importation bill, which Smith said he opposed, was the best measure against England and France that Madison could obtain from a Congress that would no longer support outright embargo. He also pointed out quite correctly that Smith had crippled the President's negotiations with England. His questioning of French sincerity in the professed revocation of the Berlin and Milan decrees made it difficult for Madison to persuade the British to repeal their Orders in Council against American shipping. If the Secretary of State did not believe the French decrees had been abandoned, how could England be convinced? Thus Smith did great mischief "in furnishing to the British government a pretext for persisting in its orders in council."

Robert Smith torpedoed his political career by his attack on the President, but whether or not he did irreparable damage to American diplomacy is hard to assess. Barlow's spirited defense no doubt helped neutralize the domestic effect of Smith's pamphlet, and it certainly earned the author a warm thanks from the President. But the British felt no compelling reason yet to end their restrictions and continued to demand proof of Napoleon's change in heart. The most immediate result of Smith's ouster was the appointment of James Monroe as Secretary of State, and when Barlow left for France he again was under the direction of the man who had sent him to Algiers sixteen years before.

For five months after his nomination and confirmation Barlow waited for his sailing orders. The President was trying to decide whether or not he really ought to send a minister to France. Madison wanted assurances that Napoleon was living up to his supposed repeal of the Berlin and Milan decrees, in return for which the United States had imposed non-importation against England. The President was waiting for his minister to England, William Pinkney, to return to America on the warship *Essex* in late spring. Pinkney would have recent dispatches from Jonathan Russell, American chargé d'affaires in Paris, and on those reports a decision could be based. Weeks went by with no news of the *Essex*, while diplomacy marked time, but finally after a forty-nine-day passage the ship reached America at the end of June. Russell's dispatches, however, were inconclusive, and the President postponed his decision a little longer. Then at length a favorable report arrived in mid-July on another ship, and the Secretary of State prepared Barlow's instructions.

Monroe wrote Barlow that the first objective of his mission was to obtain payment of American claims against France for the past spoliation of American shipping. The United States admitted the right of France to close its ports to American ships under the Berlin and Milan decrees if it wished, but Monroe instructed Barlow to demand payment for vessels illegally seized. Napoleon, for instance, had ordered all American ships confiscated that came to French ports after the Embargo Act was passed. His pretext was that because all American vessels were forbidden to sail, any American ship on the seas must be in British service. This order deliberately ignored the fact that scores of American ships were legally at sea when the Embargo went into effect. His subordinates were even more high-handed. There was one case on record in which sailors on an American ship were bribed to say that their ship had been boarded by a British warship and thus made liable to seizure under the Milan Decree.

Barlow's second objective was to obtain for the future normal trade relations with France. He was therefore to police the supposed revocation of the Berlin and Milan decrees to make certain that Napoleon did not go back on his word. He was to convince the French that trade restrictions between the two countries were mutually disadvantageous. He was to get rid of the licensing system by which French consuls in the United States granted export permits to American shippers. He was to remove the endless delays in French ports, the snarls of red tape, and the exorbitant duties levied on American goods. If France wanted to exclude all American trade, summarized Monroe in the instructions, she ought to say so clearly, but for her to ask for trade and then to harass it endlessly was an inadmissable practice between friendly nations.

Barlow's trunks were packed, and he was ready to leave the moment he received his orders. He had rented Kalorama to the new French minister, Louis Sérurier, who arrived in February, and he had put his affairs in order. His household now consisted of two additional persons: Tom Barlow, the nephew he was sending through Yale, whom he had invited to go along to finish his education in Paris; Clara Baldwin, Ruth's younger half-sister, who had been married and deserted and had come to live with Ruth and Joel the preceding winter. Besides the Barlow household, the Minister to France added two more members to his entourage: William Lee, who was returning to Bordeaux, and David Baillie Warden, the new consul to Paris.

The send-off for Europe began with suitable fanfare. The Secretary of the Navy ordered the Frigate *Constitution* (*Old Ironsides*) to Annapolis in July to stand by to take the diplomatic mission to France. Five days after Monroe wrote the instructions, the Barlows left Washington by carriage for the site of the future naval academy. They were accompanied to Annapolis by the Benjamin Latrobes, who went to see them off, and early on the morning of August first they boarded the frigate. Fifteen minutes after Barlow and his party were piped on board, the captain issued sailing orders. The *Constitution* weighed anchor and moved down the Chesapeake Bay under full canvas.

The next day, as the ship lay at anchor in Hampton Roads, Barlow wrote Fulton a poignant letter. Ruth was in excellent spirits; the captain and officers were amiable; the discipline on board the frigate was harmonious and perfect; the ship was a model of cleanliness and comfort; and they had a fair prospect for a speedy passage. "But my heart is heavy. I have left my country, possibly & why not probably forever ... I go with an ardent wish, but without much hope of doing good & with the full intention, though with a feeble hope, of living to return." He wrote again on August fifth, his last letter from the United States, dated "off the Capes of Virginia": "God bless our dear friends, Harriet & Fulton. Our health & spirits are pretty good. I wish the prospects of success in this mission were as good as that of a fine passage."

Despite gloomy forebodings, Barlow could not help enjoying the grandeur of his position. The contrast was vast between his trip to France as a penniless young man in 1788 and his return on board the *Constitution*. As he sat in the spacious wardroom at the stern of the gundeck, he must have remembered the miserable, vermin-infested, cubby hole he had occupied on the French packet and his perpetual seasickness from New York to Le Havre. On this trip he, Joel Barlow, was the reason for the special voyage of a fifty-two-gun frigate manned by a crew of four hundred and fifty. He took pride in his country's growth and determined to pour into his mission every skill and to utilize every experience he had acquired in his eventful career.

The frigate *Constitution* already had a distinguished history when it carried the Barlows to France in 1811. She had been built at Edmund Hartt's shipyard in Boston and launched in 1797 during the trouble with France. A trim, fast, graceful ship, the frigate had been fashioned from timbers of solid live oak, hard pine, and red cedar. The bolts, copper sheathing, and brasswork had been supplied by Paul Revere, and the sails were made on Park Street in Boston. The ship had taken part in the war with the Barbary pirates, and the peace treaty with Tripoli had been signed in the captain's quarters on the gundeck. When Barlow boarded the frigate, it was captained by Isaac Hull, who soon became famous in the War of 1812.

At seven p.m. on Tuesday, August sixth, the *Constitution* passed Cape Henry Light, and Barlow saw the coast of the United States for the last time. The wind stood fair for France. The next day all the passengers were seasick, but their indisposition was only temporary. The voyage was smooth and swift, and by the seventeenth the frigate was off the Grand Banks of Newfoundland making nine or ten knots. The passengers amused themselves with games and pets. Clara Baldwin and Warden took turns beating each other in backgammon, while Ruth Barlow looked after her two caged mocking birds. Though the birds died during the voyage, the wardroom also was equipped with a tame raccoon trained as a mouser. All the passengers and crew alike laughed at the antics of several loose squirrels that scampered up and down the rigging. In the wardroom with the ship's officers the Barlows enjoyed dinners that began with mock turtle soup and were embellished by madeira and claret from the captain's locker. The food was good, for the ship carried an ample supply of livestock and poultry. The most disturbing feature of the crossing was the daily sight of several hundred sailors living like ants in an anthill. While the officers and passengers enjoyed plenty of space, the crew had fewer comforts than prisoners in jail. Nevertheless, the morale was high, the gunners expert, and the ship well manned.

On September sixth the *Constitution* approached the coast of France and sighted a blockading British squadron. Captain Hull, taking no chances, beat to quarters and cleared the ship for action. There was no incident, however, and the British commander's ship, after sending a small boat alongside, waved them on to Cherbourg. Before noon the frigate dropped her starboard anchor in the French harbor and received on board the port's quarantine officers. Twenty-four hours later the yellow quarantine flag was lowered, and on the eighth Barlow left the ship for Paris. As he departed, the frigate fired a seventeen-gun salute to speed him on his way. His mission was beginning in earnest, but whether or not it could succeed, he would have to wait to find out.

2: *Failure of a Mission*

Barlow's return to Paris touched him far deeper than he expected. After a ten-day trip from Cherbourg the Minister and his lady, plus Clara Baldwin and Tom Barlow, reached the capital and moved into their old house at 50 rue de Vaugirard. The sight of the old rooms and his cherished garden made Barlow suddenly realize that France still was his second country. He had left youth and innocence in Paris, and everywhere he looked there were promptings to memory. He wrote a friend: "We have moved into our own good, convenient . . . house, which is really one of the best in Paris. The garden planted with my own hands is doubly interesting from our absence of seven years, especially as the trees & shrubs are grown up to thickets. Our old French friends too are very affectionate, & we find more of them than we expected. How much more cordial & friendly my reception is here than it was in any part of our own country [New England] except at your house & one or two others!" During the first week back in Paris they received a warm welcome from everyone, expatriate Americans, French neighbors, and former retainers. Even "our ancient servants are pressing round us with tears of gratitude & attachment," Barlow wrote.

The abundant cordiality raised Barlow's hopes that his mission might be successful after all. He immediately announced his arrival to the French foreign minister, the Duc de Bassano, and presented his credentials on the twenty-first. Because Napoleon had departed for Holland the day Barlow arrived in Paris, he could not be presented at court for some weeks, but the Duc was extremely cooperative and offered to start negotiations right away without waiting on formalities. Barlow called on the foreign minister again the next day and spent two hours patiently explaining the American point of view and outlining the objectives that he was instructed to obtain. The Duc seemed very understanding and insisted that France wanted very much to smooth relations with the United States. But having said that, he left Paris to join Napoleon in Amsterdam and turned over further discussions to a subordinate. His deputy, Jean Baptiste Petry, continued the talks but had no authority to conduct negotiations and spaced the parleys as far apart as possible. The net result of the absence of Napoleon and his foreign minister was to postpone serious diplomacy until the court returned to Paris.

In November Barlow met Napoleon face to face for the first time in many years. He had known the Emperor slightly when he was General Bonaparte preparing to lead an army to Egypt. This had been in 1797-1798 after Barlow returned from Algiers. He remembered Napoleon as an anti-social little man who scarcely talked at social functions unless he could get off in a corner to discuss military and political problems. Now Barlow prepared to confront the man who had conquered an empire, whose armies controlled Europe from the Baltic Sea to the Adriatic. To a confirmed republican the presentation at court was most distasteful.

Barlow went to St. Cloud for a private audience with the Emperor, dressed in a "plain bottle green coat" with "no ornaments or frippery about him." William Lee in full dress accompanied him as far as the *salon des ambassadeurs* where the Duc de Bassano met them. The foreign minister then went in to ask the Emperor's pleasure, after which Lee surrendered the Minister to a pair of *maîtres des cérémonies* in full regalia carrying ivory-headed, black walnut canes. These functionaries threw open the doors and took Barlow to the head of a huge flight of stairs where the head *maître des cérémonies* took over and escorted the Minister into Napoleon's cabinet. On entering the room, Barlow unbent to the amenities of the situation enough to bow at the threshold, again half way across the chamber, and a third time as he was presented to Napoleon. The American Minister then surrendered his letter of credence and delivered the platitudes expected of a diplomat meeting a chief of state.

Later Clara Baldwin, with fine republican irreverence, sent a secondhand report of this interview to a friend at home. "The great man has returned and Mr. B. has been presented to him . . . he was obliged to go through a deal of ceremony to get to him. He had a private audience, a monstrous honor, let me tell you . . . From the quantity of gold and jewels he passed through to get to him, you might reasonably suppose the mines of Peru and Golconda were in the court yard of St. Cloud where everyone loaded themselves before entering the palace." Clara went on to describe her brother-in-law's garb, the bowing and scraping, and Napoleon's response after Barlow's speech of greeting. The Emperor also made a speech "but stammered, looked on the floor, stopped, repeated, and at last finished." He paid Barlow a personal compliment and "said he was great enough to be just." Whereupon Joel "bowed and retreated and retreated and bowed till he got out of his august presence without turning. So ended the first chapter." In writing to Dolley Madison the next month, the Minister himself reported: "I have got to be a prodigious fine gentleman & a perfect courtier."

The first chapter was not really over, however, until the end of the year. Barlow was hopeful but noncommittal when he wrote a friend in November: "I have nothing decisive to say on public business. My reception by the emperor has been personally kind &

flattering, but officially neither one thing nor t'other." A month later he sent a cautiously optimistic message to Madison following a second audience with Napoleon. This time he had been to a large gathering on the anniversary of the Emperor's coronation. In passing around the circle of diplomats, Napoleon had stopped at Barlow and smiled.

"Well, Monsieur, you know how to oppose the English," he said, alluding to the recent battle between the American *President* and the English *Little Belt* off Sandy Hook. In that encounter the British ship had been badly mauled when it refused to stop for questioning by the American frigate on coastal patrol.

"Sire, we know how to make them respect our flag," replied Barlow. Napoleon completed the circle of guests and returned to the American Minister.

"Monsieur, you have presented an interesting note to the Duc de Bassano. It is going to be answered immediately and satisfactorily, and I hope the frigate waits for that reply."

"Sire, she waits only for that."

It was true. Barlow had kept the *Constitution* in French waters ever since he had arrived in September. He hoped that he could send it home with news that the French formally had agreed to pay American claims and restore normal trade relations between the two countries. The note that Napoleon referred to was a long essay reviewing Franco-American affairs in which Barlow argued the American position convincingly. Barlow added in his report to the President that the Emperor's attention to him at the public reception was so extraordinary that it seemed to mark an official change of attitude. "As it cannot be on my own account, but on that of the government, it is proper I should notice to you that he & all the grand dignitaries of the empire have taken pains to signalize their attention to me in a manner they have rarely done to a foreign minister, & never to an American."

At this point Barlow's mission seemed to be going so well that he pressed the Duc de Bassano for an immediate statement of French policy towards the United States. He drew up a memorandum on December twenty-eighth and took it to the foreign minister to sign. The paper declared that goods of the United States and the French colonies should be received free in French ports and that no future cause whatever should warrant capture or detention of American ships, except suspicion of forged papers. Moreover, the paper stated that the Emperor would release all remaining United States ships and seamen in his ports as fast as proof of American ownership and nationality could be established. This memorandum was intended to accomplish at a stroke the second of Barlow's objectives—the restoration of normal trade relations. Getting France to pay for previously confiscated property would be far more difficult and had better be negotiated separately. To Barlow's chagrin, when the Duc de Bassano was confronted with a written statement of all the assurances he had made orally, he refused to sign it. His government was not prepared to commit anything to writing.

As Barlow composed his dispatches for the Secretary of State on New Year's Eve, he had to conclude that Napoleon had no serious intention of keeping his promises. The pessimism he and Madison had shared the preceding summer in Washington was quite obviously justified. All the protestations of the foreign minister and the smooth phrases of the Emperor were worth nothing. The Duc insisted that Napoleon had agreed to everything, that the Berlin and Milan decrees had been revoked, that American property would be respected; but orders to carry out those declarations had not been given to the minister of marine or the captains of privateers. If Barlow could have read the correspondence now buried in the archives of the French foreign ministry, he would have known for sure that his mission was hopeless.

Napoleon's policy for years had been to involve England and the United States in war. He did not want a rupture with the United States because France needed American shipping to supply her with needed food and raw materials. Nor did he want England to rescind the Orders in Council which were driving the United States and England towards a break. Hence Napoleon's plan was to give just enough ground to keep America from invoking her non-intercourse act against France but not enough to give England grounds for calling off her Orders in Council. At the same time, the suspension of American trade was hurting England, and the British ministry was becoming increasingly interested in discovering a way to end the impasse. Joel Barlow found himself playing an international poker game, but Napoleon and the ministry in London held all the high cards and dealt from a marked deck. Without military power to back up his diplomacy, Barlow could only bluff.

The best course, the American Minister concluded, was to persuade the French that war between the United States and England was a foregone conclusion. Napoleon's pleasure over the *President-Little Belt* fight suggested that he interpreted that action (incorrectly) as marking the outbreak of hostilities between England and the United States. If Barlow could convince him that this was so, he might be lulled into making a specific enough commitment to the United States to induce England to end the Orders in Council. He wrote the President: "You will have perceived that the pole-star from which I have all along graduated my compass was to remove the cause of war with England. The object of this government being directly contrary, you will easily discern at least one of the causes of the delays they have practiced not only in completing the arrangements I had prepared, but in answering official letters on pressing subjects."

The year 1811 ended with the United States still caught between two fires. On New Year's Day William Lee wrote Madison privately saying that up to that moment everyone in France had expected Barlow's mission to succeed completely. Merchants in France had been buoyed up by the prospect of improved commercial relations with America, but Napoleon suddenly seemed to have changed his mind. Lee did not realize that Barlow had forced the Emperor's hand by asking the Duc de Bassano to sign a memorandum stating that the obnoxious Berlin and Milan decrees had been repealed.

Despite a brief period of optimism that hindsight proves unwarranted, Barlow turned out to be an able, tough, realistic negotiator who suffered from few illusions. Monsieur Petry, who dealt with Barlow when the foreign minister was in Holland, found him a cold, aloof, cautious adversary, who kept himself at arm's length. Another of the Duc's subordinates reported that "Mr. Barlow has a mettlesome character and is hard to handle. He does not depart from his American stubbornness." Lee wrote Madison that "Mr.

Barlow's deportment is just what a minister's ought to be; he goes to all the circles of the court, sees & hears all he can—believes as much as he ought to."

The Minister kept the tone of his official correspondence analytical and formal, but in personal letters he let his fears and anxieties show. He was intensely eager to hear off-the-record opinions from home of his conduct in France. When he sent Dolley Madison a fourteen-pound sugar beet to put in her garden, he took the opportunity to say some things he could not write the President directly. "I have been here three months at work very hard for our blessed country; yet I am afraid I shall have produced but little effect & the president may think I have been idle. If he should approve my conduct, I wish you would let me know it. For you cannot realize how much I am attached to him & his administration."

Mrs. Madison used her intimacy with the Barlows to relay unofficial information, and in the same letter that she thanked them for sending her the latest Paris fashions, she also warned Joel against indiscretion. Barlow had written of his negotiations to Postmaster-General Granger, who had promptly published the news in the paper. Mrs. Madison said: "As I promised to write you everything, personal or impersonal, you will pardon me if I say aught that gives you pain." She then reported Granger's stupidity but softened her reproach by pretending that criticism of the disclosure had come "from the people, not the Cabinet." She concluded: "Yet you know everything vibrates there." No doubt the President had prompted her to send this admonition.

The vexations of diplomacy did not stop the residents of the American legation from savoring the attractions of Napoleonic Paris. Their social calendar was filled with diplomatic dinners, official receptions, and invitations from old friends. They entertained Volney when he came to town, asked Lafayette in to dine, and during the summer of 1812 visited their neighbor Madame de Villette at her country place outside Paris. The carnival season that winter, especially brilliant, filled the streets with parades of masked figures and carriages. On February eleventh the *Boeuf Gris* circulated about the streets all day dressed with flowers and colored streamers and followed by one hundred butchers on horseback. That night the Emperor gave a masked ball that Barlow and Lee attended. While the spectators came in full dress, the court ladies wore masks and dressed as characters, and the courtiers added splashes of color in bright dominoes. Despite the gaiety, the luxury displayed at court in a country bled white by Napoleon's wars repelled the Americans.

With one exception, the Barlow menage was on the go constantly. Joel kept busy with official business and writing dispatches, while Ruth, whose good health amazed her husband, went everywhere. The Minister wrote Dolley Madison: "You cannot think how my precious wife has renewed her life since her terrible fever of last winter. She has not known so much health before in twenty years." Young Tom Barlow took to Paris with all the zest his uncle had displayed more than two decades before. Joel informed Tom's older brother: "Tom is happy as a prince." He was "sucking the milk and honey" from four colleges at once. "He takes chemistry from one, natural philosophy from another, and astronomy from a third, and . . . at the fourth . . . he takes his mathematics, his fencing, dancing, drawing, and French." Tom was living at one of his colleges but spending his week ends at 50 rue de Vaugirard.

Only Clara Baldwin, who was confined to the house with some kind of a knee injury, did not make the most of Paris. When Ruth invited Mrs. Madison's sister to visit them, she added: "Poor Clara is obliged to reserve her manslaughter for next winter." But "poor Clara" was a gay spirit whose presence, despite her disability, added seasoning to the Barlow household. She refused to let her brother-in-law take himself too seriously, and Joel in turn carried on a lively duel with her. When she went to the country to recuperate at Daniel Parker's château, Joel wrote her: "You have mistaken, dear Clara, the motive I had for getting you married. It was not precisely to get you off my hands, or out of the family, though that might be a very laudable motive considering the mischief you do in exciting your sister to rebellion. But it was rather for your own sake, to get you as soon as possible into a state of discipline, wholesome correction, regular conjugal torment for the good of your soul."

Besides the official difficulties of his mission Barlow encountered the same financial problems that always have plagued American diplomats. The Minister's salary was only half enough to pay for the scale of living he had to maintain. He wrote General Bradley, Senator from Vermont and chairman of the Republican caucus: "It is impossible to have your work well done here . . . without raising the salary of your minister . . . I have spent more than my outfit & an year's salary in furnishing my house & living here three months . . . I can stand this expense as long perhaps as most men whom the President would be likely to send. But it is not your intention to make bankrupts of your public servants." He already had written the Secretary of State soon after reaching Paris that the salary ought to be from twelve to fifteen thousand dollars. The minister either had to double his own salary, as Robert Livingston had done, or keep himself out of French society, as Major Armstrong had done. He added: "I naturally and habitually love simplicity and have an aversion to luxury, but my duty requires that in this respect I should give up my own taste."

When Barlow saw that France did not intend to satisfy American grievances, he shifted his efforts to another quarter. He now concentrated on stopping the imminent war between the United States and England. Though the Duc de Bassano would not put it into writing that the Berlin and Milan decrees had been revoked for American shipping, Barlow tried nevertheless to prove the truth of the Duc's oral assurances to Jonathan Russell, now chargé d'affaires in London. Barlow was able to make something of a case because the French actually had slackened off in their depredations. They had seized only forty-five American ships since the decrees supposedly were rescinded less than two years before. That figure, compared with the five hundred and fifty-eight ships captured between 1803 and 1810, made the French contention somewhat plausible.

Early in January Barlow sent Russell prima-facie evidence of the revoked decrees. The ship *Acastus*, which recently had been boarded by the British, captured by the French, and taken to a French port, had been restored to its owner with the cargo intact. Moreover, several other ships, which he listed in subsequent letters, had arrived in France in the past several months after touching England and had been admitted to French ports. Recently, every ship (some thirty to forty) loaded wholly with American goods and sailing directly from America had been respected. He concluded: "Since my arrival in September last, there has not been a single instance of the application of the Berlin and Milan decrees to an American vessel or cargo." Barlow also was having some success in obtaining release of cargoes and crews seized earlier. The foreign ministry's archives are filled with a bombardment of letters from the American Minister asking redress for specific cases of capture or confiscation. Barlow's dogged persistence pried loose one minor concession after another from the reluctant foreign minister.

Jonathan Russell in London relayed Barlow's information to the British ministry and hopefully waited for England to revoke her Orders in Council. British manufacturers and merchants were clamoring for that deed as loudly as the American State Department. But the Duc de Bassano must have sensed that Barlow might be succeeding in his strategy, for on March tenth he delivered a report to the French Senate in which he declared that the Berlin and Milan decrees had not been revoked. That assertion, when it was reported in London, checked Barlow's preceding gambit.

Meantime, Barlow was trying a different tack in his efforts to obtain smooth commercial relations with France. He drafted a proposed treaty and sent it to the Duc with cogent arguments for its approval. In submitting a treaty Barlow went beyond his instructions from Secretary Monroe, but he sent a copy to the State Department and asked if he could proceed with negotiations. Monroe replied that the United States did not see the need for a formal treaty; everything Washington demanded could be accomplished by unilateral French action. But if Barlow felt a treaty was desirable, he could go ahead—provided that he was able to obtain provision in it for paying the spoliation claims.

Barlow had two aims in trying to negotiate a treaty: he wanted a cover for his more important efforts to head off the war with England, and he hoped that a treaty might force France into a public commitment. If a treaty could be worked out, it certainly would put American trade on a more rational basis than before. The correspondence between French word and deed ought to be closer if a public instrument were drawn spelling out mutual obligations. The Duc de Bassano was equally agreeable to discussing a treaty, for it offered him endless opportunities to procrastinate and thus carry out Napoleon's cat and mouse game. The treaty talks began about the first of the year 1812 and went on and on.

When the British refused to repeal their Orders in Council because of the Duc's report to the French Senate, Barlow sent a sharp note to the French foreign office. He demanded to know what the Duc meant by saying one thing to the Senate and another to him. The foreign minister was in a tight spot and knew it. Napoleon was about to begin his tremendous campaign in Russia and could not afford a break with the United States. Barlow followed up his note with a visit to the ministry and insisted that proof be furnished him of the repeal of the decrees. When he pounded on the table, he finally got some action.

Confronted by the American Minister in a fine rage, the Duc picked up a paper and handed it across the table. Barlow read the document and scarcely was able to conceal his astonishment and indignation. It was the Decree of St. Cloud, dated April 28, 1811, stating unequivocally that the Berlin and Milan decrees no longer applied to American shipping. For a year the United States had been trying to get France to produce just such a document. Barlow reported this remarkable interview to Monroe: "I made no comment on the strange manner in which it [the decree] had been so long concealed from me . . . I only asked him if that decree had been published. He said no; but declared it had been communicated to my predecessor here, and likewise to Mr. Sérurier, with orders to communicate it to you. I assured him that it was not among the archives of this legation; that I never before had heard of it."

The Decree of St. Cloud, in fact, had not existed more than a few days. The Duc had manufactured it for just such an emergency as he faced when Barlow's demands could no longer be resisted. He did not fool Barlow by producing the decree, nor did he fool Madison, who was equally angry at the French duplicity: "The conduct of the French government . . . will be an everlasting reproach to it," he wrote Barlow. Unfortunately for the United States, the Duc had managed to hold off the American Minister just long enough.

Barlow received a copy of the post-dated decree on the evening of May eleventh, a day or two after his sharp exchange with the foreign minister. The next day he sent a courier to the coast where the American warship *Wasp* waited his orders. Eight days later Jonathan Russell transmitted this decree to Lord Castlereagh. The English ministry, under heavy economic pressure at home, finally had to make good its promise to revoke the Orders in Council on receipt of proof of reciprocal French action. The ministry dallied, however, and not until June twenty-sixth was Russell able to send Monroe a copy of the repeal of the Orders in Council. Meantime, in Washington on June seventeenth Congress had declared war on Great Britain.

The war which neither country really wanted was under way at last, thanks to the guile of Napoleon and his ministers and the painful slowness of communications in 1812. If the British Cabinet had acted quickly when the Decree of St. Cloud was delivered to them, the war perhaps could have been averted. With good winds a fast ship might have made the Atlantic crossing in a month, and the revocation of the Orders in Council might have been received in the United States before the fatal war resolution had been passed. The war of 1812 certainly could not have begun in an era of steamships and transatlantic cables. The failure of Barlow's mission, which had seemed almost inevitable in 1811, now became a painful reality.

3: *The Last Futility*

The Duc de Bassano sent the spurious Decree of St. Cloud to Barlow and then left immediately to join Napoleon in the East for the Russian campaign. He turned the snail-paced treaty talks over to his chief deputy, the Duc de Dalberg, with orders to keep Monsieur Barlow talking as long as possible. If any French port official, judge, or privateer captain ever heard of the St. Cloud Decree, he had to find out about it for himself. The Duc departed without giving any instructions that American ships were not to be molested. In fact, not until the end of June when he was off in Wilna did he even ask Napoleon's permission to issue such an order. By then the Emperor was so busy fighting the Russians that he could not be bothered with the United States. Thus Franco-American relations bumped along pretty much as they had for several years.

The outbreak of hostilities between the United States and England did not improve American relations with France. One might have expected Napoleon's success in embroiling England and America to make him treat the United States as an ally. But the fact was that he did not like the United States and wished to see republican government crushed. Also he regarded the United States contemptuously as a little nation that he could treat with the same high-handed tactics he might use against Holland or Denmark. Finally, he seldom gave the United States much thought at all, and at times he even exasperated his foreign minister by his lack of interest in and understanding of international trade.

The Duc de Dalberg wrote the Duc de Bassano soon after taking charge of the foreign office: "Since you left I have had several conferences with Mr. Barlow, and in compliance with the spirit of my instructions the work is not far advanced." Barlow was arguing for free commerce, and Dalberg was holding out for limited commerce. When Barlow insisted on his terms, the deputy foreign minister appeared to give in but said he would have to ask his chief before he could agree. Thus a letter that could not be answered for three weeks had to go off to Bassano in Wilna. On the matter of indemnities, which President Madison stipulated must be in the treaty, Dalberg went through the same routine. By the middle of June the deputy foreign minister reported that Monsieur Barlow was getting very impatient at this procrastination. Furthermore, he was furious because seventeen more American ships had been captured by French captains who insisted they never were told the Berlin and Milan decrees had been revoked.

By the end of August Dalberg was weary of the role he was playing and began to succumb to Barlow's charm. He wrote Bassano that France was fortunate in having such a great friend as the American minister. He felt bad about the deliberate delays, for Barlow not only was a man of refined taste and the owner of a magnificent *hôtel* in Paris, but he also was a poet whose works were more read in France than in the United States. "If your Excellency wishes to take the trouble to read the American papers, you will see that in his country they reproach him for his fondness for France."

There was more truth in the last statement than Dalberg realized, for Barlow's efforts had kept the United States from going to war with both England and France. President Madison wrote on August eleventh that quite a few people in the United States now thought a double war was the shortest way to peace. Although the President was not one of them, Congress nearly had passed such a resolution prior to voting the declaration of war with England. The double war bill failed in the Senate by only two votes and in the House by about the same relative margin. Secretary Monroe wrote Barlow that the measure's defeat had been very largely "owing to a passage in your last letter, which intimated the intention of the French government to make some proposition in favor of indemnities, to be comprised in the treaty you were negotiating."

When the President heard that the British Orders in Council had been revoked, he gave Barlow as much ammunition as possible to carry into the treaty talks. He wrote that England's act in cancelling the Orders probably would lead to reestablishment of peace between Great Britain and the United States, after which "the nation's hostility" will be "directed against France." Barlow received that letter and communicated it to the deputy foreign minister, who relayed it to Wilna. By that time the Grand Army was in serious trouble in Russia. Bassano finally realized that a commercial treaty with the United States would be highly desirable. He suddenly began acting with a sense of urgency and wrote Barlow from Wilna on October eleventh inviting him to come to Lithuania to conclude negotiations on the treaty. He promised: "When you arrive at Wilna . . . we may, sir, conclude, without delay, an arrangement so desirable, and so conformable to the mutually amicable views of our two governments."

Barlow read the Duc's letter with a sense of doom. Wilna was fourteen hundred miles away. It lay in the middle of a land ravaged by war and was linked to civilization by God-knew-what kind of roads. He was fifty-eight years old, and the time was October twenty-fifth. Though he always had liked to travel, this would be no pleasure excursion. He wrote Monroe: "Though the proposal was totally unexpected, and, on many accounts, disagreeable, it was impossible to refuse it without giving offense, or at least risking a postponement of a negotiation which I have reason to believe is now in a fair way to a speedy and advantageous close." He informed the French foreign minister that he would accept the invitation and leave immediately.

An hour before noon on Tuesday, the twenty-seventh of October, the Barlow carriage rolled out of the gate at 50 rue de Vaugirard. In it were Joel and his nephew Tom, who was going as secretary to the Minister, and on the box was Louis, the driver. Tearfully left behind were Ruth, her sister Clara, and the rest of the servants. Barlow's plan was to take the shortest possible route east, to ride night and day whenever possible, and to arrive at Wilna in about three weeks. The long, long journey started forlornly under leaden skies that soon began to dump a heavy, all-night rain on the travelers.

The road to the East lay through Château Thierry and Châlon in the valley of the Marne, then across Lorraine to the Moselle and Metz. The carriage made good time all the first day despite the nocturnal downpour, five miles an hour for twenty-one hours of non-stop travel. Joel wrote Ruth at eight the next morning while the horses were being changed that he had "slept like a top six hours this night." The next day he wrote again from five leagues beyond Metz that they were getting along very well; he had not been out of the carriage since leaving except to have a cup of coffee each morning. "I can eat & sleep & think of Darling as well in the carriage as anywhere." Besides, the weather was bad and the nights long and dark.

After leaving Metz, the road crossed the Rhine at Mainz, then led through Germany in a northeasterly direction. They reached Frankfort at ten o'clock Friday night in good health, with no colds, no fever or swollen legs, even though their boots had not been off for four days and three nights. The weather still was rainy, and

the roads were a sea of mud. It was impossible to get out of the carriage to walk for exercise. They would have reached Frankfort
half a day sooner if it had not been for the miserable weather. The
French government, however, was facilitating the trip in every way.
Orders had been given to French officers in all the garrison towns
along the road to speed the American Minister on his journey.
Barlow had not been in Frankfort half an hour before a French
diplomat there invited him to dine.

The travelers rested only two nights in Frankfort, then pushed
on towards Berlin by way of Weimar and Leipzig. The weather
cleared a little, and they were able to continue traveling non-stop.
Nine days after leaving rue de Vaugirard, they pulled into Berlin,
but paused there only overnight. By this time Barlow began to
take an interest in sightseeing and regretted he had to push on the
next day. Even so, he rode about the city and thought it the finest,
best-built town for its size he ever had seen. He accompanied the
French Minister to the theater on the one night he was in Berlin.
But the next day the last and most difficult leg of the journey began
—across the Baltic coastal plain to Königsberg, then due east to
Wilna.

Fifty miles beyond Berlin Barlow realized that he was approaching the war theater. When his carriage reached the Oder River
outside Kistrzy, he found the city gates shut at seven o'clock. He
had time that night to write Ruth a long letter: "This is the first
strong place where the rule is never to open the gates at night. So
here we stop & go to bed in the suburb with the fine River Oder
between my window and the city." Barlow loved rivers and reflected that the next great one would be the Vistula, which he
planned to cross at Thorn, birthplace of Copernicus. He was reminded of two lines from the *Columbiad*, which he quoted:

> This blessed moment, from the towers of Thorn
> New splendor rises; there the sage is born!

He never discovered if Thorn contained any towers worth noting,
because he found a short cut to Königsberg and by-passed the city
via a military pontoon bridge. As he headed towards the Vistula,

he boasted to Ruth: "I enjoy an impudent, vulgar health, fit for a wood cutter or a maple sugar maker."

The weather remained bad—eight days of rain out of the last eleven—and by the time Barlow was two hundred and sixty miles beyond Berlin, the roads became so primitive that he no longer could travel at night. The temperatures remained mild, and so far there had been frost only one night since leaving Paris. He might have welcomed a freeze, however, to escape the endless mud. From Königsberg he wrote: "The mud, the true sublime, the real majesty of mud, you know nothing about, having seen nothing of it either in Paris or Hartford or Maryland or Holland or any other country. My ideas have been expanding on this subject since I crossed the Rhine. It is thick or thin, black or brown, according to circumstances, through all the kingdom of Westphalia. Saxony is a quagmire, but the Devil's own hasty-pudding is in this great basin of one hundred and forty miles from Thorn to Königsberg . . . The horses' legs are the ladles that stir it up; the carriage wheels whirl it over your head in a black rainbow that moves as you move."

Two days was all the Minister could spare in Königsberg before jumping off for Wilna. There he bought a great pelisse in anticipation of cold weather to come. He made his purchase just in time, for a day or two later the mercury plummeted and the roads froze. Travel became faster but rougher. From the last town in Prussia he wrote that tomorrow he would cross into Lithuania, formerly part of Poland but now "to him that can hold it." He did not stop to go to bed that night but wished he had when the temperature dropped low enough to freeze the water bottle he carried in the carriage. On November seventeenth, when the travelers stopped at Kovno, Barlow wrote his last letter before reaching Wilna.

As the carriage approached Kovno, the country became barren, sterile, famine-ridden. The peasants left behind the Grand Army's locust flight earlier in the year huddled wretchedly in log huts on empty plains broken occasionally by stands of fir and pine. The travelers now slept on straw when they stopped overnight at post houses along the road, but the evening before crossing the Niemen into Kovno they arrived after the city gates had closed and had to sit in the carriage all night on the newly built military bridge. The city itself was choked with soldiers, the sick and wounded as well as the garrison, and for the rest of the journey the Americans shared the road with steady streams of military traffic.

Despite the tedium of travel, the rain, the mud, and now freezing temperatures, Joel and his nephew kept themselves occupied during the long expedition. "Tom was all the while sucking in ideas like a calf. His soul seemed to fatten," Joel wrote from Königsberg. He added: "I have given him a great many lessons on life & manners, history & politics, science & literature." He also was teaching Tom German and having him read aloud Robertson's *History of Charles V*. This work with the *Columbiad* and the *Iliad* comprised their entire traveling library. The long trip finally ended twenty-three days and fourteen hundred miles after leaving Paris, and the carriage rolled through the city gate of Wilna at eight p.m. on November eighteenth.

There is an air of unreality about Barlow's sixteen-day stay in Wilna. While the Russians were massacring the French army, life went on in the ancient Lithuanian city as though Napoleon were sitting triumphantly in the Kremlin. The Duc de Bassano had set up a temporary foreign office, and the diplomatic corps had gathered there to do business. Until the final moment of the disaster Napoleon was expected to winter in Wilna. Artificial gaiety flowered in the midst of famine and carnage everywhere outside the city. It was like the last mad whirl of a fever-wracked beauty dancing all night on the brink of a fatal collapse. Barlow observed and reported this with a premonition of the outcome, but he also filled his letters with forced levity.

Only the foreign minister's influence could have found the American Minister a place to live in that small city of thirty-six thousand. The Prussian envoy had to sit in his carriage for twenty-four hours before he could get into any house, but the Duc de Bassano took special pains to treat Barlow well. He was billeted in a house with the Danish minister, and when his special shipment of provisions and wines arrived from Paris, the two diplomats pooled their resources and dined together. There was no such thing as a restaurant "where you get anything eatable," wrote Joel, and besides the less one moved about, the better. Tom informed his aunt that even without Napoleon and his front-line troops Wilna already was so crowded that he nearly got run over whenever he walked through the streets.

Keeping house in the Lithuanian city was a problem requiring considerable resourcefulness. Barlow wrote Ruth triumphantly five days after arriving that he had just made a great bargain. He had bought ten napkins, one tablecloth, six sheets, and two blankets. "There are no more than two blankets to be had in Wilna & I believe in the whole province of Lithuania, if [not] in all Poland." Added to the one blanket he had brought from Paris in the carriage, he, Tom, and Louis had one apiece. They also had one pair of sheets each, and Joel asked Ruth: "How the deuce to contrive against washing time I don't know. When a gentleman has but one shirt he can lie abed till it is washed, but how does he do when he gets his sheets washed? I wish you would let me know by return post."

There was never a reply to that question, however. By the time Ruth received the letter Joel was escaping from Wilna for Warsaw in the midst of the great debacle. Ruth in Paris was not lulled by her husband's forced gaiety. She already had written poignantly in a letter that Joel received soon after reaching Lithuania: "O, my *precious*, take great care of your health. I fear you will fatigue too much and get cold, and of how much more consequence to me is your life than the lives of all the world besides."

Barlow was a perennial sightseer, and once he had solved the housekeeping problems, he looked about the city. Wilna seemed about the size of Boston, but it did not look anything like Massachusetts. The houses were built of brick or stone to hold multiple family units. The ground floors were left unfinished as pig pens, and the upper floors were badly laid out and barnlike. There were "no closets or snug little boudoirs where an honest wife . . . can shut in her sweetheart & shut out her husband." On the other hand, public buildings in Wilna had some charm: there were handsome churches and a famous old university. Outside the city, which was built in a valley, ran the Wilia River, a small, swift stream which was supposed to be good fishing. The hills surrounding Wilna, young Tom noted, were crowned with "the ruins of old towers or fortifications which present a scene truly romantic." Everything was covered with snow and looked like a Connecticut winter.

As news came from the front reporting Napoleon's retreat, the diplomats and court officials kept up the pretense of life as usual. On the twenty-second the Duc invited Barlow to dine with some Polish ladies but warned him to be on guard. Joel wrote Ruth that he was getting too old to have to worry about such things, for age "prevents the attack being made & preserves us against its success if it is made; so I say with Voltaire, '*Ah, Saint Père, envoyez moi la tentation.*'" After the dinner he reported to his wife that he had fallen in love with a Polish princess "whose name I can't recollect, though I know it ends in 'sky,' & the name is not the only thing celestial about her. She has a pair of eyes that, if they had been made before our solar system, would have induced the architect to make two suns instead of one." Then he went on with the banter but ended by admitting that the princess was older than he. After another dinner with the Duc he wrote that there was so much Polish beauty "I quite forgot my first *flambeau* who was not there." He continued this joke for another teasing paragraph, then suddenly stopped: "All flummery—I love my darling, first-begotten, long-beloved wife better & more & harder & softer & longer & stronger than all the Poles between the south pole and the north pole."

Barlow's real feelings during the last month of his life went into a bitter, satiric poem, "Advice to a Raven in Russia." * In it he poured out all his pent-up revulsion against the havoc Napoleon's insane ambition had wrought in Europe. If the same passionate outcry had informed the *Vision of Columbus* or the *Columbiad*, Barlow would be a major poet. "Black fool, why winter here?" he asks his fancied raven in the opening line; then he adds that Napoleon's trail of blood and carnage stretches the length of Europe. No raven need brave the frozen steppes of Russia to find carrion enough. The final lines of the poem are as moving an indictment of Napoleon as any poet has written:

* Reprinted in the Appendix.

War after war his hungry soul requires,
State after State shall sink beneath his fires,
Yet other Spains in victim smoke shall rise
And other Moscows suffocate the skies,
Each land lie reeking with its peoples slain
And not a stream run bloodless to the main.
Till men resume their souls, and dare to shed
Earth's total vengeance on the monster's head,
Hurl from his blood-built throne this king of woes,
Dash him to dust, and let the world repose.

On the next-to-last day of November a half-frozen courier arrived from Napoleon's headquarters. The Emperor was then only sixty-five leagues away and still retreating, but the foreign minister continued to assure the diplomats that the army would make Wilna its winter headquarters. He expected the Emperor in six days and insisted to the American Minister that his business then could be completed quickly. Barlow wrote Ruth his last optimistic sentence on November thirtieth: "The Duke speaks of its [the treaty's] success as a matter of certainty."

Five days later every Frenchman or diplomat who could walk or find a conveyance was crowding the roads west. The retreat from Moscow had become a rout. Joel Barlow's journey from Redding to Wilna, from the Eighteenth Century to the Nineteenth, from the New England farm to the court of Napoleon, was nearing its untimely end. Three weeks later between Warsaw and Krakow he caught pneumonia and died in the village of Zarnowiec. The marble tablet which Ruth later had placed in the porch of the parish church reads thus:

JOEL BARLOW

Plenipotens Minister

a Statibus unitis America

ad Imp. Gallorum & Reg. Italia

Itinerando hicce obiit

26 December 1812

Epilogue

The news of Barlow's death, which reached Paris about the middle of January, struck Ruth like lightning. The legation clerk wrote Monroe on the fifteenth that her plight was dreadful. But she lived through her sorrow, and in February was able to write President Madison: "You will doubtless be informed before receiving this of the dreadful event which has deprived me of the best of husbands & my country of a zealous & devoted friend. Borne down by this cruel, this unexpected stroke, I know not how to get fortitude to support my sinking health." By summer, however, she was able to travel and packed her things for the long voyage home, this time to remain. The French government obtained assurances of safe conduct from the British navy, and she left with her sister and nephew in early September.

Ruth spent the winter of 1813-1814 in New York with the Fultons while she recovered gradually from her bereavement. The following year she wrote an old friend that she was about to reopen Kalorama, "which I wrote you I never could do. All places must forever be sad to me. *That* may in time be more agreeable than any other, as everything there will recall the *image* I wish to be ever present to my still bleeding heart." To this she added: "Grief, I find, does not kill the body, though it destroys the mind."

She went back to Washington to live with her sister at Kalorama and with the Latrobes as next-door neighbors. There she died in 1818. Before her death she had the marble tablet placed in the church at Zarnowiec. But she was not able to remove her husband's remains from Europe during the final upheavals of Waterloo and the downfall of Napoleon, and Joel Barlow still lies buried in Poland. Senator Otis Glenn of Illinois in 1930 introduced a bill to erect a suitable monument in the graveyard at Zarnowiec, but his bill died in committee and never was revived. Barlow's treaty also died uncompleted, for by the time a new American minister reached Paris, Napoleon's end was in sight, and a new era was beginning in Europe.

Because Joel and Ruth Barlow had no children, Tom Barlow inherited Kalorama and the bulk of his uncle's estate, which amounted to about one hundred thousand dollars in stocks and real estate and nearly twice as much more in claims to western land. He subsequently sold the house and settled in Western Pennsylvania. Clara Baldwin, meantime, married Colonel George Bomford, Chief of Ordnance of the United States Army, and bought Kalorama where she lived until 1845. By the time she died at her daughter's home in Maine some years later American history had entered a new period. As events raced towards the Civil War, the triumphs and disappointments of Joel Barlow passed from the memory of living men to the pages of American history.

Notes

SOURCES: The primary sources for this book are MSS owned by public and private libraries from Boston to Los Angeles. There is no dearth of material. There are inevitable gaps in the record, but Barlow's adult career is abundantly documented. The major collection of Barlow MSS is at Harvard University Library, where most of the family papers have come to rest. The Harvard papers consist of hundreds of letters to and from Barlow, notebooks, diaries, and published and unpublished literary works. This material was collected by Lemuel Olmstead in the middle of the last century for a biography of Barlow that he did not live to write. These papers subsequently were used by Charles B. Todd in the *Life and Letters of Joel Barlow* (New York, 1886). All of Barlow's official dispatches from his diplomatic missions are in the National Archives, and his correspondence with public figures like Jefferson and Madison is in the Library of Congress. His mission to France is abundantly recorded in the photographic reproductions at the Library of Congress of the French foreign ministry's archives. There are other MS collections in various libraries: A significant group of family papers recently was obtained by the Huntington Library, and the collection of Barlow material at Yale University is large and important.

ABBREVIATIONS AND SYMBOLS: I have indicated MS sources in the following way:

AAS	American Antiquarian Society
Abinger	The Shelley-Godwin Collection of Lord Abinger, which is available on 16 reels of microfilm at Duke University
AE	Affaires Etrangères, Correspondance Politique, Etats-Unis. This is the material reproduced on photographs at the Library of Congress from the archives of the French foreign ministry

BPL	Boston Public Library
CHS	Connecticut Historical Society
CSL	Connecticut State Library
Harvard	Harvard University Library
Haverford	Haverford College Library
HEH	Henry E. Huntington Library and Art Gallery
LC	Library of Congress
MHS	Massachusetts Historical Society
NA	National Archives
Northwestern	Northwestern University Library
NYHS	New York Historical Society
NYPL	New York Public Library
Yale	Yale University Library

Throughout my notes I have used these symbols to refer to writers of letters and persons named most frequently:

JB	Joel Barlow
RB	Ruth Barlow
AB	Abraham Baldwin
TJ	Thomas Jefferson
RF	Robert Fulton

The following abbreviations stand for the three printed works most frequently cited:

Todd	Charles B. Todd, *Life and Letters of Joel Barlow* (New York, 1886)
Zunder	Theodore A. Zunder, *The Early Days of Joel Barlow, a Connecticut Wit* (New Haven, 1934)
Howard	Leon Howard, *The Connecticut Wits* (Chicago, 1943)

There are many supplemental printed sources on which this book is based, but these I have indicated in the notes below where appropriate.

STYLE AND FORM: Most of my quotations are taken from original manuscripts, but because many MSS have been published, at least in part, I have tried when possible to give both MS and printed sources. In some instances my text varies from the printed version because of errors in transcribing or, in the case of letters not written in English, because of my differing translation. In addition, I have not hesitated to make silent corrections of spelling or obvious slips of the pen in reproducing MSS. Also I have found no reason to preserve peculiarities of eighteenth-century spelling or punctuation, if the peculiarity draws attention to itself. My aim has been to modernize MSS where emendations seemed desirable to clarify texts. I have not altered the spirit or substance of any MS. Finally, I have silently supplied conventional days and months for letters dated from the French Revolutionary calendar.

In citing unpublished MSS, I have adopted this notational style: JB to RB, 12 Nov. 96 (HEH). Such a source would be a letter written by Joel Barlow to Ruth Barlow on November 12, 1796, and owned by the Huntington Library. Where no location is indicated in parentheses, the MS may be assumed to be in the Barlow Papers at Harvard. Probably half of all the MSS I quote or cite are among this collection.

BIBLIOGRAPHY: There is an excellent list of JB's printed works in Jacob Blanck, *Bibliography of American Literature*, Vol. I (New Haven, 1955). The bibliographical appendices in Howard and Zunder are very useful; also see R. E. Spiller, *et al.*, *Literary History of the United States* (New York, 1948), III, 396-398. There are three unpublished dissertations on JB: Milton Cantor, "The Life of JB" (Columbia, 1954); Macklin Thomas, "The Idea of Progress in the Writings of Franklin, Freneau, JB, and Rush" (Wisconsin, 1938); Hans Zinser, "Studien zu JB's *Columbiad*" (Giessen, 1944).

PROLOGUE

The main source is JB's letters to RB. He wrote frequent letters, which give a vivid, eye-witness account of the retreat as seen from the rear. "It grows worse" was written from Wilna, 18 Nov. 12 (LC). I omitted the grimmest story: the account of a soldier with legs shot off, still alive a month after the battle and still eating the flesh of the horse he had been riding.

The report of JB's last illness comes from four sources: AE, LXIX, 400-401; Tom Barlow to James Monroe, 25 Jan. 13 (NA); Todd, pp. 282-283 (Clara Baldwin to Dolley Madison, 16 Feb. 13); letter to the editor from Miecislaus Haiman, N. Y. *Times*, 10 Nov. 1929.

For data on Zarnowiec and environs, I used these works: Bronisław Chlebowski *et al.*, *Slownik Geograficzny*, XIV (1895), 741-743; Father Jan Wisniowski, *Historyczny Opis Kisciolow: Miast, Zabytkow i Pamiatek w Olkuskim* [Historical Description of the Churches, Towns, Monuments, and Memorials in Olkuski District] (1933), pp. 494, 503. This material was translated for me by Dr. Margaret Schlauch of the University of Warsaw.

CHAPTER I: THE FOREGROUND

ANTECEDENTS AND EARLY EDUCATION: My sources for Connecticut history are too numerous to list completely, but these items were particularly useful: Walter F. Prince, "An Examination of Peters's 'Blue Laws,'" *Annual Report of the Amer. Hist. Assn. for 1898* (Washington, 1899), pp. 97-138; Mary C. Crawford, *Social Life in Old New England* (Boston, 1914); Edward M. Chapman, *New England Village Life* (Cambridge, Mass., 1937); JB, "Letter Addressed to Harry Grégoire," *Monthly Anthology*, VII, 291-292 (Nov. 1809).

Anyone who writes on Barlow is indebted to Theodore Zunder for a painstaking study of JB's early days. My investigation has added only a few new facts to Zunder's study, but I differ frequently in the interpretation of the facts. JB's genealogy I have taken from Zunder. For background here, see Charles B. Todd, *The History of Redding, Connecticut* (New York, 1906). JB's verse is from JB to Oliver Wolcott, 3 May 79 (CHS); also in T. A. Zunder, ed., "Six Letters of JB to Oliver Wolcott," *New Eng. Quart.*, II, 475-489 (July 1929). A good account of social customs and the husking bee is in JB's *Hasty Pudding* (1796). Wheelock's diary is in the Dartmouth College Library; pertinent portions are in Zunder, pp. 7-8. Wheelock to Daggett, 8 Nov. 74 (Dartmouth Library; Zunder, p. 18). The wills of JB's parents are recorded in "Probate Records, District of Fairfield," XVIII, 250-251, 413 (see Zunder, pp. 11-12, 31-32).

COLLEGE: No one should write about Yale in the Revolution without reading Howard's excellent book on the Connecticut Wits. Also useful is Harry R. Warfel, *Noah Webster: Schoolmaster to America* (New York, 1936). Older histories of Yale are less useful. Zunder has mined thoroughly Yale archives. Three noteworthy sources of Yale lore, all edited or written by Franklin B. Dexter: *The Literary Diary of Ezra Stiles*, 3 vols. (New York, 1901); "Student Life at Yale" in *A Selection from the Miscellaneous Papers of Fifty Years* (New Haven, 1918), pp. 266-273; *Biographical Sketches of the Graduates of Yale College* (New York, 1907). The rules of Yale are reprinted in part in Zunder, pp. 21, 25. Washington's visit to New Haven was reported on July 5, 1775. Fitch's diary was edited by Calvin Durfee, "Memoir of Rev. Ebenezer Fitch, D.D.," *Amer. Quart. Register*, XV, 358 (May 1843). JB's letter to his mother is at Harvard. Reference to JB's first poem appears in early biographical sketches, the earliest I noted being unsigned in the *Monthly Magazine and British Register*, VI, 250-251 (Oct. 1798).

PATHS OF GLORY: Stiles on the Declaration: *Literary Diary*, II, 21. Gov. Trumbull's proclamation: reproduced in facsimile in Charles W. Burpee, *The Story of Connecticut* (New York, 1939), I, 389-390. Early biographical sketches, for which JB was direct or indirect source, agree that JB was in the Battle of Long Island. There is no record of his service either in state or federal archives, but surviving records, especially of militia companies, are fragmentary. There is no tracing all the privates who served for short periods. One key document exists, however: JB to General Assembly of Conn., 7 Mar. 81 (CSL); this letter asks reimbursement for expenses of illness after his "tour of military duty . . . at New York" in 1776; Zunder, pp. 37-38. My account of the Battle of Long Island comes mainly from *Memoirs of the Long Island Historical Society*, Vol. II: *The Battle of Long Island* (Brooklyn, 1869). This work quotes from the New England volunteer, James S. Martin, in *A Narrative of Some of the Adventures . . . of a Revolutionary Soldier* (Hallowell, Maine, 1830).

The parody of *Chronicles* is printed in Anson Stokes, *Memorials of Eminent Yale Men* (New Haven, 1914), I, 127. I have seen no MS copy of this. "I advise you": Buckminster to JB, 5 Oct. 78 (Yale); this and several later letters are in Todd, p. 10 ff. JB's commencement poem was published by Thomas and Samuel Green, New Haven, 1778. Title page is erroneously dated 1788.

CHAPTER II: CHAOS AND ORDER

YOUNG MAN IN LIMBO: "You and I": JB to Webster, 30 Jan. 79. Humphreys' opinions of JB: Zunder, p. 100; David Humphreys, *Poems*, 2nd ed. (Philadelphia, 1789), p. 89. "The discovery": JB to Buckminster, 19 March 79 (LC). Perkins' advice is in JB to Webster, 21 Oct. 79. New London is described in JB to RB [Jan. ?] 80; Todd, pp. 37-38. JB's despondency: JB to RB, 26 Sept. 79; JB to Wolcott, 4 Nov., 13 Dec. 79 (CHS; also in Zunder, ed., "Six Letters"). JB on the ministry: JB to Buckminster, 19 March 79 (LC). AB's invitation to chaplaincy: AB to JB [March ?] 80; Todd, pp. 25-27; Zunder, p. 99. "I will pull every string": AB to JB, 2 May 80. "Don't communicate a word": JB to RB, [?] June 80. Stiles' report of exam: *Literary Diary*, II, 456-458.

CHAPLAIN: A good recent, one-volume history of the Revolution is John R. Alden, *The American Revolution* (New York, 1954); the military situation of 1780 is well treated in Douglas S. Freeman, *George Washington: A Biography*, Vol. V (New York, 1952).

JB's chaplaincy is documented in letters to RB, which I have quoted from in this order: 11 Sept., 23 Sept., 10 Oct., 23 Sept., 11 Sept., 18 Sept., 23 Sept., 11 Sept., 23 Sept., 2 Oct., 18 Oct. 80; portions in Todd, pp. 31-37. The comment on JB's prayer is in James Thacher, *A Military Journal during the American Revolution War from 1775 to 1783* (Boston, 1823), p. 255. Thacher met JB less than three weeks after he joined his brigade. André's execution: JB to RB, 2 Oct. 80; Thacher, pp. 273-274. See also Freeman, *op. cit.*, pp. 196-222.

COURTSHIP AND MARRIAGE: Charles K. Bolton, *The Elizabeth Whitman Mystery* (Peabody, Mass., 1912), spins a whole book out of the meager facts of this tale. Mrs. Caroline Healey Doll, *The Romance of the Association, or One Last Glimpse of Charlotte and Eliza Wharton* (Cambridge, Mass., 1875), writes a very sticky introduction for a printing of Elizabeth Whitman's letters to JB. I have used the originals at HEH. I am greatly indebted to RB for saving JB's letters, for they are the richest lode in my source material and document the entire relationship from 1779 to 1812. Only a few of RB's letters have survived. "Precipitate yourself not": RB to Clara Baldwin, 10 June 10 (HEH).

"I move at present": JB to Webster, 30 Jan. 79; part in Todd, pp. 18-19. Todd prints large chunks of JB's letters but often transcribes carelessly or bowdlerizes. Zunder prints a good many bits of primary source material, reproducing all the peculiarities of 18th-century spelling and punctuation. His errors are few. The letters from JB to RB are quoted in this order: 8 Feb., 6 April, 26 July, [Nov.], [Dec.] 79; [June], 2 Oct., 18 Oct., 29 Oct., 26 Dec. 80; 17 Dec. 12; 5 Jan., 21 Feb., 9 March, 12 Aug., 24 Oct. 82. Miss Whitman's letters to JB are quoted in this order: 16 Feb., 17 March, 29 March, 9 Feb. 79.

Records of the marriage ceremony are lacking, but the date may be fixed from subsequent anniversary verses and letters that JB wrote. Upson's part must be inferred from JB's later reference to Upson's keeping the secret. "Do you think": AB to RB, 23 Jan. 82. "You dearest of men": RB to JB, 13 Aug. 81. "From my first acquaintance": JB to Michael Baldwin, 12 March 82. "Repentence is the only cure": AB to JB, [March ?] 82; Zunder, p. 150. The *Dauphinade*: JB to RB, 9 June 82; David Humphreys in the *New-York Packet*, 20 June 82; Zunder, pp. 151-152. Verses on sorrel mare: MS at Harvard; Zunder, pp. 153-154.

CHAPTER III: POET, LAWYER, CONNECTICUT WIT

POST-WAR PREPARATIONS: Brissot de Warville, *New Travels in the United States*, 2 vols. (London, 1792), pp. 133-135. This was translated by JB. The standard history of Hartford is J. Hammond Trumbull, ed., *The Memorial History of Hartford County*, 2 vols. (Boston, 1886).

JB's rapid composition in the winter of 1781-82 is reported in letters to RB; also in AB to RB, 23 Jan. 82. JB's *Poem Spoken at the Public Commencement . . . 1781* was published in Hartford by Hudson and Goodwin, no date. Stiles in *Literary Diary*, II, 555, reported the poem's reception. Humphreys' metrical praise is in his *Poems* (Philadelphia, 1789), p. 36. His letter to Gen. Greene is in Anson Stokes, *Memorials of Eminent Yale Men*, II, 314. JB's trip to Philadelphia: JB to RB, 2 Nov., 12 Nov., 15 Nov. 82; parts in Todd, pp. 42-44, Zunder, pp. 159-162.

JB's co-editorship of the *Mercury* is documented chiefly from the files of that newspaper. The start of the JB-Babcock partnership may be dated from JB to Babcock, 3 May 84. The prospectus is in Todd, pp. 46-47. The verses on the thunderstorm appeared on 6 Sept. 84. JB's *Elegy on the Late Honorable Titus Hosmer* was published in Hartford, c. 1782. The title page that annoyed Stiles: *Doctor Watts's Imitation of the Psalms of David, Corrected and Enlarged, by Joel Barlow, to Which is Added a Collection of Hymns.* This work supplied New England churches for years until JB's political and religious apostasy required a new revision. The *Psalms* were published 21 March 85. Stiles' criticism: *Literary Diary*, III, 156. Arnold's quatrain comes from Frances M. Caulkins, *History of Norwich, Conn.* (Hartford, 1866), p. 415. The dissolution of the JB-Babcock partnership was announced in the *Mercury* on 5 Dec. 85.

NEW DIRECTIONS AND OLD FRUITIONS: JB's legal dissertation exists in MS at Harvard. "Manners and address were not popular": *Monthly Magazine and British Register*, VI, 252-253 (Oct. 1798). JB's Fourth of July oration: *An Oration Delivered . . . at the Meeting of the Connecticut Society of the Cincinnati* (Hartford, 1787). As ex-Revolutionary officer, of course, JB was a member of the society. The best study of *The Anarchiad* is in Howard, pp. 169-205, to which my discussion is indebted. The text of the satire was rescued from oblivion by Luther G. Riggs, who edited, with introduction, *The Anarchiad: A New England Poem* (New Haven, 1861). The lines quoted here are from the first and third installments. Hopkins' verses (*Conn. Courant*, 7 Nov. 85) are quoted by Howard, p. 170.

The announcement that the *Vision* was in press appeared on 8 Jan. 87. The advance newspaper essay on the poem: "An ESSAY on American GENIUS," *New-Haven Gazette*, 1 Feb. 87. Zunder's chapter on the *Vision*, pp. 202-231, contains ample data on the poem's publication and reception, but Howard's criticism, pp. 144-165, is the only reliable analysis of it. An interesting article on the poem is Merton A. Christensen, "Deism in JB's Early Work: Heterodox Passages in *The Vision of Columbus*," *Amer. Lit.*, XXVII, 509-520 (Jan. 1956). The author thinks JB's heterodoxy is clearly evident in the *Vision*. I agree that the roots of his heresy lie in his writings before going to Europe, but these were faint clues and indirections and not apparent to his friends or enemies at the time. No one attacked the poem in 1787 on grounds of heterodoxy. There was enough flexibility in late-18th-century Calvinism to tolerate some of the ideas of the Age of Reason. The eminent scholar I quote is Howard, p. 159. Washington sent the *Vision* to Mrs. John Penn on 18 Sept. 87 with this note: "Genl. Washington takes the liberty of offering his respectful compliments to Mrs. Penn, and the Vision of Columbus. It is one of several copies for which he subscribed some years ago and received since he came to this city. To the merit, or demerit of the performance, the general can say nothing, not having had time to read it." This is from J. C. Fitzpatrick, ed., *Writings of George Washington* (Washington, 1939), XXIX, 276. The passages quoted from the poem are from these pages (2nd ed., Hartford, 1787): 194, 207, 209, 211, 257, 230, 235. The review of the poem quoted: *Critical Review*, LXV, 31-35 (Jan. 1788); reprinted in the *American Magazine*, I, 334-337 (April 1788). Alsop's lines are in *The Charms of Fancy* (New York, 1856), p. 47.

CHAPTER IV: AN AMERICAN IN PARIS

PRELUDE: The MS and printed sources for studying the Ohio Company and the Scioto speculation are voluminous. Chief MS sources are the Craigie Papers (AAS), Sargent Papers (MHS), Cutler Papers (Northwestern), Gallipolis Papers (copies of documents only; Hist. and Philos. Soc. of Ohio, Cincinnati), Knollenberg Hist. MSS (Yale), various papers (NYHS, NYPL). Chief printed sources are A. B. Hulbert, ed., *The Records of the Original Proceedings of the Ohio Company*, 2 vols. (Marietta, Ohio, 1917), which has a good introduction; A. B. Hulbert, "The Methods and Operations of the Scioto Group of Speculators," *Miss. Valley Hist. Rev.*, I, 502-515 (March 1915); W. P. Cutler and Julia P. Cutler, *Life, Journals and Correspondence of Rev. Manasseh Cutler, LL.D.*, 2 vols. (Cincinnati, 1888); T. T. Belote, "Selections from the Gallipolis Papers," *Quart. Pub. of Hist. and Philos. Soc. of Ohio*, II, 39-92 (April-June 1907); T. T. Belote, *The Scioto Speculation and the French Settlement at Gallipolis* (Cincinnati, 1907). For William Duer, see J. S. Davis, *Essays in the Earlier History of American Corporations* (Cambridge, Mass., 1917), I, 111-338, for a very adequate treatment by a competent economic historian. Cutler's letter to Platt is in *Life of Cutler*, I, 381.

ALLEGRETTO: JB's life from 25 May to 11 Oct. 88 is fully documented in his diaries at Harvard. Parts are printed in Todd, pp. 65-85, and in T. A. Zunder, "Joel Barlow and Seasickness," *Yale Journal of Biology and Medicine*, I, 385-390 (July 1929). The quotation from TJ: TJ to Edward Rutledge in Julian Boyd, ed., *The Papers of TJ* (Princeton, N. J., 1956), XIII, 377-379. JB's diary skips over his first visit to Paris. A pertinent letter from TJ to JB, 5 July 88 (not in Boyd) is in *William Winston Seaton of the "National Intelligencer"* (Boston, 1871), pp. 104-105. See also *Papers of TJ*, XI, 473; Gilbert Chinard, ed., *The Letters of Lafayette and TJ* (Baltimore & Paris, 1929), p. 123. Washington wrote letters of introduction to Lafayette and Count de Rochambeau (*Writings of George Washington*, XXIX, 503, 506-507), but if the dates (28 May 88) are correct, JB could not have carried them with him.

ANDANTE MODERATO: Trumbull's letter to Wolcott is in George Gibbs, ed., *Memoirs of the Administrations of Washington and John Adams* (New York,

1846), I, 25. Various references to JB occur in Beatrix C. Davenport, ed., *A Diary of the French Revolution by Gouverneur Morris*, 2 vols. (Boston, 1939); those quoted here: I, 133; II, 50. "The sudden and glorious": JB to RB, 28 July 89 (Yale). Several promotional pamphlets published in French pushed the Scioto speculation; one I have seen (HEH) is a 16-page pamphlet titled *Avis* (Paris: Prault, 1789). Business better "than I expected": JB to RB, 28 July 89 (Yale). "My heart goes" and "the affair goes" are in Belote, "Selections," pp. 62-65.

INTERMEZZO: The sources for this section are JB to RB, 9 Dec. 89 (Yale), 1 Jan., 2 Jan., 1 Feb., 9 March, 20 June, 29 June, 8 July, 11 July, 15 July, 19 July 90; RB to Mary Woolsey Dwight, 3 Oct. 90.

PRESTO E FURIOSO: "Demur would ruin": Craigie to JB, 24 May 90 (AAS). JB's account of his agency: JB to Benjamin Walker, 21 Dec. 90, in Belote, "Selections," pp. 72-77. "A consummate villain": Putnam to Duer, 28 Jan 91 (Northwestern). "Every exertion": Craigie to JB, 24 May 90 (AAS). Volney's report is in his *View of the Climate and Soil of the United States* (London, 1804), pp. 355-366. Walker's comment on JB: Walker to Wolcott, 26 June 91 (CHS); JB's explanation: JB to Wolcott, 6 March 91 (CHS).

CHAPTER V: POLITICIAN OF THE WORLD

There are two special sources for this phase of JB's career: Victor C. Miller, *Joel Barlow: Revolutionist, London, 1791-92* (Hamburg, 1932). This is based on original research in the British Museum and the Public Record Office. M. Ray Adams, "Joel Barlow, Political Romanticist" in *Studies in the Literary Backgrounds of English Radicalism* (Lancaster, Pa., 1947). This is a revision of the author's earlier excellent article in *Amer. Lit.*, IX, 113-152 (May 1937). My quotations from JB's writings come from *The Political Writings of Joel Barlow* (New York, 1796).

MISSION DISCOVERED: "Because Scioto": AB to JB, 15 Nov. 91 (HEH). The account of JB's life in Palais Royal Hotel is from Horace Scudder, ed., *Recollections of Samuel Breck* (Philadelphia, 1877), pp. 171-172; supplemented by some unpublished detail from the MS at the Amer. Philos. Soc. Lib. For data on JB's translation of Brissot, see *The Historical Mag.* (New York), II, 19-20 (Jan. 1858), which prints JB's letter to Nathaniel Barret of 13 July 91. There is a MS of JB's translation at CHS. After Brissot was guillotined, JB wrote a biographical sketch for a new edition of the *Travels*. About JB's hopes for a job: See JB to AB, 3 May 91; JB to Wolcott, 17 Oct. 91 (CHS). As everyone will recognize, the quotation from Paine is from No. 1 of *The Crisis*. The material on the "great debate" is from my own M.A. thesis (New York Univ., 1943) and my article, "The 'Cold War' of 1790-1791," Duke Univ. *Library Notes*, No. 20, pp. 7-18 (July 1948). "Luckless wight": JB to John Warner, 16 July 91 (Yale). A fruitful source for JB's associations at this time is Godwin's unpublished diary (Abinger). "To chin up": JB to AB, 17 Oct. 91.

PAMPHLETEER: JB's relationship with revolutionary societies and persons tried or indicted for sedition in 1794 is best seen in T. B. Howell, *A Complete Collection of State Trials* (London, 1817), XXIV, 511 ff. Twelve were

NOTES

indicted, but after Thomas Hardy and Horne Tooke were tried and acquitted, the others were released. The issue of the St. James Chronicle cited and quoted is 28 Feb.-1 March 92 (Miller, p. 7). JB's comment on Paine, "a luminary," is in Political Writings, p. 109. Advice to the Privileged Orders was reprinted by the Cornell Univ. Press in 1956. JB's two attacks on Burke: Political Writings, pp. 116, 252-258. The latter is a prose note first published with a French edition of The Conspiracy of Kings (1793). This poem was reprinted in Political Writings, pp. 237-251. TJ's note, "Be assured": TJ to JB, 20 June 92, in Andrew A. Lipscomb, ed., The Writings of TJ (Washington, 1903), VIII, 382. Both Miller and Howard deal extensively with JB's political ideas; Howard is especially good on JB's sources. Burke on the "prophet Joel": The Parliamentary History of England (London, 1817), XXX, 110. "Though one of my kings": JB to TJ, 18 March 92 (LC). JB's "mysterious mission": JB to RB, 15 April, 25 April, 20 May, 31 May, 4 June, 14 June, 18 June, 25 June 92; parts in Todd, pp. 94-96. For data on Swan's proposed tannery, see Alexander Tuetey, ed., Correspondance du ministre de l'intérieur relative au commerce, aux subsistances et à l'administration générale (16 avril-14 octobre 1792) (Paris, 1917), pp. 275-281. "I was almost disgusted": Mary Wollstonecraft to Everina, 20 June 92 (Abinger; printed in Ralph Wardle, Mary Wollstonecraft, Lawrence, Kans., 1951, pp. 175-176). "Such a situation": Mary to Everina, 25 Feb. 92 (Abinger; Wardle, p. 175). See also Mary's letter of 14 Sept. 92 (Abinger).

CITIZEN BARLOW: "I shall not": JB to Wolcott, 8 March 93 (CHS). "Glorious republic": JB to TJ, 1 Oct. 92 (LC). "Almost equal": Le Patriote François, 24 Sept. 92, p. 348. Brissot's paper recommended citizenship for six Englishmen and JB, but a check of the proceedings of the Convention reveals that JB was the only one so honored. Previously on Aug. 26 the Convention had given citizenship to Priestley, Paine, Bentham, Wilberforce, Mackintosh, Clootz, Pestalozzi, Washington, Hamilton, Madison, Klopstock, Kosciusko, and several others. For this data and for JB's connection with the Convention, I have gone to two sources: Archives parlementaires de 1787 à 1860, recueil complet des debats legislatifs & politiques des chambres françaises, Première Série (1789-1799) (Paris, 1898), LIII, 273, 286-297, 609, 636-637; Reimpression de l'ancien Moniteur, seule histoire authentique et inalterée de la Révolution Française depuis la réunion des états-généraux jusqu'au consulat (mai 1789-novembre 1799) avec des notes explicatives (Paris, 1847), XIII, 541-542; XIV, 593-594; XV, 491-492. This work contains an excellent index.

The decree of the French National Convention, No. 172, of 17 Feb. 93, making JB citizen, is in AE, XXXVII, 130; copies at Yale, NYPL. "Do great credit": John Warner to JB, 18 Oct. 92; Todd, pp. 96-97 (correspondent incorrectly identified as Joseph). "Dear Politician": 23 Oct. 92 (Yale). "Although the observations": JB to Society of Constitutional Whigs, 6 Oct. 92 (Yale); similar letters of transmittal are in Howell, State Trials, XXIV, 510 ff. The Society's reply: ibid., p. 524. JB's address to the Convention is in Annual Register (1792), pp. 73-74; Howell, op. cit., pp. 526-528. "The president gave": Howell, op. cit., p. 529. "I congratulate you": Stiles to JB, 20 March 93. Watson's offer: quoted in JB to RB, 13 Feb. 93; see also JB to Watson, 24 Aug. 93 (Yale). Fox's speech: Parliamentary History, XXX, 19-20. "I am obliged": RB to JB, 1 Jan. 93; part in Todd, pp. 108-109; Adams, "JB, Politi-

317

cal Romanticist," pp. 56-57. Other letters used in this paragraph: RB to JB, 9 Jan., 28 Jan., 1 Feb. 93; also in Todd and Adams, *op. cit.*

JB's stay in Chambéry and Paris is reconstructed from 17 letters of JB to RB, 4 Dec. 92-10 June 93; parts in Todd, pp. 97-98. The report of the Commissioners is quoted from an unpublished document in the Archives Nationales, Paris (Series C-242). I have searched French and Italian libraries without finding the Italian edition of JB's letter to the people of Piedmont, which JB wrote on 15 July 94 had been published in Nice (*Political Writings*, p. 199). The wedding verses are in Todd, pp. 292-293 (MS at Harvard). JB sent a MS of *The Hasty Pudding* to Matthew Carey (JB to Carey, 27 Sept. 94; Haverford), but Carey never published it. JB to John Fellows, 23 May 95: "As to the little poem I sent Carey, I care nothing about it. If it should come to you, you may publish it." Apparently it did not, for it was first printed as pamphlet in New Haven in 1796.

For data on the Louisiana scheme, see E. Wilson Lyon, *Louisiana in French Diplomacy, 1759-1804* (Norman, Okla., 1934); F. J. Turner, "Documents on the Relations of France to Louisiana, 1792-1795," *Amer. Hist. Rev.*, III, 490-516 (April 1898); *ibid.*, "The Origin of Genêt's Projected Attack on Louisiana and the Floridas, *Amer. Hist. Rev.*, III, 650-671 (July 1898). "The affairs of this country": JB to Wolcott, 24 Aug. 93 (CHS). JB described Brissot's execution in his introduction to the *Travels*, Vol. II (London, 1797). For JB's testimony and deposition for Miranda, see *Archivo del General Miranda* (Caracas, 1931), XII, 157-159, 248-249, 348. For JB's relationship with Paine, see chiefly Moncure D. Conway, *The Life of Thomas Paine* (New York, 1893), II, 100-108; Thomas C. Rickman, *The Life of Thomas Paine* (London, 1819), pp. 100, 131-133, 227-238; also JB to Monroe, 23 Feb. 96. "One of the most benevolent": JB to James Cheetham, 11 Aug. 09; Todd, pp. 236-239. Also see JB to John Montgomery, 18 Oct. 09, in Raleigh *Register* (date unknown but clipping at Harvard).

CHAPTER VI: COMMERCIAL INTERLUDE

For background, see A. C. Clauder, *American Commerce As Affected by the Wars of the French Revolution and Napoleon, 1793-1812* (Philadelphia, 1932); also important is Joseph Dorfman (the economic historian I quote), "Joel Barlow: Trafficker in Trade and Letters," *Political Science Quart.*, LIX, 83-100 (March 1944). This article is reprinted in Dorfman's *The Economic Mind in American Civilization.* "A set of New Englanders": Monroe to Madison, 30 June 95, in S. M. Hamilton, ed., *The Writings of James Monroe* (New York, 1899), II, 143. Letter urging boycott: JB to TJ, 2 Dec. 93 (LC). The JB-Leavenworth plan: F. J. Turner, "Documents," pp. 508-510.

JB's business affairs are hard to document. Business letters have not been preserved as abundantly as personal letters. In the Barlow Papers at Harvard there are a few items: copy of the contract chartering a ship from Bromfield; letterbooks kept during JB's mission to Algiers. The letterbooks reveal some of JB's later business dealings and occasionally refer to earlier transactions. To make this business profile, I have had to collect many casual references from widely scattered letters. The result lacks the detail I would like, but the over-all picture probably is accurate. An important printed source: Pierre Caron, ed., *La Commission des Substance de l'an II: Procès-verbal et acts* (Paris, 1925), pp. 88, 102, 662-663. For JB's dealings with Imlay, see B. P. Kurtz and C. C. Autrey, eds., *New Letters of Mary Wollstonecraft and Helen M. Williams* (Berkeley, 1937); William Godwin, *Memoirs of Mary Wollstonecraft* (London & New York, 1927), with preface and supplement by W. Clark Durant. "Mammon has always been": AB to JB, 28 May 98 (Yale).

Background detail on Hamburg comes from Mary Wollstonecraft, *Letters Written . . . in Sweden, Norway, and Denmark* (London, 1796); "Consular Letters, Hamburg, 1790-1808" (NA); Robert Batty, *Hanoverian and Saxon Scenery* (London, 1829); W. H. Bruford, *Germany in the Eighteenth Century: The Social Background of the Literary Revival* (Cambridge, England, 1935); JB's scattered reminiscences of Hamburg; A. C. Morris, ed., *The Diary and Letters of Gouverneur Morris* (New York, 1888), II, 81-90; *William Winston Seaton of the "National Intelligencer,"* pp. 69-70; W. C. Lane, ed., "Letters of Cristoph D. Ebeling," *Proceedings of the AAS*, n. s., XXXV, 272-451 (1926); JB to Stiles, 27 May 94, in *Collections of the MHS*, 2nd Ser., VIII, 269-270 (1826). "Except that it is not": JB to RB, 13 Feb. 96. "Wise friends": JB to RB, 16 Jan. 96. "The general diffusion": JB to Wolcott, 6 Nov. 94 (CHS). "His immediate neighbors": conversation with JB published posthumously, *National Intelligencer*, 21 May 19. "We leave": RB to AB, 29 June 95 (HEH). For more data on the *émigrés*, see Valentin de Vars, *Les Femmes de M. de Talleyrand* (Paris, 1891); Gilbert Stenger, *La Société française pendant la consulat: Bonaparte, sa famille, le monde et les salons* (Paris, 1905).

CHAPTER VII: DANIEL IN THE LION'S DEN

PREPARATION FOR BARBARY: The sources for this chapter are voluminous. NA contain many pertinent volumes: consular dispatches from Algiers, diplomatic instructions from the State Department, dispatches from ministers to Spain (including Portugal). Some of this material has been published in *Naval Documents Related to the United States Wars with the Barbary Powers*, Vol. I: *Naval Operations* (Washington, 1939); hereafter abbreviated as *Documents*. I have given a printed source whenever possible. The MSS are available on microfilm from NA at nominal cost. Many letters exist from JB to RB written during the mission to Algiers. Also surviving are four letterbooks and a notebook (MSS at Harvard). Another primary source of less value is T. B. Wait, ed., *American State Papers*, Class I: *Foreign Relations*, Vol. I (Boston, 1819). A good background source is Ray W. Irwin, *The Diplomatic Relations of the United States with the Barbary Powers, 1776-1816* (Chapel Hill, 1931).

"No person": *The Writings of James Monroe*, II, 378. "It has ever been": *Writings of Washington*, XXXV, 162. "Might be very useful": Pickering to Humphreys, 18 June 96 (MHS). "Louis XIV said": JB to Pickering, 20 April 96 (NA). *"Où es tu"*: JB to RB, 11 Jan. 96. "Visits me often": RB to JB, 14 Jan. 96. "Even if you": RB to JB, 6 Jan. 96. "I am poor": RB to JB, 28 Jan. 96. "Though the pigs": JB to RB, 11 Feb. 96. "Hercules went": JB to

RB, 29 Jan. 96. "I was well convinced": *Writings of James Monroe*, II, 489.
"The theater": JB to RB, 9 Feb. 96.

SUFFICIENT UNTO THE DEY: "I shall not hesitate": *Documents*, p. 138. "You
can say": JB to RB, 8 March 96; Todd, p. 125. "A menacing and insulting":
Documents, p. 146. "The affair sleeps": JB to RB, 14 March 96. "With the
exception": *ibid*. "The last debasement": JB to RB, 8 May 96. "The haunt
of pirates": JB to RB, 2 April 96. "If a Turk": JB to RB, 14 March 96; Todd,
p. 126-127. "Is it the opinion": JB to Cathcart, [April ?] 96 (Yale). "It is here
that": Notebook (Harvard). "The penalty": JB to RB, 14 March 96; Todd,
p. 127. "It is a common saying": *Documents*, p. 140. "They will then": *ibid*,
p. 141. "You are my light": JB to RB, 2 April 96. "A scene of . . . distress":
Documents, p. 143. "A huge, shaggy beast": Charles Prentiss, *The Life of
the Late William Eaton* (Brookfield, 1813), p. 59. "He seems to have": JB
to RB, 26 April 96. JB's ruse in getting rid of Cathcart: JB to Pickering, 12
July 96 (NA; Todd, pp. 133-134).

DIPLOMATIC SLEIGHT OF HAND: "I have now to add": JB to Monroe, 31 May
96; Todd, p. 132. "I am trying": *ibid*. JB's will is printed in Todd, pp. 295-
303; for another copy and discussion of it, see E. K. Maxfield, "A Newly
Discovered Letter," *Amer. Lit.*, IX, 442-449 (Nov. 1938): "To the Editors,"
ibid., X, 351-352 (Nov. 1938); M. R. Adams, "On the 'Newly Discovered'
Letter," *ibid.*, X, 224-227 (May 1938). JB's assets are summarized in this letter.
JB's account of ransoming the prisoners: *Documents*, pp. 163-165. Though
the *Fortune* was dispatched for Leghorn, the prisoners actually were landed
at Marseilles. "This will be presented": *Documents*, p. 165. "This was only
the rattle": JB to Pickering, 18 Oct. 96 (NA). "I am the only": JB to RB,
7 Sept. 96; Todd, p. 138. "Is it possible": JB to Pickering, 18 Oct. 96 (NA).
"Is it possible": *ibid*. "It is nine months": JB to RB, 25 Sept. 96. "The Dey
. . . changed": JB to RB, 12 Oct. 96; Todd, p. 141. "My lord": JB to RB,
9 Oct. 96; Todd, pp. 140-141. "Our business": JB to RB, 19 Oct. 96; Todd,
p. 143.

THOUSAND AND ONE NIGHTS: "Flattered his heart": JB to RB, 20 Nov. 96;
Todd, p. 144. Copies of all the treaties may be found in *Documents*, pp. 107-
116, 177-180, 210-214. "The Bey of Tunis": JB to RB, 20 Nov. 96; Todd, p.
143. "The Dey has sent": JB to RB, 30 Dec. 96; Todd, p. 144. The boar
hunt is described in the same letter; part in Todd, p. 145. The *Eliza* affair is
told in JB's "Declaration Relative to Captain Samuel Graves of the Schooner
Eliza" (HEH). The claims arising over Bacri's wheat taken from an American ship involved the subsequent history of the *Fortune*. JB chartered the
ship from Bacri to transport the captives, giving Capt. Calder orders to burn
his American papers as soon as the voyage was completed. This order was
to avoid what actually happened. The ship somehow sailed again with Bacri's
cargo under charter to Donaldson and was captured. Because it sailed with
American papers, the firm of Bacri was able to make Barlow, as United States
agent, pay for the cargo. "This absence": JB to RB, 3 April 97. "How much
you have lost": RB to JB, 29 April 97. "As an individual": JB to Humphreys
as quoted in Humphreys to Pickering, 17 July 96 (MHS). "At the expense":
JB to Wolcott, 12 Jan. 97 (CHS). "It has been fortunate": *Documents*, p.
183. "I have turned": JB to RB, 1 Aug. 97. "I have . . . escaped": JB to

Humphreys, 4 Aug. 97 (Harvard, Letterbook). "I wear large mustaches": JB to RB, 1 Aug. 97; Todd, p. 149.

CHAPTER VIII: TRANSATLANTIC POLITICS

POLITICAL IMBROGLIO: "I have grown fleshy": JB to Hopkins, 14 March 98 (Harvard, Letterbook). JB's notes for a history of the French Revolution are among the papers at Harvard. Dudley Baldwin's remark: AB to JB, 11 May 97 (Yale). "The nomination of Adams": JB to RB, 3 April 97. "It has been your . . . fortune": AB to JB, 28 May 98 (Yale). JB's relationship with RF (see Chap. 9 for more data) is shown in many unpublished letters and printed sources. Pertinent here is RB's memoir of RF (copies at Harvard and Yale) of 24 July 15, quoted in part in C. D. Colden, *Life of RF* (New York, 1817).

JB's observance of XYZ is recorded in JB to Stephen Cathalan, 29 Oct., 12 Nov. 97, 29 April 98, 15 June 99 (Harvard, Letterbook). The last contains the quotation: "To aid you." Also see JB to William Lee, 5 May 98 (Harvard, Letterbook); JB to TJ, 26 March 98 (LC). "Little make-weight": JB to AB, 4 March 98. This is the famous Baldwin letter. It is printed in a good text in John Dos Passos, *The Ground We Stand On* (New York, 1941), pp. 346-358. The quotations from "the frightful problem" through "when in God's name" are from this letter. I collated the text of this letter with the version printed by the *Columbian Centinel* (22 Dec. 98) and found the alterations fairly insignificant. In fact, "cant" and "royalists" were changed to "language" and "leaders," which softened JB's bluntness. The changes not due to sloppy printing were probably made by Lyon, but this cannot be verified, for no known copy of his pamphlet exists. The theft of the Baldwin letter is reported in AB to JB, 14 Feb., 30 March 99 (Yale).

For data on the Lyon affair, see J. F. McLaughlin, *Matthew Lyon, the Hampden of Congress* (New York, 1900), a poor book; yet it quotes an interesting Lyon letter of 14 Oct. 98 written from jail. See also Francis Wharton, *State Trials of the United States* (Philadelphia, 1849), pp. 333-344; *The Debates and Proceedings of Congress* (16th Congress, 2nd Session), pp. 478-486. The Lyon indictment had three counts, two based on the Baldwin letter, a third on Lyon's own writings. For background on the Alien and Sedition Laws, see J. M. Smith, *Freedom's Fetters: The Alien and Sedition Laws and American Civil Liberties* (Ithaca, N.Y., 1956).

The *Columbian Centinel's* editorial abuse is in Todd, pp. 163-165. The *Commercial Advertiser's* attack comes from an undated clipping (AAS). *The Political Green-House* appeared in the *Courant*, 1 Jan. 99, then separately at Hartford the same year. Webster's attack is in Harry Warfel, ed., *Letters of Noah Webster* (New York, 1953), pp. 187-194. "I understand . . . that you and Meigs": JB to Wolcott, 6 Oct. 00.

JOEL THE PEACEMAKER: JB to Watson, 26 July 98, is in *Memoirs of . . . Washington and Adams*, II, 111; also Watson to JB, 26 Oct. 98, and Watson's covering letter to Wolcott, 25 Nov. 98. Murray's diatribe is in W. C. Ford, ed., "Letters of William Vans Murray to John Quincy Adams," *Annual Re-*

port of the Amer. Hist. Assn. (1912), p. 478. Logan's mission is well treated in Frederick B. Tolles, *George Logan of Philadelphia* (New York, 1953); Pickering is quoted, p. 176.

JB to Washington, 2 Oct. 98, is in JB's *Letters from Paris to the Citizens of the United States* (London, 1800), pp. 35-40; also in Todd, pp. 156-160. There are various editions of JB's political letters printed both in Europe and America (see Blanck's bibliography). Washington to Adams, 1 Feb. 99, is in *Writings of Washington*, XXXVII, 119-120. Adams reply, 19 Feb. 99, is in C. F. Adams, *The Works of John Adams* (Boston, 1853), VIII, 624-626. "I . . . considered": *ibid.*, IX, 239ff. "Like the toad": W. C. Ford, *op. cit.*, p. 532. The JB-Skipwith address: AE, Vol. LI; also in JB's *Two Letters to the Citizens of the United States* (New Haven, 1806).

APOLOGIA PRO VITA SUA: JB's two political letters (March and December 1799) appear in both of the pamphlets cited above. Quotations from "every part" through "if you really have" are from the letter of 4 March. There is another pamphlet (Paris, 1798) called *The Second Warning or Strictures on the Speech Delivered by John Adams . . . in November Last,* which is unsigned but attributed by some bibliographers to JB. I do not think he could have written this. Though his opinion of Adams was low, this attack is clumsy, much inferior to JB's other pamphlets. Internal evidence suggests another author: words like "honor," "favor," for example, are given the British spelling of "honour," "favour," but JB always spelled these words in the American fashion, one matter in which he agreed with Noah Webster.

"In answer to": JB to Hopkins, 12 April 99 (MHS). Howard thinks this letter may have covered the *Second Warning,* but the date on JB's pamphlet of 4 March (his *apologia*) suggests that he sent this essay. There is a Paris edition of this pamphlet published in 1799, and my assumption is that JB had it printed between 4 March and 12 April when he wrote Hopkins. The quotations from "must be convinced" through the discussion of the "Maritime Convention" are from JB's public letter of 20 Dec. 99. "I wish to live": Howard, p. 305. "His exertions": *Two Letters*, p. iv. "Things in America": JB to Hopkins, 12 April 99 (MHS).

CHAPTER IX: RETIRED LEISURE

PATRON OF SCIENCE: *"Politicks"*: RB to Mrs. Jesse Putnam, 11 March 01. "It seems that": JB to AB, 15 Sept. oo. My data on RF, when not from letters, is taken from H. W. Dickinson, *RF, Engineer and Artist, His Life and Works* (London, 1913), the best general book on RF; James T. Flexner, *Steamboats Come True* (New York, 1944), a good book for surveying the whole topic of steamboats; William B. Parsons, *RF and the Submarine* (New York, 1922), detailed but sometimes inaccurate; Alice Crary Sutcliffe, "RF's Invention of the Steamboat," *Century*, LXXVIII, 752-772, 809-834 (Sept., Oct. 1909), important for printing documents.

"Under the pretense": JB to AB, 15 Sept. oo. "Tell Toot": JB to RB, 31 Aug. oo; Todd, pp. 178-179. "Concise and clear": JB to RF, 5 Sept. oo; Todd, p. 182. See also JB to RF, 7 Sept. oo; Todd, pp. 182-183. "The whole system": JB to TJ, 15 Sept. 01 (LC). Details of JB's househunting come from his letters to RB, 18 Aug.–8 Sept. 00 (19 letters). JB described the house to Lady Hamilton, 21 Sept. 01 (Harvard, Letterbook). "Poor Min": JB to RB, 16 Aug. 00. "Bathing & scouring": JB to RB, 17 Aug. 00. RF's studies under JB are recalled in RB's memoir cited in Chap. 7. The unfinished fragment of "The Canal" is at Yale. For RF's part in the *Columbiad*, see Chap. 10. "Remove from the mind of Man": Parsons, *op. cit.*, p. 81. "Bonaparte has thrown back": JB to RB, 19 Aug. 02. In JB's 1788 diary there is an account of Rumsey's steamboat.

TALE OF THREE CITIES: JB's reading for "The Canal" and the revision of the *Vision of Columbus* are well treated in Howard, pp. 306-309. JB's notebooks (Harvard) contain an essay on the liberty pole. "I rejoice at the progress": JB to John Fellows, 23 May 95; the MS is not extant but at Harvard there is holograph copy in contemporary hand. *Conn. Journal* printed it on 28 Aug. 99; so did the *Courant* and other papers. The quatrain to JB's sister comes from one of the notebooks at Harvard. The provenance of the Volney translation comes from Gilbert Chinard, *Volney et l'Amérique* (Baltimore and Paris, 1923), pp. 110-112, which prints the letters quoted here. "Another country": *Ruins* (Boston, 1835)', p. 55. "The mountains below": RB to Mrs. Jesse Putnam, 14 June 01.

JB's plans for the rest of his life: JB to TJ, 25 Aug. 01 (LC). "A lovely seat": TJ to JB, 3 May 02, in *Writings of TJ*, X, 319-322. For more data on Mme. de Villette, see Jean Stern, *Belle et Bonne: une fervente amie de Voltaire (1757-1822)* (Paris, 1938). There are 61 letters extant from JB to RB written between 1 May 02 and 14 Sept. 02, from which I have drawn heavily for this section. Portions are in Todd, pp. 183-203, though the transcriptions are careless and bowdlerized. Except for the quotation, "a race of hereditary masters," JB to Wolcott, 28 July 03, I have quoted from JB to RB in this order: 30 July, 3 May, 20 May, 23 May, 7 May, 6 June, 25 May, 15 Aug., 25 May, 15 Aug., 6 July, 12 July, 6 July, 16 July, 14 July (soliloquy over the trunk), 16 July. The letter of 16 July about fashions and Mme. Recamier was too Rabelaisian for Todd but is printed in Dos Passos, *The Ground We Stand On*, pp. 364-366.

FULTON'S STEAMBOAT: The Plombières drawing of the steamboat is in Sutcliffe, *op. cit.*, p. 760, and is dated 5 June 02. "I had a great talk": JB to RB, 18 July 02. (JB often wrote RB and RF in the same letter.) JB's willingness to let Livingston back Fulton is seen in the letter just cited and RF to JB, 1 March 09 (HEH). The contemporary account of the steamboat trial on the Seine is in Sutcliffe, *op. cit.*, p. 765. JB's trip to London in 1803 is reported in 8 letters from JB to RB, 1 April–10 Aug. The *Neptune* award is mentioned in two places: RF to JB, 1 March 09 (HEH), and JB to Col. William Stephens Smith [c. 1808] (Brown Univ. Lib.). "A little solid income": JB to RB, 1 April 03. "Very sick": AB to Clara Baldwin, 16 Jan. 04 (HEH). "You must not imagine": JB to AB, 2 Nov. 04.

"I am happy": JB to William Lee, 20 March 05 (Yale; LC). JB on Mackintosh: *National Intelligencer*, 28 May 19. A glimpse of JB at this time is in Benjamin Silliman's *Journal of Travels in England*, 3rd ed. (New Haven, 1820), pp. 205-216. I present RF sympathetically from JB's point of view, but I have some reservations about his motives. He was determined to make a fortune and rationalized rather too easily his principles and his weapon. This subject needs investigation; in fact, RF needs a new biography.

CHAPTER X: MR. JEFFERSON'S AMERICA

HOMECOMING: "Do not give": JB to Aaron Barlow, 17 April oo. "I intend to pass": JB to TJ, 2 Sept. o5 (LC). "Prepare yourself": RB's postscript in JB to AB, 4 Aug. o5. "A downcast look": Webster to S. Jacob, 8 Oct. o5 (BPL). A memory of JB's manner in society is in [G. C. Verplanck] "Sketch of the Life and Writings of JB," *Analectic Mag.*, IV, 152. A good survey of the United States at the turn of the century is in H. J. Carman and H. C. Syrett, *A History of the American People* (New York, 1955), I, 253-278.

"The Guillotine Song" first appeared in Peter Porcupine [William Cobbett], *A Bone to Gnaw for the Democrats* (London, 1797), p. 26. Cobbett said he reprinted the song but did not give his source. The Boston *Repertory* printed it on 15 Oct. o5; the *Columbian Centinel* on 16 Nov. o5. JB denied authorship of song in JB to Jonathan Law, 24 Oct. o9 (Yale); he said he first heard of it in Cobbett's pamphlet. I have seen an undated (c. 1811) clipping from the Baltimore *Federal Republican* attributing authorship to John Thelwall. "Philo would do": JB to Law, 24 Oct. o5 (Yale). "Knock on the empty skull": JB to Babcock, 30 Oct. o5 (NYPL). JB's address to friends in New Haven is in Todd, p. 207; it was in *American Mercury*, 7 Nov. o5. "I was actually": J. Meigs to JB, 22 Dec. o5. "I suppose": JB to Meigs, 6 Oct. oo. See also G. P. Fisher, *Life of Benjamin Silliman* (New York, 1866), I, 150.

"Jogging on slowly": JB to AB, 28 Nov. o5. "It is certain": JB to Allen, 28 Dec. 98 (Harvard, Notebook). "In all our colleges": JB to TJ, 15 Sept. oo (LC). See Tolles, *George Logan*, pp. 270-271. The *Prospectus* was published as pamphlet in Washington in 1806. It also appeared in the *National Intelligencer*, 24, 26 Nov. o6, and as appendix in G. Brown Goode, "The Origin of the National Scientific and Educational Institutions of the United States," *Papers of the Amer. Hist. Assn.*, IV, 5-77 (April 1890). See also *Writings of TJ*, VIII, 424-425, 494. RF's letter announcing his plan to marry does not survive, but a copy of JB's reply of 30 March o6 is at Harvard; partly printed in Sutcliffe, *op. cit.*, pp. 770-771. "Perhaps about the fourteenth": RF to JB, Sept. o6; Todd, pp. 209-210.

THE COLUMBIAD: Yale has two of the MSS of the *Columbiad;* the third, which I have not seen, is privately owned. Notes and fragmentary revisions are at Harvard. JB commissioned Smirke to do the paintings at 20 guineas each. See JB to John Vanderlyn, no date. "The infant republic": *Edinburgh Rev.*, XV, 24-40 (Oct. 1809). The dedicatory letter to RF, 1 May o7, is printed in the *Columbiad*. After JB went to France as minister, RF took over stock of books because Conrad and Co. no longer wanted to give it warehouse space. RF still had the books when he died in 1815 and willed them to RB. There is an excellent and perceptive discussion of the *Columbiad* in Howard, pp. 309-323. "As a poem of the Epic": JB to TJ, 23 Jan. o8 (LC). Passages quoted from the poem appear in this order: I, 1-2; VIII, 79-80, 158, 161, 363, 265-266; IX, 97-100; X, 600, 625-626.

For the Lewis dinner, see the *National Intelligencer*, 16 Jan. o7. Adams' parody is in *Monthly Anthology*, VII, 143-144 (March 1807). Though unsigned, the verses are definitely attributed to Adams by Evert and George Duyckinck in *Cyclopaedia of American Literature* (1855). "Every sentiment": JB to RB, 6 March 07; part in Todd, pp. 211-212. The AB obituary was published on 11 March 07; reprinted in *Ga. Hist. Quart.*, III, 169-173 (1919). "We belong": JB to S. Jacob, 20 May 07. Peale painted the portrait in Feb. 07 (see Peale to JB, 25 Feb. 07, in Peale Letterbooks at Amer. Philos. Soc.). JB was notified of election to Amer. Philos. Soc. by Mahlon Dickerson in letter of 30 Jan. 09 (Amer. Philos. Soc.). The account of RF's voyage is printed in Todd, pp. 233-234. His later relations with JB and RB are reconstructed from these letters: RF to JB, 5 June 08 (Yale); 1 March 09 (HEH); RB to Clara Baldwin, 7 Feb. 10, 7 March 15.

CHAPTER XI: SQUIRE OF KALORAMA

Elder Statesman: "Barlow's house": William Lee to his wife, 20 Oct. 10 (LC). "In passing over": JB to Stephen Barlow, 8 April 10. Latrobe's relation with JB is seen in Talbot Hamlin, *Benjamin Henry Latrobe* (New York, 1955). For data on Kalorama, see Mrs. Cora Bacon-Foster, *The Story of Kalorama* (Washington, 1910); reprinted in *Records of the Columbia Historical Society*, XIII (1910). Mr. and Mrs. Joel Barlow of Washington, D.C., pointed out to me the site of Kalorama. RF to JB, 1 March 09 (HEH) contains important data on Kalorama. A feature story by John B. Proctor, Washington *Star*, 21 July 1935, summarizes the history of Kalorama with illustrations. Some of my data comes from scattered remarks in various letters.

"A pleasant country residence": TJ to JB, 3 May 02, in *Writings of TJ*, X, 321. There is a wealth of data on TJ's administration in Irving Brant, *James Madison: Secretary of State, 1800-1809* (Indianapolis, 1953). RB on her radishes: RB to Clara Baldwin, 10 March 10 (HEH). See also her letter of 1 Dec. 10 (HEH). "Washington thus resembles": D. B. Warden, *A Chorographical and Statistical Description of the District of Columbia* (Paris, 1816). The British diplomat (Augustus Foster) is quoted by Brant, *op. cit.*, p. 163. The newspaper ads cited and quoted appeared in the *National Intelligencer*.

My summary of JB as elder statesman comes from too many sources to list them all, but the letters to and from TJ provide important data. The British chargé d'affaires (John Morier) is quoted by Hamlin, *op. cit.*, p. 334. "The cultivation of the sciences": JB to TJ, 4 Dec. 08 (LC). "In all our country": JB to Granger, 3 May 09 (Yale; Todd, p. 235). The account of Madison's inauguration comes from Gaillard Hunt, ed., *Forty Years of Washington Society* (London, 1906), pp. 58-63; this book is compiled from the letters of Mrs. S. H. Smith (Margaret Bayard), wife of the publisher of the *National Intelligencer*. "As the reading": TJ to JB, 8 Oct. 09, in *Writings of TJ*, XII, 323. "You owe to republicanism": TJ to JB, 24 Jan. 10, in *Writings of TJ*, XII, 351. "I am not much": JB to TJ, 15 Jan. 10 (LC). "The mountains among which": TJ to JB, 14 Aug. 05 (LC). TJ's later invitations and directions: TJ to JB, 25 July 08 (Todd, p. 240); 5 Aug. 08 (LC); 8 Oct. 09 (*Writings of TJ*, XII, 323). Since JB left no account of his visit to Monticello, I have reconstructed it from Mrs. Smith's notebook description of the visit she and her husband made in August, 1809 (*Forty Years*, p. 65 ff.)

HONORS AND OBLOQUY: The Military Philosophical Society's certificate of election (2 Nov. 07) is at Harvard. The LL.D. was announced in J. Meigs to JB, 20 Oct. 09. JB's oration was published as pamphlet and also printed in the *Monthly Mag.*, No. 194 (Feb. 1810). The dinner was reported in the *National Intelligencer*, 7 July 09, and the oration printed on 10 July. "I was doubting": TJ to JB, 8 Oct. 09, in *Writings of TJ*, XII, 323. The *Columbiad* was reviewed in *The Port Folio*, I, 59-68 (Jan. 1809), 432-450 (May 1809); *Edinburgh Rev.*, XV, 24-40 (Oct. 1809). Other reviews may be located through the extensive American bibliography at New York Univ. Lib. "Of the poem": Webster to JB, 13 Oct. 08, in Todd, pp. 220-221.

Grégoire's pamphlet and JB's reply were printed separately in Paris and Washington in 1809. Grégoire's letter is in *Monthly Anthology*, VII, 2-11 (July 1809); JB's reply, *ibid.*, VII, 290-298 (Nov. 1809). Grégoire's second letter to JB, 28 Jan. 10 (Yale) was printed in *American Mercury*, 12 July 10. See also *The Panoplist and Missionary Mag.*, III, 171-179 (Sept. 1810). "I am now perhaps": JB to S. Jacob, 1 Oct. 09 (Yale). "Hubby has been so busy": RB to Clara Baldwin, 1 July 10 (HEH). The familiar passage from TJ's *Notes* is from Query IV. "Mr. Jefferson in his notes": RB to Clara Baldwin, 6 Aug. 10 (HEH). "The bedbugs . . . swarmed": RB to Clara Baldwin, 18 Aug. 10 (HEH). "Assuring each other": JB to Clara Baldwin, 5 Sept. 10. "Husband is not yet": RB to Clara Baldwin, 19 Sept. 10 (HEH). "There is little prospect": JB to Dearborn, 28 Oct. 10 (NYHS). "The shock she received": JB to Dearborn, 11 April 11 (MHS).

CHAPTER XII: MINISTER TO FRANCE

NOMINATION AND PREPARATION: The primary sources for this chapter are extensive. They are mostly in public archives: AE, NA, LC. There is one rather surprising group of MSS at LC known as the J. Henley Smith Papers containing JB's letters to RB written during the last two months of his life. Anyone who writes about American foreign relations between 1809 and 1812 without consulting Irving Brant, *James Madison, the President, 1809-1812* (Indianapolis, 1956), does so at his risk. This work, to which I am indebted, revises a good many old judgments about Madison as President. He was far from a weak President or the mere lengthened shadow of TJ. Another good background study is Clauder, *op. cit.* (see Chap. 6). Out of date but of some use is Beckles Willson, *America's Ambassadors to France 1777-1927* (New York, 1928), pp. 102-117. Also important is Leon Howard, "JB and Napoleon," *Huntington Library Quart.*, II, 37-51 (Oct. 1938). Howard prints "Advice to a Raven in Russia" from the MS at LC. I have followed his text.

For RF's recommendation of JB as Sec. of State, see RF to Madison, 28 Jan. 09 (LC). "I owe it": Madison to JB, 7 Feb. 09, in *Letters and Other Writings of James Madison* (Philadelphia, 1867), II, 428-429. "The sacrifice of ease": JB to Dearborn, 11 April 11 (MHS). "I have seen too much": JB to TJ, 2 May 11 (LC). "Your doubts": TJ to JB, 22 July 11, in *Writings of TJ*, XIII, 64-65. The debate on JB's appointment is recorded in Pickering's journal, "Pickering Papers," XIV, 328 (MHS); also printed in *William Winston Seaton of the "National Intelligencer,"* pp. 100-108. The charge that JB speculated in American claims on France was refuted by Monroe in letter to Madison; see *Writings of James Monroe,* IV, 119. "Our General S.": Erving to James Bowdoin, 11 March 11 (MHS). For data on the Smith resignation, see Brant, *op. cit.,* pp. 265-309. "The review of Smith's address": JB to RF, 17 July 11. See also William Lee to his wife, 11 Sept. 11 (LC), which states: "The answer [to Smith] is my work corrected by Mr. Barlow." I do not take this literally; some of the arguments no doubt are Lee's, but the style is pure Barlow. JB's *Review of Robert Smith's Address* appeared in the *National Intelligencer* on 4, 6, 9, 11 July 11, before coming out as pamphlet.

Monroe's instructions to JB are in NA; also printed with other pertinent documents in *Message from the President . . . Transmitting . . . Correspondence of the Secretary of State and the Minister . . . at Paris* (Washington, 1812). The same material also is in *American State Papers,* Class I: *Foreign Relations,* Vol. III (Washington, 1832), and *State Papers and Public Documents of the United States* (Boston, 1819), Vols. VIII, IX. Monroe's letter also is in Todd, pp. 258-268. JB's voyage to France is reconstructed from the MS "Journal Kept on Board the U. S. Frigate *Constitution*" by Midshipman Frederick Baury (MHS) and D. B. Warden, "Journal of a Voyage from Annapolis to Cherbourg," *Md. Hist. Mag.,* XI, 127-141, 203-217 (June, Sept. 1916). Anyone visiting Boston should not fail to see the *Constitution,* which is kept in a good state of preservation at the Charlestown Navy Yard. "But my heart is heavy": JB to RF, 2 Aug. 11. "God bless": JB to RF, 5 Aug. 11.

FAILURE OF A MISSION: "We have moved": JB to Alexander Wolcott, Nov. 11 (Yale). "Our ancient servants": JB to Oliver Wolcott, 26 Sept. 11. JB's memory of Napoleon in 1797: *National Intelligencer,* 25 May 19. "Plain bottle green": Clara Baldwin to Anna Maria Thornton, 13 Nov. 11 (HEH). "I have got to be": JB to Dolley Madison, 11 Dec. 11, in Dixon Wecter, "JB and the Sugar Beets," *Colo. Mag.,* XVIII, 179-181 (Sept. 1941). "Dolley" has been established by Irving Brant as the correct spelling of Mrs. Madison's name. For more on JB's audience, see W. Lee to his wife, 19 March 12 (LC). "I have nothing decisive": JB to Alexander Wolcott, Nov. 11 (Yale). The conversation between JB and Napoleon is reported in JB to Madison, 19 Dec. 11 (LC). "You will have perceived": JB to Madison, 15 April 12 (LC). "A mettlesome character": Dalberg to Bassano, 3 June 12 (AE, LXIX, 138). "Mr. Barlow's deportment:" Lee to Madison, 1 Jan. 12 (LC). "I have been here": JB to Dolley Madison, 11 Dec. 11 (Wecter, *op. cit.,* p. 181). "As I promised": Dolley Madison to JB, [April] 12, in Lucia Cutts, ed., *Memoirs and Letters of Dolly Madison* (Boston and New York, 1886), p. 87.

For an account of the *Boeuf Gris* and the masked ball, see Lee to his daughter, 11 Feb. 12 (LC). "You cannot think": JB to Dolley Madison, 11 Dec. 11 (Wecter, *op. cit.,* p. 181). "Tom is happy": JB to Stephen Barlow, 21 Nov. 11; Todd, p. 272. "Poor Clara": RB to Dolley Madison, 4 March 12 (copy at Harvard). "You have mistaken": JB to Clara Baldwin, 13 June 12. "It is impossible": JB to Bradley, 2 Jan. 12 (Yale). "I naturally and habitually": JB to Monroe, 21 Nov. 11 (NA). "Since my arrival": JB to Russell, 2 March 12, in *Message from the President.* See also JB to Russell, 29 Jan. 12 (*ibid.*), for data on the *Acastus.* Monroe wrote JB about the proposed treaty on 23

Feb., 23 April 12 (NA). "I made no comment": JB to Monroe, 12 May 12, in *American State Papers*, III, 603. "The conduct of": Madison to JB, 11 Aug. 12, in *Letters and Other Writings*, II, 540.

THE LAST FUTILITY: "Since you left": Dalberg to Bassano, 28 May 12 (AE, LXIX, 78). "If your excellency": Dalberg to Bassano, 27 Aug. 12 (AE, LXIX, 231-232). "Owing to a passage": Monroe to JB, 16 June 12, in *American State Papers*, III, 617. "The nation's hostility": Madison to JB, 11 Aug. 12, in *Letters and Other Writings*, II, 541. "When you arrive": Bassano to JB, 11 Oct. 12, in *American State Papers*, III, 604. "Though the proposal": JB to Monroe, 25 Oct. 12, in *ibid.*, p. 603. The journey to Wilna is recorded in a sequence of 20 letters (MSS at LC) from JB to RB written between 28 Oct. and 30 Nov. 12. In addition, I have used Tom Barlow's letter to Clara Baldwin of 20 Nov. 12; JB to Clara, 12 and 26 Nov. 12; Tom to RB, 29 Nov. 12 (Todd, pp. 278-279); RB to JB, 12 Nov. 12 (HEH). The inscription on the marble tablet I copied from a photograph in the Barlow Papers at Harvard. It also is printed in Wisniowski, *op. cit.*, p. 503 (see Prologue).

EPILOGUE

"You will doubtless be informed": RB to Madison, 10 Feb. 13 (NA). "Which I wrote you": RB to Mrs. Jacob, 2 March 14 (Haverford). For Sen. Glenn's bill, see *Congressional Record, Index: 71st Congress, 2nd Session*. JB's successor was William Crawford, who reached Paris in the late summer, 1813. JB's last will was the same one he made in Algiers in 1796 giving everything to RB. Her will subsequently bequeathed all the property to Thomas Barlow except for specific bequests of $24,500. There are copies of both wills at HEH; there is a copy of JB's will at Harvard. The day before JB left Paris he made a financial statement showing holdings of $115,540 in bank, manufacturing, and canal stock and debts of $34,000. This did not include real estate in Washington or Paris. In addition he estimated that his western lands were worth about $180,000. He had claims to tracts in Mississippi, Missouri, Illinois, and New York.

Appendix

THE HASTY PUDDING

Canto I

Ye Alps audacious, through the heavens that rise,
To cramp the day and hide me from the skies;
Ye Gallic flags, that o'er their heights unfurled,
Bear death of kings and freedom to the world,
I sing not you. A softer theme I choose,
A virgin theme, unconscious of the muse,
But fruitful, rich, well suited to inspire
The purest frenzy of poetic fire.

Despise it not, ye bards to terror steeled,
Who hurl your thunders round the epic field;
Nor ye who strain your midnight throats to sing
Joys that the vineyard and the stillhouse bring;
Or on some distant fair your notes employ,
And speak of raptures that you ne'er enjoy.
I sing the sweets I know, the charms I feel,
My morning incense, and my evening meal—
The sweets of Hasty Pudding. Come, dear bowl,
Glide o'er my palate, and inspire my soul.
The milk beside thee, smoking from the kine,
Its substance mingled, married in with thine,
Shall cool and temper thy superior heat,
And save the pains of blowing while I eat.

329

A YANKEE'S ODYSSEY

Oh! could the smooth, the emblematic song
Flow like the genial juices o'er my tongue,
Could those mild morsels in my numbers chime,
And, as they roll in substance, roll in rime,
No more thy awkward, unpoetic name
Should shun the muse or prejudice thy fame;
But rising grateful to the accustomed ear,
All bards should catch it, and all realms revere!

Assist me first with pious toil to trace
Through wrecks of time, thy lineage and thy race;
Declare what lovely squaw, in days of yore,
(Ere great Columbus sought thy native shore)
First gave thee to the world; her works of fame
Have lived indeed, but lived without a name.
Some tawny Ceres, goddess of her days,
First learned with stones to crack the well-dried maize,
Through the rough sieve to shake the golden shower,
In boiling water stir the yellow flour:
The yellow flour, bestrewed and stirred with haste,
Swells in the flood and thickens to a paste,
Then puffs and wallops, rises to the brim,
Drinks the dry knobs that on the surface swim;
The knobs at last the busy ladle breaks,
And the whole mass its true consistence takes.

Could but her sacred name, unknown so long,
Rise, like her labors, to the son of song,
To her, to them I'd consecrate my lays,
And blow her pudding with the breath of praise.
If 'twas Oella whom I sang before,
I here ascribe her one great virtue more.
Not through the rich, Peruvian realms alone
The fame of Sol's sweet daughter should be known,
But o'er the world's wide climes should live secure,
Far as his rays extend, as long as they endure.

Dear Hasty Pudding, what unpromised joy
Expands my heart, to meet thee in Savoy!
Doomed o'er the world through devious paths to roam,
Each clime my country, and each house my home,
My soul is soothed, my cares have found an end;
I greet my long-lost, unforgotten friend.

For thee through Paris, that corrupted town,
How long in vain I wandered up and down,
Where shameless Bacchus, with his drenching hoard,
Cold from his cave usurps the morning board.

London is lost in smoke and steeped in tea;
No Yankee there can lisp the name of thee;
The uncouth word, a libel on the town,
Would call a proclamation from the crown.
For climes oblique, that fear the sun's full rays,
Chilled in their fogs, exclude the generous maize;
A grain whose rich, luxuriant growth requires
Short, gentle showers, and bright, ethereal fires.

But here, though distant from our native shore,
With mutual glee, we meet and laugh once more.
The same! I know thee by that yellow face,
That strong complexion of true Indian race,
Which time can never change, nor soil impair,
Nor Alpine snows, nor Turkey's morbid air;
For endless years, through every mild domain,
Where grows the maize, there thou art sure to reign.

But man, more fickle, the bold licence claims,
In different realms to give thee different names.
Thee the soft nations round the warm Levant
Polanta call; the French, of course, *Polante.*
E'en in thy native regions, how I blush
To hear the Pennsylvanians call thee *Mush!*
On Hudson's banks, while men of Belgic-spawn
Insult and eat thee by the name *Suppawn.*
All spurious appellations, void of truth;
I've better known thee from my earliest youth:
Thy name is *Hasty Pudding!* thus my sire
Was wont to greet thee fuming from his fire;
And while he argued in thy just defense
With logic clear he thus explained the sense:
"In haste the boiling caldron, o'er the blaze,
Receives and cooks the ready powdered maize;
In haste 'tis served, and then in equal haste,
With cooling milk, we make the sweet repast.
No carving to be done, no knife to grate
The tender ear and wound the stony plate;
But the smooth spoon, just fitted to the lip,
And taught with art the yielding mass to dip,
By frequent journeys to the bowl well stored,
Performs the hasty honors of the board."
Such is thy name, significant and clear,
A name, a sound to every Yankee dear,
But most to me, whose heart and palate chaste
Preserve my pure, hereditary taste.

A YANKEE'S ODYSSEY

There are who strive to stamp with disrepute
The luscious food, because it feeds the brute;
In tropes of high-strained wit, while gaudy prigs
Compare thy nursling, man, to pampered pigs;
With sovereign scorn I treat the vulgar jest,
Nor fear to share thy bounties with the beast.
What though the generous cow gives me to quaff
The milk nutritious: am I then a calf?
Or can the genius of the noisy swine,
Though nursed on pudding, thence lay claim to mine?
Sure the sweet song I fashion to thy praise,
Runs more melodious than the notes they raise.

My song, resounding in its grateful glee,
No merit claims: I praise myself in thee.
My father loved thee through his length of days!
For thee his fields were shaded o'er with maize;
From thee what health, what vigor he possessed,
Ten sturdy freemen from his loins attest;
Thy constellation ruled my natal morn,
And all my bones were made of Indian corn.
Delicious grain, whatever form it take,
To roast or boil, to smother or to bake,
In every dish 'tis welcome still to me,
But most, my Hasty Pudding, most in thee.

Let the green succotash with thee contend;
Let beans and corn their sweetest juices blend;
Let butter drench them in its yellow tide,
And a long slice of bacon grace their side;
Not all the plate, how famed soe'er it be,
Can please my palate like a bowl of thee.
Some talk of hoe-cake, fair Virginia's pride!
Rich johnny-cake this mouth has often tried;
Both please me well, their virtues much the same,
Alike their fabric, as allied their fame,
Except in dear New England, where the last
Receives a dash of pumpkin in the paste,
To give it sweetness and improve the taste.
But place them all before me, smoking hot,
The big, round dumpling, rolling from the pot;
The pudding of the bag, whose quivering breast,
With suet lined, leads on the Yankee feast;
The charlotte brown, within whose crusty sides
A belly soft the pulpy apple hides;
The yellow bread whose face like amber glows,
And all of Indian that the bakepan knows—
You tempt me not; my favorite greets my eyes,
To that loved bowl my spoon by instinct flies.

332

APPENDIX

Canto II

To mix the food by vicious rules of art,
To kill the stomach and to sink the heart,
To make mankind to social virtue sour,
Cram o'er each dish, and be what they devour;
For this the kitchen muse first framed her book,
Commanding sweats to stream from every cook;
Children no more their antic gambols tried,
And friends to physic wondered why they died.

Not so the Yankee: his abundant feast,
With simples furnished and with plainness dressed,
A numerous offspring gathers round the board,
And cheers alike the servant and the lord;
Whose well-bought hunger prompts the joyous taste,
And health attends them from the short repast.

While the full pail rewards the milkmaid's toil,
The mother sees the morning caldron boil;
To stir the pudding next demands their care;
To spread the table and the bowls prepare;
To feed the household as their portions cool
And send them all to labor or to school.

Yet may the simplest dish some rules impart,
For nature scorns not all the aids of art.
E'en Hasty Pudding, purest of all food,
May still be bad, indifferent, or good,
As sage experience the short process guides,
Or want of skill, or want of care presides.
Who'er would form it on the surest plan,
To rear the child and long sustain the man;
To shield the morals while it mends the size,
And all the powers of every food supplies—
Attend the lesson that the muse shall bring,
Suspend your spoons, and listen while I sing.

But since, O man! thy life and health demand
Not food alone, but labor from thy hand,
First, in the field, beneath the sun's strong rays,
Ask of thy mother earth the needful maize;
She loves the race that courts her yielding soil,
And gives her bounties to the sons of toil.

A YANKEE'S ODYSSEY

When now the ox, obedient to thy call,
Repays the loan that filled the winter stall,
Pursue his traces o'er the furrowed plain,
And plant in measured hills the golden grain.
But when the tender germ begins to shoot,
And the green spire declares the sprouting root,
Then guard your nursling from each greedy foe,
The insidious worm, the all-devouring crow.
A little ashes sprinkled round the spire,
Soon steeped in rain, will bid the worm retire;
The feathered robber with his hungry maw
Swift flies the field before your man of straw,
A frightful image, such as schoolboys bring
When met to burn the Pope or hang the King.

Thrice in the season, through each verdant row,
Wield the strong plowshare and the faithful hoe;
The faithful hoe, a double task that takes,
To till the summer corn and roast the winter cakes.

Slow springs the blade, while checked by chilling rains,
Ere yet the sun the seat of Cancer gains;
But when his fiercest fires emblaze the land,
Then start the juices, then the roots expand;
Then, like a column of Corinthian mold,
The stalk struts upward and the leaves unfold;
The bushy branches all the ridges fill,
Entwine their arms, and kiss from hill to hill.
Here cease to vex them; all your cares are done:
Leave the last labors to the parent sun;
Beneath his genial smiles, the well-dressed field,
When autumn calls, a plenteous crop shall yield.

Now the strong foliage bears the standards high,
And shoots the tall top-gallants to the sky;
The suckling ears their silky fringes bend,
And pregnant grown, their swelling coats distend;
The loaded stalk, while still the burden grows,
O'erhangs the space that runs between the rows;
High as a hop-field waves the silent grove,
A safe retreat for little thefts of love,
When the pledged roasting-ears invite the maid
To meet her swain beneath the new-formed shade;
Her generous hand unloads the cumbrous hill,
And the green spoils her ready basket fill;
Small compensation for the twofold bliss,
The promised wedding, and the present kiss.

Slight depredations these; but now the moon
Calls from his hollow tree the sly raccoon;.
And while by night he bears his prize away,
The bolder squirrel labors through the day.
Both thieves alike, but provident of time,
A virtue rare, that almost hides their crime.
Then let them steal the little stores they can,
And fill their granaries from the toils of man;
We've one advantage where they take no part—
With all their wiles, they ne'er have found the art
To boil the Hasty Pudding; here we shine
Superior far to tenants of the pine;
This envied boon to man shall still belong,
Unshared by them in substance or in song.

At last the closing season browns the plain,
And ripe October gathers in the grain;
Deep-loaded carts the spacious corn-house fill;
The sack distended marches to the mill;
The laboring mill beneath the burden groans,
And showers the future pudding from the stones;
Till the glad housewife greets the powdered gold,
And the new crop exterminates the old.
Ah who can sing what every wight must feel,
The joy that enters with the bag of meal,
A general jubilee pervades the house,
Wakes every child and gladdens every mouse.

Canto III

The days grow short; but though the falling sun
To the glad swain proclaims his day's work done,
Night's pleasing shades his various tasks prolong,
And yield new subjects to my various song.
For now, the corn-house filled, the harvest home,
The invited neighbors to the husking come:
A frolic scene, where work, and mirth, and play,
Unite their charms to chase the hours away.
Where the huge heap lies centered in the hall,
The lamp suspended from the cheerful wall,
Brown, corn-fed nymphs, and strong, hard-handed beaux,
Alternate ranged, extend in circling rows,
Assume their seats, the solid mass attack;
The dry husks rustle, and the corncobs crack;
The song, the laugh, alternate notes resound,
And the sweet cider trips in silence round.

The laws of husking every wight can tell;
And sure no laws he ever keeps so well:
For each red ear a general kiss he gains,
With each smut ear she smuts the luckless swains;
But when to some sweet maid a prize is cast,
Red as her lips and taper as her waist,
She walks the round and culls one favored beau,
Who leaps the luscious tribute to bestow.
Various the sport, as are the wits and brains
Of well-pleased lasses and contending swains;
Till the vast mound of corn is swept away,
And he that gets the last ear wins the day.
Meanwhile, the housewife urges all her care,
The well-earned feast to hasten and prepare.
The sifted meal already waits her hand,
The milk is strained, the bowls in order stand,
The fire flames high; and as a pool—that takes
The headlong stream that o'er the milldam breaks—
Foams, roars, and rages with incessant toils,
So the vexed caldron rages, roars, and boils.

First with clean salt she seasons well the food,
Then strews the flour, and thickens all the flood.
Long o'er the simmering fire she lets it stand;
To stir it well demands a stronger hand;
The husband takes his turn; and round and round
The ladle flies; at last the toil is crowned;
When to the board the thronging huskers pour,
And take their seats as at the corn before.

I leave them to their feast. There still belong
More useful matters to my faithful song.
For rules there are, though ne'er unfolded yet,
Nice rules and wise, how pudding should be ate.
Some with molasses line the luscious treat,
And mix, like bards, the useful with the sweet.
A wholesome dish, and well deserving praise,
A great resource in those bleak wintry days,
When the chilled earth lies buried deep in snow,
And raging Boreas dries the shivering cow.

Blest cow! thy praise shall still my notes employ,
Great source of health, the only source of joy;
Mother of Egypt's god—but sure, for me,
Were I to leave my God, I'd worship thee.
How oft thy teats these pious hands have pressed!
How oft thy bounties proved my only feast!
How oft I've fed thee with my favorite grain!
And roared, like thee, to see thy children slain!

Ye swains who know her various worth to prize,
Ah! house her well from winter's angry skies.
Potatoes, pumpkins, should her sadness cheer,
Corn from your crib, and mashes from your beer;
When spring returns, she'll well acquit the loan,
And nurse at once your infants and her own.
Milk then with pudding I should always choose;
To this in future I confine my muse,
Till she in haste some further hints unfold,
Well for the young, nor useless to the old.
First in your bowl the milk abundant take,
Then drop with care along the silver lake
Your flakes of pudding; these at first will *hide*
Their little bulk beneath the swelling tide;
But when their growing mass no more can sink,
When the soft island looms above the brink,
Then check your hand; you've got the portion due;
So taught our sires, and what they taught is true.

There is a choice in spoons. Though small appear
The nice distinction, yet to me 'tis clear.
The deep-bowled Gallic spoon, contrived to scoop
In ample draughts the thin, diluted soup,
Performs not well in those substantial things,
Whose mass adhesive to the metal clings;
Where the strong labial muscles must embrace
The gentle curve, and sweep the hollow space
With ease to enter and discharge the freight,
A bowl less concave, but still more dilate,
Becomes the pudding best. The shape, the size,
A secret rests, unknown to vulgar eyes.
Experienced feeders can alone impart
A rule so much above the lore of art.
These tuneful lips that thousand spoons have tried,
With just precision could the point decide,
Though not in song; the muse but poorly shines
In cones, and cubes, and geometric lines;
Yet the true form, as near as she can tell,
Is that small section of a goose-egg shell,
Which in two equal portions shall divide
The distance from the center to the side.

Fear not to slaver; 'tis no sin.
Like the free Frenchman, from your joyous chin
Suspend the ready napkin; or, like me,
Poise with one hand your bowl upon your knee;
Just in the zenith your wise head project,
Your full spoon, rising in a line direct,
Bold as a bucket, heeds no drops that fall;
The wide-mouthed bowl will surely catch them all!

ADVICE TO A RAVEN IN RUSSIA

Black fool, why winter here? These frozen skies,
Worn by your wings and deafen'd by your cries,
Should warn you hence, where milder suns invite,
And day alternates with his mother night.
You fear perhaps your food may fail you there—
Your human carnage, that delicious fare,
That lured you hither, following still your friend,
The great Napoleon to the world's bleak end.
You fear, because the southern climes pour'd forth
Their clustering nations to infest the north,
Bavarians, Austrians, those who drink the Po
And those who skirt the Tuscan seas below,
With all Germania, Neustria, Belgia, Gaul,
Doom'd here to wade thro slaughter to their fall,
You fear he left behind no wars, to feed
His feather'd cannibals and nurse the breed.

Fear not, my screamer, call your greedy train,
Sweep over Europe, hurry back to Spain,
You'll find his legions there; the valiant crew
Please best their master when they toil for you.
Abundant there they spread the country o'er
And taint the breeze with every nation's gore,
Iberian, Lusian, British widely strown;
But still more wide and copious flows their own.

Go where you will; Calabria, Malta, Greece,
Egypt and Syria still his fame increase,
Domingo's fatten'd isle and India's plains
Glow deep with purple drawn from Gallic veins.
No raven's wing can stretch the flight so far
As the torn bandrols of Napoleon's war.
Choose then your climate, fix your best abode,
He'll make you deserts and he'll bring you blood.

How could you fear a dearth? have not mankind,
Tho slain by millions, millions left behind?
Has not CONSCRIPTION still the power to wield
Her annual faulchion o'er the human field?
A faithful harvester! or if a man
Escape that gleaner, shall he scape the BAN?
The triple BAN, that like the hound of hell
Gripes with joles, to hold his victim well.

Fear nothing then, hatch fast your ravenous brood,
Teach them to cry to Buonaparte for food;
They'll be like you, of all his suppliant train,
The only class that never cries in vain.

A YANKEE'S ODYSSEY

For see what natural benefits you lend!
(The surest way to fix the mutual friend)
While on his slaughter'd troops your tribes are fed,
You cleanse his camp and carry off his dead.
Imperial scavenger! but now you know,
Your work is vain amid these hills of snow.
His tentless troops are marbled through with frost
And change to crystal when the breath is lost.
Mere trunks of ice, tho limb'd like human frames,
And lately warm'd with life's endearing flames,
They cannot taint the air, the world impest,
Nor can you tear one fiber from their breast.
No! from their visual sockets as they lie,
With beak and claws you cannot pluck an eye.
The frozen orb, preserving still its form,
Defies your talons as it braves the storm,
But stands and stares to God, as if to know
In what curst hands he leaves his world below.
     Fly then, or starve; tho all the dreadful road
From Minsk to Moskow with their bodies strow'd
May count some Myriads, yet they can't suffice
To feed you more beneath these dreary skies.
Go back and winter in the wilds of Spain;
Feast there awhile, and in the next campaign
Rejoin your master; for you'll find him then,
With his new million of the race of men,
Clothed in his thunders, all his flags unfurl'd,
Raging and storming o'er the prostrate world!
     War after war his hungry soul requires,
State after State shall sink beneath his fires,
Yet other Spains in victim smoke shall rise
And other Moskows suffocate the skies,
Each land lie reeking with its peoples slain
And not a stream run bloodless to the main.
Till men resume their souls, and dare to shed
Earth's total vengeance on the monster's head,
Hurl from his blood-built throne this king of woes,
Dash him to dust, and let the world repose.

Drawing by Laura Thoe

Kalorama, Barlow's house in Washington from
1807 to 1811

Index

INDEX

INDEX